The I AM America

SACRED FIRE

A Handbook for Spiritual Growth and Personal Development

ALSO BY LORI TOYE

A Teacher Appears

Sisters of the Flame

Fields of Light

The Ever Present Now

New World Wisdom Series

I AM America Atlas

Points of Perception

Light of Awakening

Divine Destiny

Sacred Energies of the Golden Cities

Temples of Consciousness

Awaken the Master Within

Soul Alchemy

Building the Seamless Garment

Golden Cities and the Masters of Shamballa

Freedom Star Book

I AM America Map

Freedom Star Map

6-Map Scenario

US Golden City Map

I AM AMERICA TEACHINGS

SACRED FIRE

A Handbook for Spiritual Growth and Personal Development

I AM AMERICA PUBLISHING & DISTRIBUTING
P.O. Box 2511, Payson, Arizona, 85547, USA.
www.iamamerica.com

© (Copyright) 2020 by Lori Adaile Toye. All rights reserved.
ISBN: 978-1-880050-41-5

All rights exclusively reserved, including under the Berne Convention and the Universal Copyright Convention. No part of this book may be reproduced or translated into any language or utilized in any form or by any means, electronic or mechanical, including photocopying, recording, or by any information storage and retrieval system, without written permission from the publisher. Published in 2020 by I AM America Seventh Ray Publishing International, P.O. Box 2511, Payson, Arizona, 85547, United States of America.

I AM America Maps and Books have been marketed since 1989 by I AM America Seventh Ray Publishing and Distributing, through workshops, conferences, and numerous bookstores in the United States and internationally. If you are interested in obtaining information on available releases please write or call:
I AM America, P.O. Box 2511, Payson, Arizona, 85547, USA. (928) 978-6435, or visit:

www.iamamerica.com
www.loritoye.com

Graphic Design and Typography by Lori Toye
Editing by Dawn Abel, Elaine Cardall, Felicia Megdal, and Betsy Robinson

Love, in service, breathes the breath for all!

10 9 8 7 6 5 4 3 2 1

"Climb that mountain of the inner self!"

~ SAINT GERMAIN

Contents

FOREWORD *by Lori Toye* — XIX
PREFACE *by Lenard Toye* — XXI

CHAPTER ONE
Courage to Heal ♦ 25

Doubt and Spiritual Challenge 25
Expansion of Natural Law 26
Law of Attraction and Evolution of Divine Will 28
A Divine Leap 29
Law of Rhythm 30
Law of Surrender and Non-judgment 30
Law of Love 31
Take Action 33

CHAPTER TWO
The Inner Garden ♦ 35

We Are Awakening 35
Freedom Exchanges and Expands Energy 37

"Walk with Me" 39
"Now We Join as ONE" 40

CHAPTER THREE

Perfect Plan of Purity ♦ 43

The Consciousness of Choice 43
Crystiel, the Archangel of Clarity 45
You Will Always Be ONE 46
You Are Lighted by Acceptance 47
The Flower of Life 48

CHAPTER FOUR

Earth Healing ♦ 51

A Transmitter of Light 51
Time of Peace 51
Live the Law of Harmony 52
A Change of Heart 52
One Life 53
Cooperation, Choice, and Action 53
Assist the Acceleration 54
Karma Lifts, Joy Begins 55
Seventh Manu 55
Involution Equals Evolution 55

CHAPTER FIVE

Golden Ray, Stream Forth! ♦ 57

Spiritual Wealth 57
The New Environment 58
Light in Full Measure 58

Balancing the Dark Side 59
Experience and Choice 60
Call Upon the Golden Ray 60
Cleansing Karma, Facing Darkness 61
Law of Balance 61
Collective Consciousness 61
Use of the Violet Ray 62
Awareness and Vibration 63
Humanity's Scheme of Evolution 64
Vibration and the Gold Ray 65
The Next Step 65
A Lesson Learned 66
Call Upon the Violet Ray 67

CHAPTER SIX

Ascension of Consciousness • 69

Cause and Effect 69
Alignment and Harmony 69
"Love in Action" 70
Healing and the Ascension 71
Spiritual Education 71
Karmic Patterns 72
"The Reward Is Immeasureable" 72
Review Your Patterns 73
The Heart and Sacred Fire 73
Beyond Illusion 74
Invoke the Flame 74
Taming Emotions 74

Growth through Experience 75
The Mighty I AM Presence........................76
The Awakening Point 76
Beyond the Physical 77
The Ascension Process 78
Ascension and Diet 78
Divine Love 79
Action and the Violet Flame 80
Emotional Attachments 80
Energy for Energy 81
Emotions and the Violet Flame 82

CHAPTER SEVEN

All Is Love ♦ 83

The Violet Ray 83
A Fresh Perspective.............................84
Choice and the Process of Change 84
Karma and the Violet Flame......................85
Fear and Love 86
Spiritual Growth through the Law of Love 86
Love Drives Evolution 87
Higher Love and Consciousness 88
Two Suns......................................89
The Ancestors..................................90
A Hidden, Guiding Planet 92
The Non-dual Christ Force 93
Love, Consciousness, and Prophecy.................94

Possibility and Probability 94
"A Change of Heart" 95

CHAPTER EIGHT
The Master Within ♦ 97

The Metaphysical Law of Reciprocity 97
A Teacher Lifts Emotional Burden. 97
Gentle Leadership 99
Within the Silence 99
Out-picturing Perfection. 100
Integration, Compassion, and Enlightenment 100
Absolute Self-knowledge. 100
Opening the Heart 101
Choosing the Thought 101
Be Ready to Receive 102
Awaken the Master Within. 102
The Spiritual Paths 103
We Are Always ONE 105

CHAPTER NINE
The Mighty Violet Flame ♦ 107

Call the Flame into Activity 107
The Great Change. 108
Justice and the Violet Flame 109
Use of the I AM and the Violet Flame 110
Higher Vibration 112
The New Consciousness. 112
The Earth Plane and Planet. 113

The Heavenly Lords 114
A Plane of Consciousness 115
Beyond Imagination 115
Awakening from Darkness 116
Silicon-based Consciousness. 117
The Gift 117
Trust the Process 118
Interaction of the Elemental and Deva Kingdoms 119
Opening the Gate 119
Immersion into the Divine 120
Violet Flame Mantra 121
Judgment Is a Trap. 121

CHAPTER TEN

The Heart of Peace ♦ 123

All Events Are in the Divine Plan 123
The Time of Testing. 124
The Violet Flame and the Tube of Light 124
Evaluate Your Choices. 125
Rest in the Christ Consciousness 126
Keep the Flame of Love in Your Heart. 126
The Action of the Mighty Flame. 127
From the Inner to the Outer 128
Perception and Reality 129
The Loving Christ. 130
The Lower Frequency of Fear 131
Earth, Our Divine Mother 131
A Gentle Birth of Consciousness. 132

Stars of Golden City Vortices 133
The Gateway Point Masters 133
Temples of Consciousness. 134
Golden City Gateway Point Retreats 134
When the Student Is Ready. 135

CHAPTER ELEVEN
Unified Plane of Understanding ♦ 137
We Are by Your Side 137
A Simple Choice 138
The Mirror of Duality 138
Unite the Dual Forces 139
A Unified Plane. 140
From the Center Point. 141
For Those Who Suffer 142
Quieting Mind and Heart. 142
Groups of Seven 143
Forcefields and Momentum 144
Stars of Protection. 144
Focus and Discipline 145
Doorways of the Golden Cities 145
Many Masters of Service. 146
Activation 147
A New Energy. 147
The Great White Brotherhood and Sisterhood. 148
The Divine Temple. 148
Choice and Co-creation. 149
Beliefs 150

The Master Within.................................150
Tolerance 151

CHAPTER TWELVE
Science of Solutions ♦ 153

Preparing the Mind...............................153
Building Consciousness...........................153
The I AM Presence................................154
Camaraderie on the Path 155
Crisis and Problems..............................156
Problem and Solution Are ONE 156
Juxtaposition of Perception 157
Conscious Recognition 157
Removing Blocks with the Violet Flame 158
Solution Comes with Many Choices.................158
Empowerment through the I AM.....................159
Shifting Negative into Positive..................160
Awakening Divinity...............................160
The Work...161
Infectious Optimism 161
Paradigm of Twelve...............................162
Learning through Levels of Consciousness.........162
Pluto, an Ancient Moon...........................163
The Two Suns 162
Sunday Peace Meditation 164
Golden Star Mudra................................164
Earth Healing through the Golden Cities 165

CHAPTER THIRTEEN

I AM Awareness • 167

Vibration and Consciousness 167
You Create Your Vibration 168
When Life "Happens" 169
Balance 169
Relationship of Consciousness to Spiritual Growth 170
The Power of the Great I AM 170
Harmony's Blessings 171
I AM Awareness 171
The Interconnectivity of the I AM 172
Cultivate Tolerance and Patience 173
Call Forth the I AM Awareness 174
Divinity Exists in All Things 175
Out-picturing, Focus, and the Universal Flow 176
Pain, the Equalizer 176

CHAPTER FOURTEEN

Eternal Balance • 179

Law of Correspondence 179
The Clarity of the Teaching 180
"The Difference Is Experience" .180
Compassion and the Open Heart 181
Beyond "Right" or "Wrong" 181
Love for All 182
The Law of Forgiveness 182
Spiritual Stagnation 183
Wahanee and the Violet Flame 183

The Schools of Light.............................184
The First Seven Golden Cities......................185
Forgiveness and Perception 186
Golden City Activations............................187
Divine Intervention of the Golden Cities.............188

SPIRITUAL LINEAGE OF THE VIOLET FLAME	191
GLOSSARY	193
APPENDIX A: Saint Germain, the Holy Brother	217
APPENDIX B: Lord Sananda	221
APPENDIX C: Inner Garden Meditation Technique	223
APPENDIX D: El Morya	225
APPENDIX E: The Violet Flame	227
APPENDIX F: Prayers from the Ascended Masters	229
APPENDIX G: Decrees	235
APPENDIX H: The Gold Ray	237
APPENDIX I: Sunday Peace Meditation	239
APPENDIX J: Write and Burn Technique	243
APPENDIX K: Step-down Transformer	245
APPENDIX L: Mother Mary, Archetype of the Feminine	247
APPENDIX M: Mantra	251
DISCOGRAPHY	253
INDEX	255
ABOUT LORI AND LENARD TOYE	275
ABOUT I AM AMERICA	280

Foreword

I have yet to experience a trance channeled lesson from Saint Germain that does not include essential instruction and suggestions regarding the use and application of the Violet Flame. Throughout our many years of working together, this revered Spiritual Master of the Violet Flame has shared numerous insights, esoteric knowledge and wisdom, along with practical "how to" advice on accessing and applying this miraculous energy of rejuvenation, strength, and spiritual fortification.

The Violet Flame is the holy invocation of God's sublime transmutative energy of forgiveness and transfiguration for past mistakes and the misuse of our Divine Co-creative Energy. The Violet Flame is used as a decree, sometimes spoken with force as fiat, applied in creative visualization or in silent meditation, or internally directed through our energy system as a vibrant breath technique. Its metaphysical provenance is ancient, and this magnificent spiritual practice is credited with burning away the negative psychic residue left from harmful epochs on Earth experienced in both the times of Lemuria and Atlantis. Since the energies of the Violet Flame can induce a point of transition to a new octave of pure, unadulterated God force, the dynamic spiritual fire prompts the miraculous, transmuting power of Spiritual Alchemy. This valuable life changing strength has been used by many of the spiritual avatars and adepts of the ages, and is the treasured connection to humanity's evolution, transcendence, and spiritual liberation engendered in the Ascension Process. In the *I AM America Teachings* it is claimed that the essence of this sacred fire is held on the altar of the ethereal Temple of Mercy, placed eons ago by the Elohim Arcturus and Diana. The lineage of the Violet Flame in the *I AM America Teachings* is held through the compassion and mercy of Kuan Yin, and the transformation and alchemy of Saint Germain. This book of selected teachings shares numerous insights and teachings of how to apply this essential and ageless wisdom.

This collection of spiritual teachings that you are about to read also includes a selection of important prayers, numerous decrees, meditation techniques, and specific spiritual practices designed to hone and perfect your spiritual light. The first lesson begins the essential instruction of how to enter the solace of the Inner Garden. You will also learn how to identify repeating karmic patterns and release them through invaluable write-and-burn techniques. As each spiritual practice and method is revealed, your inner and outer light evolves, and you will advance into a seasoned Step-down Transformer of the Gold Ray. The service of the Gold Ray assists humanity's Great Awakening, and shepherds our Earth Mother—also known as Babajeran—into the wonder of the New Times.

Most importantly, apply and practice the valuable knowledge contained in this soul-freeing assemblage of teachings. Seasoned mystics and Spiritual Masters alike state, "Truth is not told . . . it is *learned*." Engage and develop a daily spiritual practice and gain the most valuable commodity of spiritual growth—vital, essential, personal *experience*.

Love and Blessings,
Lori Toye

"Let the wise hear and increase in learning,
and the one who understands obtains guidance."
Proverbs 1:5

"What is the difference? The difference is experience!"
~ *Lord Sananda*

Preface

This book is a compilation of *I AM America* spiritual techniques that can help you to achieve Ascension. As you perfect each practice, the methods set up dynamic energies that create new HU-man brain connections. These important energetic networks are never-ending and are retained even if your Ascension is not fully realized in your current lifetime. Should you choose re-embodiment, your soul will pick up where you left off with these vital soul-freeing systems still intact. These are the unique and complex soul-structures that guarantee the rebirth of great souls and Avatars to teach and free humanity. Remember, this is a step-by-step process that assures your Ascension.

Throughout the years I have had the opportunity to meet many different types of spiritual students. I remember Ray, an older gentleman who thought that everything in life should be, "easy." He also preached the "Law of Attraction." Unfortunately, his expectations always fell a bit short and he was constantly dissatisfied with his consequential outcomes. The Ascended Master precept of Energy for Energy was a vague concept for him. The fruit that he harvested was indeed effortless to produce, but it was tasteless and lacked the spiritual nourishment he desired. When you are cultivating a spiritual technique be sure to weed out impatience, develop devotion, and don't forget the rich nutrients found in diligence and persistence.

Does being a good and decent person grant one the Ascension? Undoubtedly, good karma helps one along the spiritual path, but the sole practice of "love and light" seems a bit incomplete. Spiritual practice is engaged to help us deal with reality, to retrieve the memory of our immortal soul, and to activate the process of balancing our karmas—both good and bad. This, too, is the hidden knowledge found in the Law of Energy for Energy. There is a lot of work involved in being "good" or "bad." The goal of an astute spiritual practitioner is the *balance* of karmic forces. According to the Ascended Masters this is the conscious state of harmony.

Right now, the time we are experiencing and will continue for thousands of years is the promised Golden Age. During this period the Gold Ray bathes our planet with spiritually nourishing light from the Great Central Sun, and the worldwide Golden Cities calibrate and expand these beneficial energies. This is a rare and precious anomaly and spiritually invaluable. This is humanity's *Time of Ascension* and the Time is Now! The techniques described in this compilation of teachings are designed to fortify and strengthen this light throughout your light bodies, accelerate your Ascension Process, and free you from the endless rounds of reincarnation.

This book is a workbook of how to begin a spiritual practice. I suggest you identify the spiritual techniques that you resonate with and find simple to apply. After you've gained confidence with one or two techniques, build your practice to include a bit more. If you have difficulty with meditation and cannot turn off your thoughts, find a picture of a beautiful landscape and hang it on the wall where you sit and can view. As you observe the picture imagine yourself in the setting ... sitting near a rock, tree, or stream ... maybe place a small bed of flowers ... or, a cottage or cabin. As you gaze into the picture, place whatever mind construct that engages your consciousness into the landscape. Yes, this takes practice. This activity stills your mind in a manner like meditation. And in the soft stillness, your brain responds to your landscape meditation, builds new brain connections and engages a new spiritual network.

I suggest you speak Violet Flame Decrees aloud. When you state your intention, the sound resonates into your aura. Your light fields continue to attract the transmutation of the Violet Flame for many hours after you have applied the decree. There are many different Violet Flame decrees in this book to choose from. The most effective Violet Flame method is repeating the decree seven times seven, for forty-nine times, total. This process effectually treats the seven chakras and the seven layers of the human aura. But don't believe a word I say, as Saint Germain states, "Take it unto the laboratory of self." Through your own personal experience, you will begin to know; and knowledge, through discipline and discernment, becomes wisdom. Philosophers often affirm, "Knowledge comes, but Wisdom lingers."

In the Light of God that never fails,

Lenard Toye

CHAPTER ONE

Courage to Heal
*Saint Germain and Sananda
on the healing process.*

Greetings, in that mighty Christ Light. I AM Saint Germain and I request permission to come forth into your energy fields.

Response: "Please come forward, Dear one."

DOUBT AND SPIRITUAL CHALLENGE

In the work upon the Earth Plane and Planet it would appear at times that you are conforming to meet with what another one desires but those who have entered this path of Mastery know this path is narrow and yet so focused. We request and ask that each of you, chelas and students of this mighty path of Mastery, always remain upon this path and understand that your asking is also your choosing. Many of you have wondered, "Is this the proper choice? Is this the proper way that I shall go?" Understand, Dear ones, that when you remain true and solid with that inner voice, that mighty I AM streams forth to bring Divine Laws of Manifestation. Remain true to that Source, that inner source that gives you the refreshment that never fails.

Many of you become questioning, "Is what I am hearing true? Is what I am hearing proper? Is what I am hearing a truthful connection to that mighty I AM?" Even your doubt instigates a moment that will separate you from that internal wellspring of information, power, and authority that shall lead you into the victory of the Ascension of the mighty I AM. Please, Dear chelas, understand that conformity is also another form of doubting that mighty inner strength. So take the time, pull back for a minute when you are doubting and call your mighty I AM Presence into its eternal and infinite action. There you will find that this power, this Divine Authority, is ready and willing always to give you that capitulation into the world of the Ascended Master.

Yes, the path of the Ascended Master is a narrow and disciplined focus but you are the student who is willing to take that mighty leap. There are few trails that lead to what we call the highest mountains of the Himalayas. They are narrow trails and filled with many rocks and crevices. Around the corner you go and the trail becomes narrower and narrower and you notice above you, a peak that pierces above the cloud and sees all—the mighty all-seeing Eye of God. You have no choice but to climb that challenging trail. Then would you consider another route? Of course not, Dear students and chelas, for that is the only route to obtain that peak.

When the inner voice speaks to you and asks you to complete or to go and challenge that being within yourself, that being so wants his Mastery and freedom in the Light of God that Never Fails that he is asked, in a sense, to travel this narrow path. Would you at any time divert from your heart's desire so deep within? Dear ones, forget this foolishness and stay upon this path. Climb what we shall call that mountain of the inner self. Pierce above the clouds and go into the all-seeing Eye of God.

EXPANSION OF NATURAL LAW

Our discourse for the day shall address what we call the courage to heal, for each one of you, when traveling this narrow path, forgets that it takes much strength and courage to call upon this path of Ascended Mastery. Ascended Mastery addresses not only the Mastery of natural law but addresses a Mastery, so that you may ascend out of this world of illusion. Ascended Mastery takes you into a world where you shall know the glories of the heavens. These laws shall set you free from the cycle of death. The courage to heal is the courage to live, for then you shall make that internal commitment or decision and say "I no longer accept death as part of my pattern."

> Away with death and mighty world come alive!
> In the breath of I AM, I command this!

Do you see, Dear one, when you call that mighty I AM Presence into action, you are then applying what we call the infinite and eternal laws of all of creation? Yes, there are laws that address your planet and these are called the natural laws. For instance, if you are to take ice and place it in the sun, it melts. This is a natural law. You have observed this and now you know this. Your consciousness has accepted this as a reality. What about the ice that can stay in the Sun and never turn into the pool of water but sustains its focus in whatever condition it may find itself in? That is a law that has taken a natural law and extended it into the principle of all being. In this principle of all being is the law that understands that all that is contained streams forth from a mighty universal principle, a cosmic law.

These cosmic laws lead us on to what we call a Mastery of the natural law. This moves onward to the law that serves the Divine Will and knows only the breath of the mighty I AM. Each one of you has seen how energy arcs from one point to another. This has been shown through your use of electricity upon the planet. Has not each of you understood how energy arcs to your own beloved mighty lifestream? This arcs through what we call the mighty I AM Presence and it is this I AM Presence that allows your own heart to beat.

Planted within your heart is that Unfed Flame of Love, Wisdom, and Power. This is known throughout many eons as that mighty Monad. This is the receptor of the blessings from the I AM Presence. It is only through your conscious call and conscious effort that this mighty Monad, the Unfed Flame of Love, Wisdom, and Power, can expand into the infinite eternal light and lift you into what we call the Laws of Ascended Mastery.

Of course, as you have been sent on a mission from your mighty I AM Presence, you have Mastered many natural laws. Many of you have understood how to control temperature. Many of you have understood how to make your way in this world, keeping your bodies clothed, keeping your vehicles running, and having a certain adeptship of the mind and Mastery of experience. The time has come upon the Earth Plane and Planet that the evolution of humanity is at stake.

Sacred Fire 27

Who shall be that noble one that will say there is another law that supersedes the natural, sensate law that can only see, touch, feel, and smell. The time has come for that stalwart being, whoever he or she may be, to take these natural laws and understand the underlying principle and expand them into Ascended Mastery Laws. Now you have known these throughout history as being occult laws but for reference and the belief system of humanity at this moment, we shall call these the Ascended Mastery Laws.

LAW OF ATTRACTION AND EVOLUTION OF DIVINE WILL

One of these first laws that understands the courage to heal is known as the Law of Attraction. You attract to yourself as you think. It is only through this thinking mechanism that any energy force comes to you. All moneys that come to you, all situations that come to you, all events, joyful or sorrowful that come to you, come through this natural occult law called the Law of Attraction. This is a law that we ask for you to command and demand by what we shall call arcing energy through the mighty I AM Presence to the receptor or receiver of life, the Monad, the flame in the heart.

The chela who has the courage to heal, accepts responsibility for all events that have occurred within his life. He realizes that through conscious and unconscious activity, that he has attracted all events to him. He accepts this responsibility by understanding that each one of these events has performed what we call a service to the Divine Will. Every event of your life, when you accept this grander plan of Mastery, this grander plan of law, understands the Divine Will underlying everything that occurs within that lifestream's continuum of experience.

The courage to heal is the one who understands that he is not a victim, that he is truly and absolutely a Co-creator with his life. The courage to heal is one who understands that things do not happen to him but things happen with him. Now granted, I use this word him in addressing all genders of life. I hope this will bring a greater understanding to you, Dear chelas of mine. Because the courage to heal is one who recognizes that a grander plan faces this planet, please consider this Law of Attraction and then you may accept your healing.

A DIVINE LEAP

Now let me discuss healing. It is that magical transformational moment when Alchemy occurs, or what is called a miracle. You shift your thought and leap from one plane of reality into another plane of reality. Please understand that all experiences stream from the focus of your thought. When your focus and your thought are being fed by the mighty I AM Presence, your thoughts only create what we call a perfected experience. Shifting your thought from one plane of existence to another plane of existence requires but one leap. That leap sincerely and absolutely asks for you to become Co-creators and the mighty Divine Inheritors of this kingdom.

Now suppose there was a ruler of a great kingdom and he had four bags of gold. Would he keep one of these bags of gold away from his sons and daughters, his inheritors? Of course not. He would give each bag to inheritors of this kingdom. He would give them that opportunity to use all that is in and within the kingdom that they are part of. Now you are a part of this kingdom and you are given every opportunity that is available here. You, Dear ones, have risen in a sense to this occasion and you have come to this point where you are being given an opportunity to learn another set of laws.

The courage to heal takes a great mind. It is a mind that is willing to shift at any given point, to adjust a perception, to bring forth a series of events or experiences that leads one into a greater union and harmony with being and the rest of creation. This is a simple task but harder when one has a hoe in his hand. To look across this garden and see a few acres that need to be perfected, hoed, and weeded takes one who is willing, day by day, earnestly taking this task, earnestly and rhythmically.

LAW OF RHYTHM

The second natural law is the Law of Rhythm. Everything happens in an order and in a timeliness and we would suggest that all that you do in understanding these Ascended Master Laws is to take a course of rhythm. Those chelas who walk that path to obtain that peak, to pierce above the cloud, and to be the all-seeing student of God, are ones who realize that step by step they have established a rhythm. In that rhythm is a momentum and from that momentum is the infinite source of energy that is ever present.

Have you not noticed that when you do not have a steady and constant rhythm in your life that an element of dysfunction and chaos then follows? It is time to take a rhythm, Dear students and chelas, for this is one of the Ascended Master Laws. All that occurs upon the Earth Plane and Planet and within this mighty universe is the Law of Rhythm. Those who have the courage to heal will understand that their healing will occur in an infinite rhythm.

LAW OF SURRENDER AND NON-JUDGMENT

Now, the third law we will discuss is the shifting of the perception of healing. It is a harder law for the human to understand but it is one of the most important. It is the Law of Surrender and Non-judgment. This is the one law that will pierce above all illusions of your separation with your mighty I AM Source. Take a chance. Take a risk, Dear student. Leap beyond what you do not know and fall into the loving arms of the universe, for you are of it and it is of you. Inside your being is contained every planet of this cosmos and outside your being is every planet of this cosmos. Understand that—as above so below—inside you are, outside it is. How can we activate this mighty law? Only through surrendering to it and allowing it to be without a judgment.

To give up what we would say the preconceived notion of what God is, is the greatest gift that any human can achieve. God is everything. God is within all. Every ordered event that happens throughout the cosmos is an event of perfection, for when you give up this idea that you must judge anything, you accept Divine

Perfection in all. You hold what Beloved Mary has always called an Immaculate Conception of all beings and all things within creation. You then accept this gift of creation given to you—a Divine Inheritor. You have all four bags of gold. Do you understand how these laws all merge to bring forth a great synergy that allows you to heal. The courage to heal rests within these three Ascended Mastery concepts. Do you have questions?

Response: "No, Dear one."

I shall take my leave at this time and I would like to introduce Beloved Brother Sananda.

Sananda steps forward.

Greetings, Dear children of the Golden Flame. I AM Sananda and I carry the Dove of Peace within my heart. As usual, Dear ones, I must ask permission to come forth.

Response: "Please, Dear one, come forward."

LAW OF LOVE

I am most thankful for Beloved Saint Germain's discourse outlining these laws of how you may heal. Perhaps my largest concern is that one law of the universe, which is the Law of Love. How many times have you heard this? Over and over we give this law: Love one another. Perhaps you, Dear Brothers and Sisters, are understanding love at another place than we understand the Law of Love.

Law of Love rests within the surrender of the being to the infinite ALL. For the Christ Consciousness to come within your heart, one must be willing to accept another completely and absolutely as oneself. You are an extension of me and that is why I come to give you this information, for you are me and I am you. Do you understand that every step you take is a step you take with me? Do you understand that every word, prose, and comment that comes from your mouth are my words. We all beat as one great mighty Oneship.

You separate yourself by saying I can only love this person with these particular conditions and agreements and I can only love another with these particular conditions and agreements. How can you love your little finger more than your middle finger? Do you not need both fingers to make your hand function? How can you love your foot more than you love your throat? Don't you need your foot and your throat to function? See this extended body as ONE body. Your Brother and your Sister are you. You are your Brother and your Sister. This is the Law of Love.

All material and energy and being that surround you is you, the bed that you sleep in, the chair that you sit on, the food that you eat. Dear ones, these are all extensions of that mighty you. Beloved Mother Mary has discussed what we call the Anugramic Universe. We would ask for you to review the content of this material, for you will never understand how thought creates until you put to use that mighty principle that underlies all creation. That is that principle of love.

Love is that principle of intention. It is a principle that intends to let all be what it is: supreme, absolute, wonderful energy of the Source. You are all one body of light. You are all one planet. You are all one mighty hierarchy. When you understand this and experience this day by day by day, you will then begin to understand and Master these first three laws that Beloved Saint Germain has given to you. Uplift humanity . . . exercise your faith . . . love not only through what you see but love through your hands that are willing to do . . . and take a plan into absolute action. Do you understand?

Response: "Yes."

I shall take my leave from your frequency and I thank you and hold you in the golden light of the ONE.

Response: "I thank you also. I AM you."

TAKE ACTION

Greetings, Beloved chelas, I Am Saint Germain and before we close this discourse, I would like to remind you of those mighty laws known as the Twelve Jurisdictions. Each one of those laws is a law that you may call into action through your mighty I AM Presence. Each one of those has the potential and the opportunity to lift burdens from your life. If you feel you do not have enough money, call upon this Law of Abundance:

> Mighty I AM, stream forth the abundance
> that is needed for me to fulfill the Divine Plan.
> Let this plan stream forth for the best and
> highest good for all those concerned.

It is the same if you are suffering from a sense of disharmony. Call upon your Laws of Harmony and Cooperation. If you feel weak, call upon your Laws of Faith. If you feel harried, call upon your Laws of Stillness. If you feel unfulfilled, call upon your Laws of Creation. Each one of these laws is a law that is given to you as an opportunity to feast here in this kingdom. Please use them, as they will bring such a delight and wonderful effect into your life. Please use them, as they can lift you from any trying circumstance.

As Beloved Sananda has said: you are ONE with the Source. And the time has come to stop your suffering. All it takes is that action by you, commanding and demanding your I AM Presence to handle all circumstances through these mighty laws. What can be much simpler? Are you tired of the struggling? Are you tired of the strife? Then lift yourself into the radiance of the Ascended Master Law, for there you shall be set free.

> Death to the old way of doing things!
> All life come alive with the vibrant efficiency
> of the Divine Plan, almighty I AM!

The courage to heal lies with the one who has the courage to see this, to say this, and now to do this. I also encourage you, Dear chelas, to remember your rhythmic use of the Violet Flame. This law will gain a mighty momentum in your life and will lift you into the glory and freedom of the Ascension.

Remember, you are walking this path because you have chosen to do so. Stay firm and strong in that choice and you shall never fail. I shall take my leave from you now, Dear students. Bless all that you come in contact with today. Send them the radiance of the Ascended Master's Law of Love. Accept all who are around you. Love all who are around you and remember always that I am here to uplift mankind and you are held within that mighty law. I AM Saint Germain.

[Editor's Note: For information regarding decrees and their use, see Appendix G.]

CHAPTER TWO

The Inner Garden
Teaching from Saint Germain and Sananda.

Welcome, my Beloved chelas. I AM Saint Germain and I stream forth on that mighty Violet Ray of Mercy and Forgiveness. This Violet Ray is that mighty ray of service and as usual, Dear hearts, I ask permission to come forth into your energy fields.

Response: "Please, Dear one, come forward."

Greetings, in that mighty Christ. I AM Saint Germain and today we shall discourse on that known as freedom of service. The time comes upon the Earth Plane and Planet when those who have the eyes to see and the ears to hear will open them and say, "I have a great freedom in my heart." This great freedom is indeed a choice. It is a choice that leads one to say, "I have a destiny as an immortal being of light and I also have a destiny that is here to serve." You, Dear chelas, are to bring this service to the Earth Plane and Planet for the Spiritual Awakening is at hand among those of humanity.

WE ARE AWAKENING

There are those who are awakening at all different levels, at all different times. You say among yourselves, "Well, I am here to serve this and I am here to serve that." Dear ones, I remind you that you are here to serve that vast and mighty ALL . . . I AM. There are many who are awakening, shall we say, at levels where they only wish discovery of their past lives. There are also those who are awakening to find out what is the true nature of God. There are others upon awakening say, "Buddha is my path . . . Christ is my path . . . Mary is my path . . . and even I am your path." Those who come are those who are ready to honor that great Flame of Freedom within their hearts, which is the flame that has held the continuum for spiritual development and evolution upon the Earth Plane and Planet.

You, Dear ones, are called to expand your aggregate body of light. As this aggregate body of light expands, one naturally encounters that great Flame of Freedom, that mighty Monad that carries the blueprint of your spiritual evolution. In this time upon the Earth Plane and Planet, we ask those who are aware of this mighty Monad, Flame of Freedom within their hearts, to serve. Hold a space for the evolution of your Brothers and Sisters. Of course, there are times that you weary with that which you would seem to be detailed and endless stories about another one's evolution to this spiritual work. We ask you, Dear ones, to have patience.

Offer yourself as that true healer and teacher of the esoteric law. We ask you to be as we have been. Listen with an open ear. Keep an open mind, for all energy brought to you is also energy that will free you from your own bondage. It is the same as when you offer yourself to do what we shall call this healing work. Each time that you exchange in energetic work, you also receive full benefit of the healing energy surrounding you and the recipient. Each time you hear these continuous stories, they expand your own vision, adeptship, and ability to serve the great cause of spiritual freedom upon this Earth Plane and Planet.

It has been a long journey, Dear chelas. We realize that at times you feel tired and worn but as we review the history of this great Monad upon the Earth Plane and Planet, you will see a great continuum. Soon a leap, a quantum leap, into a mighty consciousness will free all upon the Earth Plane and Planet. This will be known as the shining star of freedom. You, Dear ones, are chosen in this sense, to alert those upon the Earth Plane and Planet that this Spiritual Awakening is at hand. This is not a time for fear but a time for courage and strength. It is also a time for love and a time for compassion.

The hierarchy of the Great White Brotherhood and Sisterhoods of Light dispensed the I AM America material as early as 1983 and 1984, to be used as an awakening tool and to call for those who would feel this vibrational frequency and ready themselves to walk into that great Monad of freedom. "So what is freedom?" You may ask yourself. "If I am so awakened and ready to do, what is freedom?"

FREEDOM EXCHANGES AND EXPANDS ENERGY

There are many freedoms, Dear ones, but at its best, freedom represents balanced energy that exchanges from the inner to the outer. When we say, "As above, so below," we are honoring that Law of Freedom. There is an equal exchange always in freedom and there is never a suppression but rather a demonstration of expansion. Freedom is also that natural law that allows a continuous consciousness to expand among the species. If you were to view yourself as a species for one moment, you would see that you too have gone through a great expansion or freeing of energy. When we speak of the idea of free energy, we are not necessarily addressing what you know as a technique. However, we are addressing what is a Law of Consciousness.

Freedom constantly and steadily expands energy and is held with what we call that Law of the Best and Highest Good. For you, Dear ones, are made in the image and likeness of God I AM and the expansion of energy proves your mighty divineship. Freedom is also seen throughout many of the natural and esoteric laws. It is continuous and ever present. However, we have noted that during the last 2,000 years of mankind's epoch upon this Earth Plane and Planet, they have Mastered building many walls against this law. As this trumpet sounds, it is the law that takes apart these walls brick by brick and you expand into that mighty Oneship that is that Law of Freedom.

The highest application to understand at this time with a third dimensional body is that this mighty application of freedom shall raise you into that Ascension of light and sound and, yes, to expand the mighty energy, your God-given energy. First, expand it through service to your Brother and Sister. This is the concept of the Seventh Ray and it is also this concept that Beloved Kuan Yin so perfected upon the Earth Plane and Planet. It is the concept that I have worked towards as a perfection of diplomacy. Find the expression and individualization of your form of service upon the Earth Plane and Planet, Dear chelas. Then you can raise your consciousness and vibration with this mighty Seventh Ray and honor the Law of Freedom.

First, allow our Brothers and Sisters absolute expression and allow their expression without your judgment. Allow them to release their expression. Allow their release without your judgment. During this time upon the Earth Plane and Planet, there are many characteristics of suppression, characteristics that you see demonstrated through disease and through layers or levels of chaos. Crime and pestilence run through your streets, your newspapers, and from mankind's mouths. Are these then not ways that suppression, or that wall–brick by brick–is taken apart? Applaud, Dear chelas, and realize that as each brick is taken down, two are taken down for the expansion of the mighty Monad of consciousness. If you have questions, Dear ones, I am now available.

Response: "There are no questions, my love."

Now I should like to step back and welcome Beloved Brother Sananda.

Welcome, my Dear children of the Golden Flame. I AM Sananda and I request permission to come forth and bring this teaching.

Response: "Come forward, Dear Brother and Master."

These teachings of this Flame of Freedom can also be simply stated as that teaching of that mighty Circle of Oneship, for as these bricks are taken down one by one, there is also this great circle that extends. That flame within each one of you that you share, now becomes a flame that is ONE flame. As you ready for the vibrational frequency of Unana, let me tell you–each one of you–allow your healership to move in, through, and around you. Healership is not only to participate in a constant and steady demonstration but healership is indeed a consciousness. It is a thought, feeling, and action that always blends within the world that you live. It is taking that peace that you feel as you travel to the infinite garden and valley of life and carrying that with you always. Your healership becomes your seamless garment and vibrational frequency of service.

"WALK WITH ME"

Come with me, Dear children, to this garden. Walk with me for one moment. Do you not hear the birds singing, the slight breeze in the trees, the scent of roses, honeysuckle, and lilac? Off to the background is the music of falling water. It is in this garden that each of us contacts that which Saint Germain calls that mighty Monad. It is there that each of us realizes that we are free to be as we are, infinite, holy, unioned. Yes, this is what we are, Dear children. We are placed within this garden to express with this Oneship, this Oneship that is healing in all vibration. As we travel in this garden, let us sit for a moment and observe. [Editor's Note: See Appendix C, *The Inner Garden Meditation Technique*.]

Are not all the sounds and frequencies harmonizing? Do not all components cooperate? Do you not feel a vortexing circle surrounding the vibration of your own garden? Are you not safe, secure, and serene?

This is the vibration of the healer, one who accepts all conditions as harmony within the world. If you perceive them as chaos, then let it be so. Let me assure you, Dear chelas, Brothers and Sisters of my heart, that if you would perceive every situation like the bird who sings in this garden, you will enter into that great freedom that expands consciousness and prepares the Oneship of Unana. Even as I pluck this fruit from this tree and I take a bite, inside there are seeds and pits. Do I perceive these as brick walls taken down one by one, each brick a problem, a toil, and a labor for me? Or do I see these seeds and pits exactly as they are, not hard masses of suppression but a great centralized focused energy that contains within it the potential to multiply and sprout this energy repeatedly. Have we not said, Dear students, that all is a self-perpetual energy? If you are having a problem in carrying the vibration and sustaining the consciousness of healership, return to the garden of freedom and remember this lesson.

A time comes upon the Earth Plane and Planet that the vibrational frequencies will all be raised. You will wonder at this time, when you were so separated from one another but you are all gathered as one great family and your consciousness enfolds that which you know as this Earth. Please do not see yourself separate, even from the most heinous crimes that you hear on the news but understand that he or she who has committed the crime is you. Understand that even the victim is you. This vibrational frequency is all here for you. It is your garden. Qualify it with a Mastery of consciousness and continue to hold that vibration of perfection and then all that you perceive will be as the trickling of water within your garden. Do you have questions, Dear one?

Response: "No. I thank you."

The mighty dove of peace is ready to land. Its breast is ready to arc that White Ray of Purity and crystal consciousness upon the Earth Plane and Planet. Archangel Crystiel is ready to bring forth the service of perfection for all who desire to hold this consciousness of healership. Are you ready, Dear ones, to face your infinite glory? Honor that mighty Law of Freedom. As Saint Germain has said, "I AM."

Saint Germain steps forward.

"NOW WE JOIN AS ONE"

And now I return, Dear chelas. I AM Saint Germain and I thank you, Dear Brother Sananda. Dear ones, see us standing together, our arms around one another while we come through and individualize our consciousness to speak. Now we join as ONE. When these words come to the Earth Plane and Planet, "Mighty Christ I AM," you supposed through your perception that these are the words of Saint Germain. These mighty words travel through a Brotherhood and a Oneship. They travel as our arms, hands, and consciousness joined as ONE. Now, we have doubled the energy. Now, are we not an expression of free energy?

Consider this, Dear children, Dear students, who so desire their Ascension, just for this day, with all that you encounter, consider your union and Oneship with them. Consider the mighty Laws of Freedom and how they will expand the consciousness for you and your neighbor, this one who joins their hand with yours.

Each one of the Vortices of the planet is prepared to accept this grander consciousness that serves the destiny of freedom. Practice this today and see and feel for yourself its vibrational effect. It is a consciousness that is, of course, Alchemical and lifts the vibrational fields into that mighty Oneship of light and sound.

If you are having trouble with your judgment, use the laws of science ingrained in you. They are designed to bridge the physical world into that world of the true spirit. Consider that your aggregate body of light is the same as your neighbor's aggregate body of light. Consider that all is light and all is sound and then you will be able to accept your Oneship.

> I AM ONE with my Brother and Sister,
> I AM ONE with the Spiritual Awakening of humanity,
> I AM ONE in the service of the breath, light, and sound.
> I AM this mighty law manifest–Freedom!

I AM Saint Germain. Hitaka!

CHAPTER THREE

Perfect Plan of Purity
*Saint Germain, Archangel Chrystiel,
and Mary on the Eighth Ray.*

Greetings Beloved Children. I AM Sanctus Germanus, the Holy Brother, and I ask your permission to come forward.

Response: "Always Dear Brother, come forth."

It is again that we bring balance to this perfect plan of purity. It is again that we bring forth the great compassion, the great heartfelt yearnings, the great desire of all perfection coming forward. It is once again that the Monad, that is ONE, comes forward. And now we ask you to give this Monad its choice—the choice of perfection.

THE CONSCIOUSNESS OF CHOICE

The choice that we have spoken of as service is a service of perfection of desire. It is truly this perfection that comes forward in your daily lives of thought, in your daily lives of feeling, in your daily lives of action. It is this perfection, this focus, that we ask you to consider as being your heart, as being your desire, as being your action. You and I and all on this planet are ONE Monad, and it is the individual expression of this Monad that gives service to the consciousness of choice. It is the personal expression that you and I have individually chosen, that all our Brothers and Sisters express and act upon in accordance to this Divine Monadic Activity.

Through the perfection of choice is brought this balanced harmony. For as one fits to the other, for as one expresses to the other, so too does this balanced harmony bring forth the great desire of Unana. It is the Oneness that we all truly desire. It is the ONE thought, the ONE feeling, the ONE action, the ONE breath, the ONE Light that we truly are.

Our service comes to this awakening and it is a step-by-step path each of us takes. As you step from one step to another for the higher expansion, look about you and see those who have found the step with you. Look through the great garden ... look through these great mountain ranges ... look through these great expressions of this planetary thought, feeling, and action. Look, feel, experience; it is this experience, one step at a time, that each of us brings to you for your consideration. Look, feel, and experience on your own; for then, you may in turn bring this to others. We, as this ONE Body of Light, this ONE Body of Thought, this ONE Body of Being, had this choice. In this choice we individualize, but the choice does not separate our family, does not separate our beingness. Choice only expands our family.
ONE LIGHT, ONE SOURCE

When you look to a molecule, there are many atoms, but it is one molecule. When you look to this one organ, there are many molecules, but it is one organ. When you look to this one human body, it is one body, but there are many organs, many molecules, and many atoms. Likewise, the ONE Monad that we are, is expressed in the same pattern. The one body, the one organ, and the molecules and atomic structures are all the expression of this ONE Body of Light. For as you come to this fulfillment, the fruit of this understanding is your only nutrition ... is your only expression ... is your only breath ... is your only understanding that all life is ONE. You are ONE body of this ONE Earth. You are ONE thought of the ONE spark of creation, the ONE Light. Consider that it is all of these expressed individually.

It is the choice of each to bring this expression to this outer experience, but the outer experience flows within and inner experience is still ONE. We ask you to reconsider again and again your Oneness. When you speak to your Brothers and your Sisters, this great Unana that you are is the expression that refocuses inward. It is through this expression that creation will flow once again back to the ONE Light, the ONE Source. In that flowing, there is truly a path. There are many steps; there are many experiences; there are many understandings. It is the fleet of foot who complete this path in a timely manner. It is only the great desire, the great inwardness, the great inner joy that brings this path to its fruitful expression.

Is it not that we plant the garden to reap the fruit? It is only the fruit, once again, that sustains the garden through its seed. The garden expands. So as this expands, so too does the consciousness, one step, one experience, one expansion at a time.

CRYSTIEL, THE ARCHANGEL OF CLARITY

Now, with your permission, I ask you to accept this imprinted pattern that brings forward this Eighth Ray. This furthers the great arcing energy of the pure angelic realm, which contains and sustains the focus of all beingness. I ask you to accept our Dear one, our Dear Brother, whom you know as the great Angel Crystiel. The clarity of service, that which makes all clear in its crystal purity, I ask you to accept this great love of expression. For each Ray is an expression of this Monad; each Ray is an understanding of the quality that the consciousness may take in this focus. You, I, all creation are Unana, the ONE.

Response: "Welcome Beloved Crystiel."

Dear one, I AM Crystiel, the Archangel of the clarity of thought, of action, and of feeling; the clarity that brings to the full octave the understanding that all cycles have completion and sustainment in this cycle. With your permission, may we bring this completion of cycle, so that the seed of this cycle is completed?

Response: "You have permission. So Be It."

In the perfection that you are, that all creation is, is the clear understanding that the expressions are choice, and the expression of choice brings forward the comprehension of consciousness. However, comprehension is only one vibration or rate of spin, just as feeling is only one vibration or rate of spin. It is the integration, the blending, the Oneness of each of these expressive patterns that you call light, sound, breath, life, thought, action, and feeling. These too are contained in each of the Rays. These too are contained within each other, and so there is always the balance that is maintained.

It is the clear expression of this eighth octave that brings its cycle to its completion, and in this completion, all life comes forward with the clear balance of choice, with the clear balance of desire, with the clear balance of feeling, with the clear balance of action. For it is this Eighth Ray that brings the golden clarity of light, life, thought, feeling, action, Oneness, breath, infinitely to be sustained. One chooses to express on a Ray until this balance is sustained, this harmony is sustained, this plan of Unana is sustained. It has been in these choices of expression that the Oneness has been, as you would say, neglected. It is in these choices of expression that the Source, that deep river as you call it, the root, the vine of all, has been neglected.

If you look to all you have brought forth in your life, many like yourself, and we who have traveled the same path as well, have neglected to see and to experience all from the perspective of the Source. It is in this choice that you have brought forth each and everyone to this planet. It is in this choice that this neglect and separateness have grown in the consciousness. In the expression of lower energetic pattern there is no need to be separate, for it is only an expression.

YOU WILL ALWAYS BE ONE

So this Ray that now comes forward and anchors its seed in your heart of hearts, anchors its seed in your Monadic Flame, that comes forward and now completely expresses on the final holographic pattern of your perfected self, brings all this creation full circle again. From this moment on, you will always remember. From this moment on, you will always be ONE. You will see, you will think, you will feel, you will act, you will breathe, you will experience all from this focus of ONE.

Golden clarity is the decree of this Eighth Ray. It is the decree of this focus that all creation, whether you think it is the most evolved or the least evolved, is now aware of its Source. No longer will this separation come forward. No longer will the expression on your plane of consciousness in this planet of perfection be separate from Source. It is decreed in this moment that none shall forget. This has always been the plan, and as you are now ONE, so are we, so am I, so is all creation ONE; this ONE focus, this ONE beingness, this ONE expression. All angels are now here. We are available for every question.

Response: "Thank you Beloved Archangel Crystiel. One question: How is it that we can all best serve the awakening of humanity and bring forth a consciousness of healing for all upon the planet?"

YOU ARE LIGHTED BY ACCEPTANCE

The pivotal word for your consciousness is acceptance. This word of acceptance—to allow, to not judge, to accept the "Be-ingness" of all—is a pivotal point in the expansion of your consciousness. Acceptance is a consideration for all non-judgment to flow. As your Beloved Brother has brought forth to you the Laws of Non-judgment for the expansion of consciousness, it is a tiny seed of compassion that accepts all human frailty. All that you consider dark, all that you consider wrong, evil, or inappropriate is just an expression. As one can make a choice, so too can this choice change second by second in your world. It is the acceptance that each expresses, what they comprehend and experience.

That which you call dark may be instantaneously lighted by your own acceptance. That which you call wrong may be instantaneously balanced by your own acceptance. In this pattern, the conflicts, the walls that diminish the freedom, collapse. In this pattern, the separation dissolves. For in this pattern, the joy that you all are expresses.

There are times in your path when you will stand forward and firm and not accept, but in the not accepting, you must only hold the focus of your own chosen creation and allow the focus of another's chosen creation; for each chosen creation may not harmonize, but each chosen creation must be allowed. If these choices reach further through the Law of Acceptance, which is your natural law, the higher Law of Non-judgment may take root. As this higher Law of Non-judgment takes root, it flowers, and the great fragrance that you find in your garden will be expressed in your outer world.

We ask you to consider that the greatest service to be brought at this moment is this natural law, for all to accept and allow individuals and groups to be as they are. Also know that it is your choice for your own path that you may also accept. Come forward now, Dear ones, in your daily lives! Let the breath, the spirit, the light, the life of all creation come forward in this natural Law of Acceptance! None of you are separate. You are Unana.

Sacred Fire

Response: "Thank you Crystiel."

Dear Child of this Golden Flame, I AM known as Mary and ask for your permission to come forward, for you are the flower and the light of all life.

Response: "Thank you Beloved Mary. Come forward."

THE FLOWER OF LIFE

As our Dear Brother Crystiel has expressed acceptance, we ask that the Flower of Life be the expression of All. For, as the Dove is the messenger of this New World that you now choose, the Flower of Life is the expression of your Oneness. And from your flower will come many fruits and the seeds which will again grow to create the flower. You have stepped from the path of fruit and seed to the path again of the flower. This flower we ask you to place in much of your work, for it is this pattern which will bring forward the Oneness for all who see and experience your daily lives.

> Come gently into your garden when you are troubled,
> And I am there for you.
> Come gently into the garden of your heart,
> And you will find you are never without this
> great Flower of Life.
> You are always ONE.

Come forward, as you have been requested by your Brother Sananda, to step into this garden anytime there is a conflict in your life. As you come to this place of serenity, these great flowers and fragrances will breathe a breath that brings a new life, a new focus, and a new acceptance. These Flowers of Life will always bring that which you know as prana, will bring that which you have as Source. It is the continual breath of this wondrous fragrance that you become as you step into your garden. It is in this redirection of your focus in your day that brings this Oneness infinitely. It is but a small turn on your inner path to find your garden. As this Oneness comes forward, all connects in the breath of this garden. We ask you to breathe these gentle flowers and I surround you always.

Dear Mary steps back from the frequency and Beloved Saint Germain speaks.

Dear Child of my heart, I AM Saint Germain. Do you have questions before we take our leave?

Response: "Dear Brother, no questions, but much gratitude for your service. Thank you."

Then let perfection stream forward on all Rays of expression, Unana.

[Editor's Note: For a collection of Ascended Masters' Prayer, including Mother Mary's *Flower of Life Prayer*, see Appendix F.]

CHAPTER FOUR

Earth Healing

Saint Germain assists a Healing Ceremony.

Greetings in that Mighty Christ Light, I AM Saint Germain. I stream forth on the Mighty Ray of Mercy and Forgiveness. As usual, Dear hearts, chelas, and students, I must ask permission to come forth.

Response: "Please come forth, Dear one."

A TRANSMITTER OF LIGHT

The work upon the Earth Plane and Planet is one where we shall say, tarry not. For this Time of Transition that comes is indeed, as we have said, a time when that Lady shall open her legs and you would perceive, in essence, a birth scream or a howl. But yet, we see this as that Time of Awakening, a Time of Transition, and a time for the opening of the Prophecies of Peace and Grace. May peace stream forth into your hearts, Dear ones, and be forever your infinite and eternal decree. Peace and grace, that which is, shall we say, that Law of the Best and Highest Good, that which streams forth from that Ray of Divine Will and that Ray of Divine Love.

We ask for you, Dear ones, dear Brothers and Sisters, chelas and students. Those who are gathered here for the ushering in of that Mighty Law of Grace. To hold within their hearts, that Mighty Light of God that never fails. We ask for you at all times to see yourself as that transmitter, that generator, that mighty servant of light, who allows these energies to come and bring forth an enactment of the Divine Will upon the Earth Plane and Planet.

TIME OF PEACE

Dear hearts, the Time of Peace now comes to the planet. And, you as forerunners, as lovers of this peace, we ask you to play them as a grand symphony, one string harmonizing one with the next. Or have we not taught that the first law that streams forth, is the Law of Harmony? And now, we as members and as servants of lovers of peace and grace, ask that each of you consider that not only is this a Time of Change and Earth Change for that matter, but also a time which will be a Time of Peace and Prophecies of Peace.

The Spiritual Hierarchy of this Lodge has, for some time, decided that Earth Changes Prophecy will no longer be given for a short time. However, we will now allocate this time to bring forth what are known as those Prophecies of Peace.

For Dear ones, as you have known, your attention is where energy flows! Have you not noticed this in all Co-creation and manifestation? And, have you not noticed this in the work-about world in which you live?

LIVE THE LAW OF HARMONY

Each and every one of you asks daily, "How is it that I can apply these teachings and utilize them for my life? How can I serve this Spiritual Awakening? How can I best serve my Brothers and Sisters?" I say to you, each and every one of you, that it is as simple as living in that Law of Harmony.

But first, that Law of Harmony is built upon agreement. That is, again, that harmonious response to thought—for it is the thought that is the premise of all Creation. And we would ask that each and every one of you consider to align your thoughts to that plan of the best and the highest good. Allow a frequency and a vibration to come forth that serves that mighty plan of the Divine Will!

A CHANGE OF HEART

In the days to come, yes, there will be the shaking and the rattling of the Earth forces. Not only shall we see eruptions in that Cascade Range, but also into the Sierra Madres, and in a counter-clockwise positing of that Pacific Rim. These were all the prophecies that we have dispensed in the I AM America material and we will continue to give brief updates on.

However Dear chelas and students, we ask for you to place your attention not only on the element of change, but to look deep within the heart of your own being and recognize the change that is happening within your heart. Are we not now in the middle of a spiritual transition? Are we not now in the middle of a Spiritual Awakening? I ask you Dear stalwart students of the Mighty Flame of Truth, to come forward in that breath of the Mighty ONE; come forward in that breath of that Mighty ONE Peace.

The Time of Transition is a time when we are transiting not only from the Third Dimension, but onward into the Fourth and the Fifth dimension. For it is, shall we say, in the harmony of the spheres, where peace is gained; and the bitter cup is taken from your lips. You have sought the sensation of this elusive reality and have found so contained within that duad, that form of clay, your body; and now we move into that Time of ONE, that Time of Monad, that Time of ALL Interconnectiveness of All Life!

ONE LIFE

Your emotions, your feelings, even your thoughts, Dear ones, run rampant at this time. And we would ask that you discipline them through enacting that first Mighty Law of Harmony. Call forth harmony in all your agreements; call forth harmony in all your transactions. Remember, you are a Oneship as beloved Kuan Yin has stated, "Each and every one of you shares this life." This ONE life that is contained upon the planet is ONE that is contained in your own being. You have studied the energetics of change and also the energetics related to not only the human or electromagnetic field, but also study Dear chelas and students, that electromagnetic force that is of the planet itself. Understand that each of the fifty-one Vortices, which have been brought forth in service to the awakening of humanity, are also those mighty focuses of energy contained upon the planet—and for her transit into what we would call, a quantum leap in Collective Consciousness.

COOPERATION, CHOICE, AND ACTION

The positing of your location at this moment is the location of one of those older Vortices of the planet. And yes, while you carry forward a readjustment and re-alignment of, that electromagnetic body, the impulse body, a natural feeling body of the planet, you are also assisting in anchoring in the energies which align to the Golden City Vortex known as Klehma. And we would ask that in your heart and in your thought today, that you hold forth that thought of Continuity, Cooperation, and Balance.

As members of this Lodge, Dear hearts, remember at all times we hold within our hearts, first, that Mighty Law of Cooperation. And we would ask each and every one of you to become not only a symbol of this cooperation, but also to carry it forward in your daily demonstration. Choose and you shall act; act and you shall choose.

As we have stated before, Dear ones, "as above so below." We ask for this Divine Will to stream forth in you—this day. And with these Prophecies of Peace, carry them forward not only in your heart, but also in that active hand.

ASSIST THE ACCELERATION

In the times to come, after that time where that polarization of energy is balanced, we shall see not only changes in government, but also within the social structures, these, first starting with the family unit. The Time of Equity now comes to the planet, and that inner marriage or marriage of the Kundulini energies will now be woven, not only as male and female, but the activation of the Christ.

In the family units, even conception as you have understood it, will come forward in a different manner. You have worries of the clay vessel and the carrying forth of energies in the human duad. We ask for you to consider forms of sponsorship of energy that are carried forward in consciousness and in thought.

Beloved Mother Mary brought forward, that first idea of Divine Conception. Held first immaculately in her inner eye, in her inner vision. We ask you now, Dear students, to hold that forward, to hold that perfect thought.

To assist the accelerations of energies upon the Earth Plane and Planet, we will encounter what is known as holo-leaping or the movement between the Third and Fourth Dimensions. How do we do this, Dear ones? Through what are known as our energy fields. How do we direct our energy fields? Through creative thought.

KARMA LIFTS, JOY BEGINS

Many lifestreams from other planets now seek entry into the Earth Plane and Planet. However, at this time, we are seeing the ending [lifting] of the Mighty Law of Cause and Effect. This, you have known through many lifestreams, and through some, shall I say, even limited teachings as karma. But we ask you to consider this as dharma. For is it not joyful now to be ending this portion of the path, Dear hearts, this portion of the journey?

Now we have climbed to this new positing. And we look over the valley and we say, "It is good." Is it good for you, Dear ones? Is this, in that Law of the Best and the Highest Good? These are the choices that lay in front of you in this Time of Transition.

SEVENTH MANU

During these times that await us, as I have stated, many lifestreams are preparing themselves now to come upon the planet known as the Seventh Manu. I have spoken of them in previous discourse. Not only do they await entry through your conscious thought, but also through those Mighty Vortices on the planet.

They come to bring their service, Dear ones, and to bring their service not only to humanity, but to those other kingdoms of creation: Devas, Elementals, and Elohim. They come, in essence, to raise the vibrational frequencies of the planet, for these are the Times of Peace that await us!

Will a time come when humanity will again live in harmony with its environment? This I say—so! [yes] In this illusion, there is always an element of chaos! You are blessed, Dear ones, as Co-creators, inheritors that possess, that mighty spark, the Monad, the ONE.

INVOLUTION EQUALS EVOLUTION

As all life contains within it that One Mighty Breath, we ask for you to consider, Dear chelas, stalwart students of truth, that it is held within the frequency and the Vibration of your thought, the development of your consciousness.

These small exercises, the gathering of a group to hold collective thought, to hold Collective Consciousness, are those first steps that allow that involution of consciousness to become an evolution of humanity.

And then those higher frequencies are allowed, conceptualized and To Be. We fear so often, as when taking the human form, that the extent of all reality is contained [only] within that vessel of clay. Yet, Dear ones, your true life, your true inner spark, is made of neither. It is the pure consciousness from that which we have known as Helios and Vesta—that which is known as the Source—planted eons ago upon your planet by those Mighty Lords of Venus, those who have brought forth their sponsorship for your evolution.

A time now comes where you will assume these new positions as members of this Lodge, a Brotherhood and a Sisterhood of light and love. I ask for you to consider, Dear students, that you too shall become as the elders have become. And in this time that awaits us—a Prophecy of Peace—you shall become [as] those Elohims of Tranquility, Elohims of Peace. You shall hold the spark, the Jiva, the Monad of Consciousness for those residing in kingdoms of lesser consciousness and for those who await us, those beloved dear children of the Seventh Manu, who hold within their heart that spark and consciousness for your own evolution.

I shall take my leave from your frequency and ask you to carry the prayer of the ONE throughout the day. Understand that even though we enter into a time of limited turmoil and chaos, that this is also a Time of Peace and a Time of Awakening.

Response: "Thank you."

CHAPTER FIVE

Golden Ray, Stream Forth!
Saint Germain on the Gold Ray.

Greetings Beloved chelas, in that mighty Violet Flame, I AM Saint Germain and I stream forth on that mighty Violet Ray of Mercy, Compassion, Forgiveness, and Transmutation. Dear hearts, Dear ones, I request permission to come forth.

Response: "Please, Saint Germain, you are most welcome. Come forward."

SPIRITUAL WEALTH

There is much work upon the Earth Plane and Planet. Yes, work not only of education . . . work not only of compassion . . . work not only of forgiveness . . . work not only of transmutation and transformation, but also that mighty work of building consciousness. For you see, Dear ones, Dear hearts, at this time in the history of the Earth, the great flood of consciousness is scheduled to come forward. This has been spoken of by beloved Brother Kuthumi as the Golden Ray. Of course, what we are speaking of is that power from the Great Central Sun itself arcing to your solar system. It is this Golden Ray that will bring forth a dawning of a new consciousness. It is this Golden Ray that will bring that great leap in consciousness, which will bring enhanced spiritual understanding, enhanced spiritual knowledge, and enhanced spiritual wealth.

You see, Dear ones, Dear hearts, it is this growth in consciousness that will bring the New Times, the Golden Age, a Golden Crystal Age, shall I say. That time, or consciousness within man itself, will grow to a level that it has not known for many thousands of years. You see, Dear hearts, you have been bound into the darkness of Kali Yuga and have not known, shall we say, the light of the Great Central Sun falling upon the true face of knowledge, your true consciousness for some

Sacred Fire 57

time. It is through this work of the Golden Ray that this consciousness is then opened up, or shall we say, bursts forth, as when there is a paradigm shift, or as you call it "pushing the envelope." It is now time for us to open this consciousness, for you to become aware of it and bring about its total and complete enhancement.

THE NEW ENVIRONMENT

This consciousness that comes forward will bring about many new changes in your technology. Not only will it bring forth new plans in laser technology, new plans in the computer industry, and new plans in the growth of medical knowledge, but it will also bring about the complete and total awareness of the environment. There will be many businesses and focuses within social and economic climates that will understand the great importance of the environment and the need for it to be impacted in a more perfect way with any type of technology.

The time that you have entered out of, which is the Industrial Age, was a time of great pollution of Mother Earth, beloved Babajeran. Of course, now through the new knowledge and information, it is important to understand that much of this pollution needs to be cleaned up to pave a pure pathway of consciousness for the Age of Information.

This Age of Information shall also be guided and directed by this Ray of Consciousness known as the Golden Ray. The Golden Ray brings a complete and total understanding of the true HU-man, the true human who is indeed divine. It is as simple as accepting the divinity within, is it not? So, Dear hearts, Dear ones, know that this Golden Ray comes forward for the benefit of all. It does not come forward just for the benefit of the spiritual elite. Indeed, it is meant for all and is about a complete and total understanding that will pave the way for the New Times.

LIGHT IN FULL MEASURE

The Golden Cities themselves are also affected by the Golden Ray. Of course, their activation has a timing and intention with each Ray Force that it represents within itself, but the Golden Ray itself plays a role in their activation at higher levels. A portal of cleansing karma opened at the last lunar eclipse and with the Golden Ray working alongside it, will lift you into a stream of new consciousness. It is most important that we work towards bringing this new stream of consciousness forward, so that all may understand and utilize the work of the Golden Ray.

> Mighty Golden Ray stream forth now
> into the heart of the consciousness of humanity.
> Mighty Golden Ray bring forth new understanding.
> Bring forth a new Spiritual Awakening.
> Bring forth complete and total divinity
> in the name of I AM THAT I AM.
> So be it.

It is through this work of the Golden Ray that even the Spiritual Hierarchy has been able to access, shall we say, deeper levels of consciousness and obtain greater points of contact. In this time of duality upon the Earth Plane and Planet, where darkness seems to produce an all-time low, as I have stated before, it is also the opportunity for light. This light may now come forward in full measure, so that the darkness is also understood.

Since you have read and understood the cycles of the Yugas, when you understand a descending culture, then you can also understand an ascending culture. What is this information all based upon but that of vibration, vibration within itself and how vibration serves not only for all past memory but all present and, subsequently, future experience. Vibration serves within the complete and total cycles the Laws of Harmony. As we have always stated before in the Hermetic Laws, it is within these cycles, as you have understood through beloved Kuan Yin, that perfect harmony is then absolute.

BALANCING THE DARK SIDE

In this dual experience, as you see a great deal of darkness, is there not then also that opportunity for a great deal of light? The middle way has been brought forward to understand both of these teachings simultaneously. To live and to walk in balance is to accept the work of the Golden Ray. The Golden Ray brings a higher form of consciousness which understands why your past has been what it is. One may understand this simply as understanding the dark side. But perhaps, there are those who do not reach at all into the dark side that is part of them. Instead, it remains suppressed and therefore its expression is out-of-control.

EXPERIENCE AND CHOICE

Of course, the work of the Spiritual Hierarchy is always to bring the emotions into complete and total understanding but one cannot bring such into control until they have had the complete and total experience of them. So, that is why you, the soul in the sojourn of the physical body, have come here and put on the physical body . . . the emotional body . . . the astral body . . . the mental body. Each of these bodies brings their own service of the Rays forward and their own unique set of experiences. These experiences build one to the next, one on top of the other. These experiences then allow one to feel . . . allow one to take action . . . allow one to have complete and total experience.

But do we randomly create, randomly experience, have these actions, these feelings, these thoughts? No. Dear ones, Dear hearts, that is why you have been given the vehicle of choice, or the will. The chela who travels along the spiritual path then begins that spiritual tutelage of aligning that will to the Divine Will. In that greater alignment of that will comes the Golden Ray of Consciousness. This is most important, for the Golden Ray enters through the seventh chakra and runs along the Golden Thread Axis. It is most important to understand that the Golden Ray is in alignment to the Divine Will. It is that greater understanding that all experiences, good and bad, come together into a greater understanding, that of divinity.

CALL UPON THE GOLDEN RAY

All things work together for ONE, which is indeed, Unana or Unity Consciousness. Therefore, the Golden Ray is also identified with Unity Consciousness and those who call upon and use the Golden Ray will notice this affect immediately. They herald in a new consciousness even through the invocation of its presence. This great new consciousness allows for a greater acceptance and tolerance of one another.

Brotherhood and Sisterhood reign supreme and you shall face that New Day cloaked in the glory of the Sun. Dear ones, Dear hearts, please consider this short lesson upon the Golden Ray. And now, I shall open the floor for your questions.

Question: "The Golden Ray is now making its appearance in our plane?"

CLEANSING KARMA, FACING DARKNESS

This is so, Dear ones, Dear hearts. Its presence has been here from time immemorial; however, at times its pulsation, or shall we say, vibrational effect, is felt at greater levels. As you have been experiencing Kali Yuga, or a time of lesser light, it has been hard to identify and therefore utilize. But, Dear ones, Dear hearts, as I have explained in my last discourse on the opening of this time period, which is a portal for the cleansing of all past karma, as the Golden Ray comes forward, simultaneously, one faces the dark side of their soul. It is also in the dual expression that one finds the light side of eternity.

LAW OF BALANCE

Question: "So, what you are saying is that no matter how much darkness is present, the Law of Balance will prevail?"

The Law of Balance is the Law Eternal.

COLLECTIVE CONSCIOUSNESS

Question: "I see. So, the Collective Consciousness, does it have only one heart?"

There is one consciousness and ideally one heart of consciousness; however, in the dual expression, there are many individuals with their individual expressions ... their individual lives ... their individual matrix of light and sound ... which comprises a greater global matrix of light and sound. In the same way, in the physical body, there are cells that exist within the skin itself; however, upon the skin exist nails or hair, even different colors, freckles, moles. You see, Dear one, it is the same as understanding a microcosm within a macrocosm.

Question: "So all the souls present on this planet and in this plane are of one Collective Consciousness?"

There is one Collective Consciousness indeed and that Collective Consciousness is guided and led through the Laws of Vibration, so that a series of souls can attract a lesson unto themselves. Let me explain. You see, at this time upon the Earth Plane and Planet, those souls have attracted unto themselves those life experiences for the timing and intent of this present hour; but individually, there are many different paths of life, many different choices that have been made. There is, however, when one attunes to it, that greater alignment to that greater Divine Will and Divine Plan. That is the consciousness of Unana. That consciousness of Unana comes under the Jurisdiction of the Golden Ray.

USE OF THE VIOLET RAY

Response: "So, now we are in this time period where the Golden Ray is expressing at a greater degree."

It is so. Dear ones, Dear hearts. However, the proper preparation is the use of the Violet Ray of Mercy, Transmutation, and Forgiveness. This is how you can bring a greater alignment and preparation for the assimilation of this new Ray Force. As I have stated before, this Ray Force settles itself not only along the Golden Thread Axis but what you would know as the Kundalini current of the body. Therefore, it affects all cells of the body and performs, shall we say, a great acceleration. However, it is most difficult to feel until you can bring about that greater understanding of the Violet Ray.

Mighty Violet Ray, come forth in all transmuting action.
Mighty Violet Ray, come forth now and dissolve all discord
and the cause and effect of all that is holding me
from understanding and moving forward into the new Golden Age.
I call this forth in the name of that mighty Christ I AM.
So be it.

Response: "So be it."

Call forth that mighty Violet Ray in action . . . call it forth within your voice . . . call it forth within your emotional body . . . call it forth within your mental body . . . call it forth in your daily action.

AWARENESS AND VIBRATION

Question: "Does the Golden Ray affect those who are visiting our planet?"

The Golden Ray is brought forward at a vibrational level for those who are ready to receive its gift. You see, Dear ones, Dear hearts, those who are visiting the planet, some are of a higher vibration, some are of a lower vibration, so your question would be contingent then on those who are ready to receive.

Question: "I see. So when we refer to the alien influences that are not necessarily for the evolution of humanity, the Golden Ray will not affect them?"

Nor would there even be an awareness of it. In the same way, in your many lifetimes in the lesser light years of Kali Yuga, you were not even aware of that mighty Violet Ray in action. Mercy, Compassion, Forgiveness, and Transmutation were not any of the qualities that you carried forth in those embodiments. But subsequently, through application and Divine Intervention, this Violet Ray has been brought forward. It can now be used to serve and assist humanity at this most wondrous time.

Sacred Fire 63

HUMANITY'S SCHEME OF EVOLUTION

Question: "What about those who are being influenced by this alien force?"

They would not be affected at all by this mighty Golden Ray. You see, Dear ones, Dear hearts, it is brought forward for the evolution of humanity. Even though those of higher vibration would know of its influence, humanity within itself has its own scheme of evolution, which moves forward with its own Divine Timing and Intent.

Question: "Is this scheme of evolution also in the genetic code and structure of our physiology?"

It is not only carried within that genetic code but let us go one level deeper, to the choice of the soul. In the choice of the soul is engendered that Golden Thread Axis, which then aligns itself to a greater Plan Divine. The soul existed long before the physical body; however, it has been attracted not only through karma and purposes but is also attracted through mental activity and the thoughts that are held. These thoughts manifest themselves through choices. Choice manifests itself as a will, as a current of electricity that aligns itself then to a greater Plan Divine.

To understand this most simply, know that the soul itself has charted the course that it will now travel through in the world of duality, known as time. The soul moves forward in its sojourn in duality, putting on body after body, as one would change a set of clothes and yet at times, feels a discontent in some activities and a conclusion in others. But it is most important to understand that there is a plan that is moving forward and being fulfilled. Growth and evolution of this human soul is then achieved. This comes under a timing, a planning, and an intention. The Rays bring forth their service to bring this evolution and this essential schooling forward. So, understand, Dear ones, Dear hearts, that the Golden Ray then comes forward to bring this greater understanding and evolution. Questions?

VIBRATION AND THE GOLD RAY

Response: I see. So the Golden Ray will really only affect a certain group of people on the planet.

Again, it is at that level of vibration that it brings its affect. Understand it as simply, when you enter school as a young one, you understand only the rules of kindergarten. You understand how to make objects from clay; how to paint; how to draw; a time to rest; a time for a snack. These are the things, are they not, that are contained within a kindergarten schedule?

Response: "True."

But as one proceeds through the grades, one moves upward and soon that schedule as a small or younger child is not suitable for the older child. Again vibration, shall we say, changes as the soul moves, grows, and learns. This of course is very simplistic and is only a model to grasp and to understand this concept. Questions?

Question: "Many. So in essence, the Golden Ray is a blessing coming forth to aid and assist the evolution of humanity?"

THE NEXT STEP

Indeed, it brings a greater blessing forward, for it allows an understanding of a greater reality . . . a greater reality that exists in the consciousness of Unana . . . a greater reality that exists beyond a dual consciousness. It is the next step that lies within the Violet Flame. Now, you will notice those who apply and use the Violet Flame on a regular basis will begin to have a gold tinge to the outside of their aura. This is the activation of the Golden Ray. However, it has been decided that in the next opening, this portal of entry that we have spoken of, that the Golden Ray will be flooded forth from our consciousness in complete and total harmony with beloved Babajeran, to bring an assistance for the evolution of humanity.

Now of course, if there are those who have not utilized the Violet Ray in their daily applications, it will be more difficult for them to recognize and understand this higher consciousness. But there are those who apply and use the Violet Flame on a daily basis and they will begin to notice a higher vibration. Some of these signs will be a high-pitched frequency, which at this moment you too can hear. There will be the sensation of music upon awakening from sleep or falling into sleep. This calls forth the greater harmony of the spheres; for you see, you have entered into a new dimension of sound frequency and a new level of understanding. Hence, it has its own light and its own sound vibration. Do you understand?

Question: "Yes I do. May we proceed with questions?"

Proceed.

Question: "I have some health questions to ask you with regard to a former secretary and her husband. Would you be able to do a scan and give us a course of action?"

[Saint Germain offers specific dietary suggestions for the individual's medical problems. This is followed by a spiritual cause discussion with general applications.]

Let us talk about the spiritual cause, for perhaps if we approach that first, the physical body will take suit, will it not?

Response: "Usually it does."

A LESSON LEARNED

The spiritual lesson is one of forgiveness, to completely forgive others for the way that they have behaved in the past and to not see that it was any result of this individual. This individual has harbored long-term resentments, which are deep-seated in the subconscious. This resentment has gone towards the self and has been seen within a mirror of self-hate and self-loathing. Dear one, Dear heart, understand that you attracted that lesson to learn complete and absolute forgiveness and compassion and now it is time to move forward and face the New Day. This lesson has brought forward great strengths and greater harmony within the soul, which are now achieved. These lessons now must be released for they are learned and completed. Questions?

CALL UPON THE VIOLET RAY

Question: "I see. So, when following these suggestions, there will be great changes to the physiology and to the spiritual outlook of each chela?"

And as I always suggest, calling upon that mighty Violet Ray of Mercy, Compassion, and Forgiveness always brings about a most refreshing drink, a most high vibration, and a greater understanding of that mighty will in Divine Alignment.

Response: "I completely understand."

Questions?

Response: "At this time I do not have any further questions."

I shall take my leave now from your frequency and shall return at the given time.

Response: "One other question . . ."

Proceed.

Question: "Next week, we may not be available at the specific time. May we set this back one day?"

This shall work; however, I caution you, for you see, Dear ones, Dear hearts, we work always upon that ideal of rhythm. However, we shall return at the given time that you select.

Sacred Fire 67

Response: "I understand. Thank you."

Om Manaya Pitaya Hitaka.

Response: "Hitaka."

[Editor's Note: For more information on the Gold Ray, see Appendix H.]

CHAPTER SIX

Ascension of Consciousness
Saint Germain on the heart, mind, and emotions.

Greetings Beloved chelas in that mighty Violet Ray. I AM Saint Germain and I stream forth on that Violet Ray of Mercy, Compassion, and Forgiveness. As usual Dear hearts, I request permission to come forward.

Response: "You have our permission Saint Germain, please come forward."

CAUSE AND EFFECT

There is much work for us to continue with Dear ones, Dear hearts, within this dispensation, not only of that Mighty Violet Ray but also of that Mighty Green Ray. The work that you are bringing forward, while it contains many aspects of that mighty Violet Ray of Transmutation, Alchemy, ultimate Compassion, and Forgiveness, it also contains within it that Green Ray of Understanding. For you see Dear ones, Dear hearts, it was long decided that there would be brought forth a dispensation to bring an understanding of cause and effect to humanity. This has now been brought forth in the teachings of prophecy but also in the teachings of the energetic grids, the layers of the field of the aura and the layers of the field of the Earth. When all of this is brought to a greater understanding, then healing can come forward. This healing that comes forth from the heart of the Central Sun, that mighty logos, aligns to the Divine Plan, to that mighty will. OM MANAYA, PITAYA, HITAKA!

ALIGNMENT AND HARMONY

Dear ones, Dear hearts, this healing work that comes forward brings a greater alignment of that mighty will among the collective consciousness of humanity. It is this alignment of the will that is of most importance and you know that this has been the focus and the intention of the work in Gobean and the work of beloved Master El Morya. This mighty Blue Ray, as it streams forth from the heart of the Central Sun, arcing through the solar system to the core of your own Earth, brings with it an understanding and an intention to bring others to that greater plan . . . to a greater alignment . . . to their own purpose in this embodiment.

When one enters into this path of greater purpose and alignment to that Divine Plan, a greater harmony then ensues. This harmony brings forth an easing in the collective consciousness. The tensions begin to ease and balance begins to come forth from the great heart of compassion. This balance, when it is understood, brings a greater opening of the heart of love and a greater peace and tolerance is the end result. This grand alignment brings a greater energy over the Earth. This energy, when it is understood as a greater cosmic unity, begins to align with greater ease to the solar system. That alignment to the solar system brings forth a greater alignment to the Great Central Sun.

"LOVE, IN ACTION"

As you see Dear ones, these three actual physical locations are always working to bring a greater harmony for the evolution of those on planet Earth. This alignment also brings a greater understanding of the positioning of the Earth as a schoolroom. As it has always been said, "To do, to dare, and to be silent." Those who enter into the Earth Plane understand the great need to bring demonstration into the physical . . . understand the great need to bring forth action . . . understand the great need to put love into complete and total action. As we have always stated before, it is love in action, is it not, that brings about that greater understanding, that greater education?

When one begins to understand the intention of their heart and brings this intention further into its greater plan and awareness, the schoolroom becomes, shall we say, a great flora and fauna of experience. To love brings about a completion, does it not? To love brings about a greater understanding of the emotional fields and a greater understanding of higher intelligence and how this higher intelligence can be brought into greater thinking and arenas of experience.

Through this greater plan, the Law of Love, all is brought to greater alignment and to greater harmony and ultimately, a greater abundance. This grand alignment upon the Earth Plane and Planet brings about a graduation of souls upon this schoolroom. This graduation of course is not just a graduation in consciousness but also a graduation that leads one to a greater understanding of the Ascension.

HEALING AND THE ASCENSION

The Ascension, as you see Dear ones, Dear hearts, is the movement, yes, inter-dimensionally but it is also a greater and higher awareness of experience. The Ascension of consciousness brings a greater understanding of the purpose of the Law of Love and the inter-connectivity of all in your path. Compassion, which is an element and an aspect of that mighty Violet Ray, brings forward a greater understanding of the Law of Love. One then is readied and able to see that great inner working in all situations and circumstances. As I have said before, there is never a mistake, ever, ever, ever. When one enters into that mighty Law of Compassion, one is then able to see how this mighty law works in the Earth Plane and Planet and brings one into a higher awareness, into a higher experience of consciousness. This of course is the path of Ascension and many who work on that mighty White Ray understand and know that the healing of many wounds is always essential in order to bring one to a higher consciousness. But this healing, does it not come forward through the letting go of past experience?

SPIRITUAL EDUCATION

This letting go is not forgetting the lesson but forgetting the pain and moving beyond the experience that is encoded in the memory. The memory is then viewed with the end result, as I have always said, of education. This grander education exists for all upon the Earth Plane and Planet. It is the purpose of life here ... it is the purpose that one is moving towards ... moving to a greater education ... having a greater knowledge of the inter-connectivity that exists within that mighty Law of Love. When you call upon that mighty Violet Flame, it leads you into a greater awareness, a greater tolerance of experience, and expands one in that mighty heart of love into the consciousness of Unana, into the consciousness of that all and mighty ONE.

KARMIC PATTERNS

In the consciousness of the all and mighty ONE, lies the memory eternal, lies the true memory that exists in all situations and circumstances. This is important to understand as one enters into that focused path of Ascension, that all experiences are inter-connected, each to the next. Yet, all experiences are seen for the unity that they contain, seen through that one thread or path of demonstration that they hold. This path of course is the path of love, for one then sees the tolerance, the open giving. The open door, as Dear Sananda has always expressed, is contained in all experiences. When the soul is non-detached from these experiences, it is very hard to let go of the wounds of the past and the soul is held back in its own evolution. The soul is then called upon to repeat the experience over and over again. While some might see this as a punishing effect of karma, know Dear ones, Dear hearts, it is no punishing affect at all but only the exercise of your will and your choice. These repeat performances, shall we say, of experiences are seen at a point in evolution as a pattern.

"THE REWARD IS IMMEASURABLE"

These patterns of course are very important for the development of the will and the soul. Through this experience and demonstration of end results, one is then able to align through choice to a higher experience. This higher alignment and the use of that mighty Blue Ray brings transformation. This transformation is always essential Dear ones, Dear hearts, in order to move to a greater understanding of a pattern. These patterns of past experience are held by all who tread the spiritual path. All will begin to understand through that end result, education. Being led through the experience of a painful existence, education always comes to the forefront, does it not? For we have always stated, it is never promised to be easy but the reward is immeasurable. That is why those who tread the path to higher knowledge . . . who seek Ascension of their own consciousness . . .

who seek an Ascension of any situation or circumstance are then led into the embrace of the mighty Violet Ray.

REVIEW YOUR PATTERNS

When one reviews, through meditation or in calmness of their day, the past karmas, or actions of that day, one then can see the result of patterns, many patterns of the past that are held at many levels. These patterns are held in the physical body, yes, but they are also held in that most important body of understanding, the mental body. For in that mental body is contained, at all times, the mighty builder of the physical form. It is true Dear ones, when you put your focus there, you shall see the end result. I have taught this many, many times in my precipitation and manifestation techniques.

It is important to understand that thoughts do create physical end results. Of course, this being a primary entry lesson for those upon the path of the Ascension, it is always important to give this great review, to understand that there is always an end result to an action. The action, does it not always come from the mental functions? Does it not come forth through thinking such a thing first? Thoughts must be held to be more sacred, Dear ones, Dear hearts. Thoughts that are held then seek a manifestation through that natural law. All thoughts will contain an end result. Of course, then one says, "How do I capture the mind? How do I keep the mind from traveling and racing into undesired areas? How do I harness the energy of my mind? How do I bring my mind forward into a greater alignment to the Divine Will?"

THE HEART AND SACRED FIRE

The mind itself is always balanced through that mighty heart of love and in that heart of love is the consciousness of the ONE, Unana. The mind is brought to a quietness, is it not, through the use of that Sacred Fire, the mighty Violet Ray? This is why we have brought these techniques forward at this time, Dear ones, Dear heart, so the mind can be tamed as it travels through the experience of illusion. Illusion is indeed a topic to be understood, is it not? For then one sees the temporal illusion of the creation of the mind and the temporal illusion of the experiences of the physical.

BEYOND ILLUSION

Illusion exists, Dear one, to bring the education of the truth . . . to bring you into the alignment of the mighty Law of Love . . . to bring you into the alignment of that Plan Divine. One then begins to peer above illusion, when having the experience of Divine Love. One then begins to have experiences beyond illusion, when seeing the cause of unity demonstrating in all experience. These indeed are the true treasures that await the one who ascends upon the spiritual path . . . who ascends in consciousness . . . who ascends in understanding . . . who ascends to that mighty alignment – the love of all – that guides humanity.

INVOKE THE FLAME

This mighty Violet Ray streams forth too as the Blue Ray comes forward. This mighty Violet Ray streams forth from the heart of the Great Central Sun, arcing itself to the solar sun, then to core of the Earth. As you invoke its substance, it comes forth from the ethers. As it appears, coming from each layer of the field of the Earth, it is contained within its own manifestation. When you command and demand a Ray Force into action, you are calling, not only upon that Law of Love, but also upon a law that exists within the physical. For you see, all the rays in their action come forth at every level, as well as the same level of your experience of mind into physical manifestation.

TAMING EMOTIONS

Then one is led to ask, "What about the emotional field? Is not all thought, then feeling and action?" Of course, Dear ones, it is but the feeling is brought more to bridge the thought and the action. It is always that great impetus that then brings the will to action, does it not? The emotions have always been so important to understand and the taming of the emotions is as important as the taming of the mind. For the mind, when we see with crystal clarity, we can see each individualized thought as it passes through the mind. But it is the nature of the human to get trapped upon occasion in the fields of emotional experience. Why is this so?

Held within the genetic coding is the genetics of the animal in the experience upon the Earth Plane and Planet. This is not to say that the human is animalistic but, at times, can behave and act in an animal behavior or modality. It is always a matter of choice, is it not Dear ones, Dear hearts? Calling upon that Will Divine, raises one to a higher understanding, to a greater knowledge. Then in that greater knowledge, one begins to understand that the travels among the illusions are indeed controlled through the mental out-picturing.

GROWTH THROUGH EXPERIENCE

All experiences come, of course, through the mental conduit of out-picturing. This is the basis Dear ones, Dear hearts, of manifestation and experience. Through this out-picturing, the soul in its sojourn in the Earth Plane and Planet grows, learns, and receives the most precious gem of all – education. Where does this all fit in, one may ask, lifetime after lifetime? The soul, ascending upon the spiritual path, learns that education is the highest reward.

Dear ones, Dear hearts, as you understand, the Earth schoolroom is a place where you grow only by experience, only by demonstration in the physical. The astute student begins to understand, through these experiences, that there is a higher order which brings about the patterns, demonstrating great physical laws. There is indeed a higher intelligence, is there not? There is indeed a higher order, is there not?

When one begins to see this higher order, they begin to understand the Ascension of consciousness and that there is much more that lies beyond physical demonstration and the Maya or illusion. There is the eternal truth that lies behind all such things, even behind that of the mind . . . a Divine Order that is being orchestrated beyond a great central intelligence. Dear ones, Dear hearts, when one begins to seek this great higher order, they are then ready to meet the I AM THAT I AM.

THE MIGHTY I AM PRESENCE

The first of the I AM THAT I AM is the God-self that dwells within. It has always been there but it lies, shall we say, asleep within so many people. It is not yet awakened, not yet put in its proper authority. When one begins their contact with this mighty I AM, one then begins to see the spiritual laws that lie underneath all activity ... the true realities that lie within all situations and circumstances. When you travel in the physical experience in contact with the mighty I AM Presence, one then is led beyond illusion and into truth eternal. The contact with the mighty I AM indeed is the Akashic Record ... indeed is the silent witness ... indeed is that wellspring of eternal truth. The mighty I AM, Dear ones, Dear hearts, strives in the Ascension of consciousness to gain emotional and ultimate contact. The mighty I AM is contained within all. It contains within it, not only the universal mind but the universal heart of love. It contains within it all experiences, so it can lead you into new experience. Questions?

THE AWAKENING POINT

Question: "Yes. It is my impression that Ascension can only be taught to a mortal person by an already Ascended Being. Is this true?"

It is very difficult for the consciousness to be brought into its ascending order without the guidance of one who has been there before. However, within healing is the ultimate authority. That ultimate authority longs to be awakened ... longs to be brought to the complete, full podium of consciousness. This awakening is always fostered by one who has been there before. As we have always said: To do, to dare ... and then that great silence is the mighty witness.

Response: "I see. Then truly, Ascension occurs when the individual soul is sponsored by one who has already ascended."

It is true Dear ones, Dear hearts. As you have understood before, there is always the sponsor who comes forward to begin that awakening process within the human. First, the animal behaviors are taken to the forefront, so that one may then be able to see the action of such.

It is only through seeing ones animalistic instincts and behaviors that one is then able to call upon the mighty Divine Nature of choice and the engendering of the will. It is important Dear ones, Dear hearts, that when the sponsor comes forward, it is brought, shall we say, in the silence of a whisper. That awakening point, the birth of conscience, is most important.

BEYOND THE PHYSICAL

Response: "Yes, I understand. So, as I present some of the principles that you have shared with me with others, it will still require someone such as yourself to sponsor them in the Ascension."

It brings one to a higher understanding of Unity Consciousness. For you see Dear ones, Dear hearts, in the awakening process, one is always at odds with the ego. Of course, the ego works for the greater purpose of presenting the mirror, or shall we say, the duad, to the soul in its educational process. It is important of course to be able to see how all is inner connected to the ONE. When one is not bound through the physical and not bound through time and space, there is an opportunity for a greater intervention. This greater intervention comes forward in its own timing and intention. There is not one, bound in the physical, who could completely understand this in its entirety.

To work beyond physical constraint and beyond time and space, you begin to understand, through the help of your sponsor, your Master Teacher, that relationship of the guru to the chela. Has it not been brought to you Dear ones, Dear hearts, that you can see what exists beyond time and space and what exists beyond the physical? You see these demonstrations brought forth daily and while each is brought with a physical result, you can also understand its intention and purpose behind and beyond the physical. It is important to understand that when one is not bound by these constraints, there is a fresh perspective. One is then allowed, as you so well know, to "hang on to that elephant" in a whole different manner.

THE ASCENSION PROCESS

Question: "Then as I understand it, the Ascension process is ongoing; it is not just from this realm but from the realm that you are residing in, by your sponsors?"

It is indeed, Dear ones, Dear hearts, for consciousness is ever expanding and growing. It moves beyond, even from its point of birth. And while this principle is taught in the physical, it is not a principle from the physical. The physical was given, Dear ones, as a great gift, so you could see each spiritual principle and how it is applied.

ASCENSION AND DIET

Response: "I understand. With regard to the mental body, emotional body, and action body, it's my impression and observation that the emotional body seems to be infinitely more active and overpowering than the mental body or the action body."

As I have said before, the time period that the Earth is in, which is a time of lesser light, the emotions run quite rampant. These emotions are held in animalistic behavior and animalistic activity. That is why we have asked for the chelas, who wish to bring their consciousness to a momentum of Ascension, to limit their intake of animal products. The day-by-day ordered routine of Ascension necessitates the control of animalistic behavior and the animalistic genetic coding, a coding that has occurred through the intervention of other Star seeds upon the Earth Plane and Planet. You see Dear ones, Dear hearts, this control can be brought about through the simple principle of energy flows where attention goes. Now, how would this relate to the food that you eat? It is very simple when one understands a spiritual principle brought into physical order, is it not?

Response: "This is true. If you are partaking of animal products, then you are going to increase the energy of that within your own system."

As I have explained before Dear ones, Dear hearts, to bring the consciousness to a higher order, to a higher understanding, we have brought this law eternal. Of course there are those who feel a great restriction in this. However, as I have always assured you, often through restriction, one then begins to become fully free. This freedom is one that is not understood until one has had the experience. I have always said Dear ones, Dear hearts, take this into the great laboratory of the self. Bring it into at least a six-week experiment and see for yourself if your consciousness does not have a higher and a finer quality. Is this not true?

DIVINE LOVE

Response and question: "I can attest to this being true in my own life. I have a question in regard to Divine Love. It has been my impression that, though ever present, Divine Love needs to be accepted to be activated in the consciousness. It seems that so many people deny this acceptance or seem to be attached to the concept of being unworthy. Could you comment on this?"

Divine Love always brings forth a greater enlightenment, does it not? For through the experiment and experience of Divine Love, one then is brought to a higher level of acceptance and a higher level of tolerance. This allows the thoughts then to become freed. Thoughts are freed beyond restriction . . . thoughts are freed beyond doubt . . . thoughts are freed beyond superstition . . . thoughts are freed beyond fear. Divine Love brings forward, in its emotional quality, a freeing of the mental body. Creations then can come forward from a higher order and a higher understanding. When one accepts this higher Law of Divine Love, one then begins to expand in their mental characteristics and expand in their day-to-day thoughts and thinking. These day-to-day thoughts then begin to create new experiences, do they not? These new experiences then begin to reflect and mirror back a greater order, a greater understanding beyond the ego, beyond illusion.

It is through Divine Love and the acceptance of Divine Love that all are loved, accepted, and needed . . . that all have their right to be here . . . that all have their right to have this experience . . . that all have their right to come forward in their own evolution. Divine Love sustains, maintains, protects, nurtures, and ultimately qualifies all to a higher order. Only through Divine Love does all then exist, does it not Dear one?

ACTION AND THE VIOLET FLAME

Response and question: "Yes, without a doubt. I have come to accept that the Divine Plan, Divine Will, and Divine Love are always in action. Another question, if one wishes to go forward and create something new, we have talked about the out-picturing process, but if one wants to be released from something, the only process that I am aware of is the utilization of the Violet Flame. Does this work completely with paying a debt or eliminating karmic attachments that you may find unpleasant?"

There are those who are more attached to their experience of pain than to the education contained therein. It is important of course to always call forth that mighty Violet Ray into any situation and circumstance where you wish to be freed. However, there are also many lessons that come forward, do they not, through the physical? Many lessons are able to be shown to you clearly and succinctly. Money or, shall we say, the attachment to money, is one of these. The attachment at the mental level and through the emotional experiences of feeling secure or insecure, are one way that one becomes over attached. Money is given, shall we say, to clarify the emotional body, so that one may become more clear in their intention with the physical.

EMOTIONAL ATTACHMENTS

It is important, when you are working to become free from such emotional attachments, to not only call upon the Violet Ray, but to use all write and burn techniques. The write and burn techniques not only call upon a level of transmutation and Alchemy but they require a physical action to begin to overcome the circumstances and situations brought about through emotional imbalance. When one becomes, shall we say, stuck within this muck and mire of emotion, it is important then to take action at a physical level. This physical activity is focused and directed always through the intention of the mind. Calling forward the higher order of the mind to identify the emotional response can bring a greater level of physical activity. Do you understand?

Question: "It is a form of out-picturing that will then take the life into an action, is what you are saying?"

It is true Dear one. Work first with the Violet Ray to identify the emotional responses, then use the write and burn techniques to eliminate these emotional responses that are overplaying in patterns. Man and money becomes stuck in emotional securities . . . stuck in power plays . . . stuck in happiness or unhappiness, contingent upon the amount of security contained in the physical world. Now, for the one who is traveling along the path of ascending consciousness, can you clearly see how this would indeed impede and hold one back?

Response: "It most certainly would."

Do this work, Dear chela of mine, and I shall bring forth further assistance.

Response: "Yes."

[Editor's Note: For more information regarding the Write and Burn Technique, see Appendix J.]

ENERGY FOR ENERGY

As you have understood Dear one, all comes forward from the Master Teacher energy for energy. It is true indeed through Divine Love that the sponsor comes forward and fans that flame, awakening the I AM to a greater level of understanding. But it is the Master Teacher who comes forward then and helps through this mighty Principle Divine.

EMOTIONS AND THE VIOLET FLAME

Question: "I see. Isn't it the emotional body that brings up memories and keeps us from being lulled into a state of unawareness and non-sensitivity?"

The emotional body plays its role in allowing the patterns to come forward, that then indeed spark the will to greater action and activity. But the emotional body itself can become out of balance with experiences that are judged as negative or positive. As I have stated before, it is important to use the Violet Flame to allow this sense of judgment of good versus bad, good versus evil, or negative versus positive, a greater understanding. That experience is there for the engendering of the will and moving the soul further on the path into the Ascension of consciousness.

Response: "That would make the most sense. At this point, I have no further questions."

I should also like to remind you Dear ones, Dear hearts, that I will bring forward more information upon the Green Ray. For you see, today I have laid a template down which shall explain to you the beginning of the Blue Ray and the ultimate Alchemy of the Violet Ray. We have also introduced the premise of the mind, which is enlightenment brought from the premise of Divine Love. Now, we have the building blocks for that Mighty Green Ray of healing, do we not Dear ones, Dear hearts? In our next discourse, I shall bring further explanation. In that mighty Christ, SO BE IT!

Response: "So Be It!"

CHAPTER SEVEN

All Is Love
*Saint Germain shares insights on
the evolutionary force of love.*

Greetings Beloved chelas, students of mine, in that mighty Christ. I AM Saint Germain and I stream forth on that Violet Ray of Mercy, Compassion, and Forgiveness. As usual Dear hearts, I request permission to come forward.

Response: "Please Saint Germain, come forward. You are most welcome."

THE VIOLET RAY

As usual Dear ones, Dear hearts, there is much work for us still to complete, much work still to be dispensed upon that Green Ray of Ministry and Service to mankind. But also, there is that work of the Violet Ray, that which I represent, the Violet Ray of Mercy, Compassion, Forgiveness, Transmutation, and Purification. The Violet Ray comes forward to give that most refreshing drink in the hour of need. It comes forward to set you at a new pace. It comes forward to give you a new perspective. It comes forward to lead you, shall we say, to a greener pasture.

Dear ones, Dear hearts, in this respect, the Violet Ray is indeed a great purveyor for adjusting perception; for in the work of the Violet Ray, when one applies it and uses it with great earnestness, one is then able to see, know, and apply with a fresh perspective what waits ahead. The fresh perspective then allows one to see with a new vision . . . to hear with new ears . . . to speak with a new voice . . . for the heart to open and truly unite with the one consciousness. The one consciousness that I speak of is indeed the consciousness of the Christ, but it is also the consciousness of unity, of Brother to Brother, Sister to Sister, Mother to Father, child to parent. It contains within it all relationships. It exists in a greater scope of understanding. It is unity, Unana, the ONE.

This energy force that exists cannot be seen in duality; for indeed, it exists beyond duality. However, it is felt, shall we say, as a great invisible rush. This rush or force of energy that you feel Dear ones, is indeed one that you feel when you invoke and use the Violet Flame. And while in this moment, I can see that Violet Flame flickering about you, you only can sense it through, shall we say, a higher awareness. Of course, there are those who have the opening of the Third Eye and see a purple light that tinges about the energy fields. But you must understand Dear ones, Dear hearts, that the consciousness that I speak of is one that does not exist within the field of duality; however, it is that next realm of consciousness where your evolution and growth lies.

A FRESH PERSPECTIVE

In the growth of this higher consciousness will come, shall we say, the "aha" of many new ways of seeing things. It is like unwrapping a new gift . . . seeing the birth of a new child for the first time . . . witnessing spring. It is a greening effect in that respect Dear ones, Dear hearts, for it is alive and comes again with a fresh perspective. Working towards this new, fresh perspective is important Dear ones, Dear chelas, Dear students, to allow yourself to see something in a different way.

Very often we get stuck in ruts. We get stuck in seeing things in just one way. We get stuck seeing things from just one perspective. But it takes only a movement, this energy movement, happening first from inside, is then expressed in its outer condition. This outer condition is then recognized as change. But the change has happened in the heart first, has it not? And then, the will is invoked and this great change that brings about a fresh perspective is known as choice.

CHOICE AND THE PROCESS OF CHANGE

The pivotal point of choice is always important in all spiritual growth; for choice, you see, is engendered in that movement of the Violet Ray . . . in that movement of transmutation . . . in that movement of forgiveness . . . in that movement of purification . . . in that movement of Alchemy . . . and, yes, the ever-present, shall we say, hope of the magic. Now, when I say "magic," I speak indeed, not of illusion, but I speak of the magical moment of the mystic mystery. Dear ones, Dear hearts, mystery always surrounds growth. There is always, shall we say, stepping into the pool of the great unknown, always moving forward, not knowing exactly what lies in that void. But know this Dear ones, Dear hearts, trust within the heart . . . trust within the Mastery of the self . . . trust within the process of change itself.

Know this, that change is always a positive movement. Change is always for positive growth. Change moves always in that spiral of upward motion, especially for those who seek the Divine Will. Know and understand, Dear ones, Dear hearts, that change is always positive, change that happens in many arenas of life. Change has happened to the Earth, has it not? Change happens to your own children as they grow. Change happens in all of the Laws of Nature, in the seasons and in the weather. But beyond all of the change lies choice and there, choice becomes engendered with that greater Will Divine. There, choice leads the chela onward and upward on the spiritual path. There, onward and upward, one foot at a time, they are led towards the ultimate goal of spiritual liberation.

KARMA AND THE VIOLET FLAME

The other dimensions await you Dear ones, Dear hearts. They are for you at your choosing. They are for you at your spiritual growth. The Third Dimension, as you well understand, was brought to you through the Law of Attraction; your vibratory rate would state in the Laws Divine that like can only seek like vibration. It is so, that the Laws of Cause and Effect draw one to the field of physicality, to bring balance to situations of the past. This is also why I have given you the work and the use of the Violet Flame, for the Violet Flame allows you to bring balance into many karmic situations that might hold you from your forward movement, that might keep you from your own choice toward that Divine Will, that greater alignment into seeking the experience of the ONE.

FEAR AND LOVE

Karma indeed holds man back with great fear, holds one back from understanding and expressing the true divinity that lies within. Fear, you see Dear ones, Dear hearts, is always that energy that binds one to the physical plane, for it seeks release through its counterpoint, which is love. Love is indeed the only energy that can move the spiral forward. Stopping on the spiral always brings great pain to the chela, for they know that there is so much more that awaits them in the Temple of the Heart.

One seeks the peace and the solace that comes through the inner knowing and the inner knowing is brought to lead one further along the path . . . further along the path of change . . . further along into the unknown. Dear ones, Dear hearts, when I speak of this great unknown, is it really as such? For in your travel and sojourn in learning and understanding the levels of consciousness that await, how could there be fear? How could there be any that would hold one back from this greater evolution and development. Before I proceed, are there questions?

Question: "When you speak of evolution and development and being held back on that spiral, isn't that a choice though, a choice to not go forward?"

SPIRITUAL GROWTH THROUGH THE LAW OF LOVE

Indeed, all is choice Dear ones, Dear hearts. One is always choosing the emotions and the thoughts that create the actions. From those actions, choices are understood and expressed as the creation comes forth. So indeed, it is true Dear one, that there is a choice, even in no forward motion, but it is also understood, that in the lack of motion, especially in the field of duality, there comes that process, shall we say, of stagnation. This stagnation, lack of growth, or lack of forward motion, brings a sense of pain to the heart, for the heart expresses all in great knowing. The heart moves beyond the field of duality and understands that all comes into a greater balance; that left and right unite as ONE; male and female unite as ONE as well. All become reconciled in this sense,

Dear ones. But, as it has been stated before, until you reach the destination, you must still use the map. You do not throw the map away until you have reached that destination of where you wish to go. So, do we stop reading the map along the journey? No Dear ones, Dear hearts, we return to the basic principles, based upon the ever-present Law of ONE, the Law of Love. Questions?

Question: "So when one is being tested, the pathway through that test is the Law of Love, is it not?"

Always there is that most refreshing drink, is there not Dear heart? Only in love can things be seen through a greater lens of perception. Through the Violet Ray, one is able to adjust the force of the mind and train it to begin to see through a new lens of forgiveness, through a new lens of transmutation. This is indeed, as I spoke before, the magic of Alchemy. In that moment, you are able to see with crystal clarity. What you once thought was your lack of movement was indeed your tenuous growth. Proceed.

LOVE DRIVES EVOLUTION

Response and Question: "It is apparent to me, that without that sense of love motivating us through these daily tests of life in this schoolhouse, we would seem to wither, shrivel up as a vine that didn't get enough nutrient. Is this so?"

The heart of love, Dear one, as you know, moves beyond the dual expression. True love, in its understanding as the true open heart, moves beyond the restrictions of duality. Its energy force moves beyond that which you know as the physical. It is indeed that grand invisible force, which many at times want to call as God . . . want to call as the savior . . . want to call as even the Master Teacher, that comes forward to give that most refreshing drink. It is an energy that exists beyond time. It exists beyond belief systems. Love is indeed the basis of the next dimension, that next evolutionary leap in consciousness. This love that I speak of is not an emotion; however, it is expressed through the human as an emotion. But understood in this context, it becomes a thought, a feeling, and an action, moving into ONE as a unified field of activity. Questions?

Question: "So, what you are saying is that love is not dual?"

Indeed it is not. Love is that healer that soothes all disease. Love gives understanding in trying situations. Love is indeed a peace that passes all understanding of those in the dual expression. Love is the one that gives hope. Love is the one that gives charity. Love is the basis of all of faith. Love contains harmony and abundance. Love is indeed a great equalizer of all forces. Dear ones, Dear hearts, love is the basis of your growth and evolution. And yet, at times, the pangs of love give such pain, do they not? Bring such stresses to the mind? Lead one into a greater arena of choice? But this forward movement, it is good. This forward movement is, indeed, leading you to a greater understanding. This level of consciousness is known as the Christ. Continue.

HIGHER LOVE AND CONSCIOUSNESS

Question: "And so, am I to understand that throughout creation, that love is the great motivator for the existence of creation and the completion of it?"

Love is indeed desire, but in its higher form. It is as a motivator. It is the great inspiration, is it not? But love cannot be categorized or catalogued as belonging to just one situation. It is an energy force that comes in and ties all together as ONE. Now throughout this whole discourse, I have given you many examples of love. I have shown you many different ways these examples are seen. Remember, the individual perception or experience of love is somewhat limited, but when I speak of love at these levels, it moves one ahead into a different understanding, a different consciousness. This new consciousness contains healing. This new consciousness moves beyond time. This new consciousness brings one to the deathless and the birthless body. For Dear ones, Dear hearts, love is one of the keys to conscious immortality. Love, you see Dear one, Dear heart, is that breath that breathes the breath for all, does it not?

Answer: "Yes, this is true, it does breathe the breath for all. So regardless of how trying a situation may be, when one can search for the love in yourself or in the situation, then you can walk that path through it."

Always, Dear one, Dear heart. As Dear Sananda has often said to you, "All is love Dear heart. When all is said and done, that is the one that is remaining."

Question: "This is very true, as has been explained to me many times. Is there time to ask questions now from those who have had questions from the last discourse?"

I have come forward specifically for this purpose.

Question: "Then I have a question from someone who asks, 'Can you please expand on the ancient race of highly evolved inhabitants who contributed to the development of Earth civilizations. Who are they and are they here now?' "

TWO SUNS

All is present now, as all that has ever been and all that will ever be. All is contained, shall we say, within that mighty Law of Love, within that greater unity. Know and understand this first as the eternal law. But what is spoken of here is from the annals of another time, another frequency, for that brings a greater understanding. As I have said so many times, there is no mistake, ever, ever, ever. What this is indeed, is the statement of vibration, of like seeking its like, of water, shall we say, seeking its own level.

The Galactic Center, the Great Central Sun, has served as a pivotal point for the evolution of your solar system, streaming forth, arcing in light and sound consciousness, moving to your own Sun. This brought a birth, at one time in a different period, shall we say, of vibration. During this time, this force brought and birthed

Sacred Fire 89

another Sun, which moved alongside the Sun, almost in equal light and intensity. This brought a greater and a higher consciousness to the Earth. But as I stated before, there was indeed another planet that came through this which is known now in your time as a dark Sun. These beings resided very closely to both of the Suns. In fact, at one moment in that time period, the planet was located between the two dual Suns.

THE ANCESTORS

The Sun, from your own experience, is hot and will burn away with great intensity but this was a planet of sorts that thrived from the energy of the light. The bodies that were of the beings upon this planet were not restricted through duality, instead their consciousness resided at higher levels of understanding. They took on bodies at will and dropped them at will. These beings understood completely the birthless and the deathless body. They encapsulated, if you could understand this, a greater purity and a greater harmony. They moved forward Dear ones, Dear hearts, as those entrusted, in a sense, as ancestors to this life stream. When I speak of this life stream, I speak now of life on Earth, as you now know it. As you know, life is continually evolving the same way that you are continually changing, moving, and growing. Your body reflects these changes through emotions . . . through smiles . . . through tears . . . through the expression of all feelings. You see these changes and feel these changes. As time moves on, you understand the growth process that your soul is making, do you not?

It is important to understand that this growth process is guided and directed by a greater consciousness. This is not to say that your own will is not developed, for indeed it is Dear ones, Dear hearts. And it is not to say that there are those controlling your choices, for indeed you are engendered with your own will. But there are influences Dear ones, Dear hearts, as you well know and understand; these influences known as light and sound play a part. They play a part in bringing you to the pivotal point of applying your will for greater good, of applying your will for choice made within and through the Law of Love.

These beings have worked throughout the whole solar system. They (can) reside within the frequencies of duality of light and sound. This is perhaps the easiest way for you to understand. They bring a greater guidance towards the Great Central Sun. They help to dispense karma; now when I say this, I say this not as an action of retribution. Indeed, they work in a greater arena, a greater scope, to allow dispensations of events, history if you will, to come forward to the Earth Plane and Planet. They will continue, Dear ones, Dear hearts, to be present and guide humanity, guide the schoolrooms of all of the solar system. This guidance comes forward Dear ones, Dear hearts, through that great understanding of the Law of Love. It comes forward, Dear one, Dear heart, in that great alignment to the Divine Plan, in the Divine Will.

It is true, as your Earth grows in light and sound frequencies, the presence of these greater beings will be known and understood. However, as you understand, like vibration can only understand like vibration. So there is some limitation presently, for lack of a greater explanation, for you to thoroughly know and understand that of which I speak. Questions?

Question: "So these great beings are, in essence, your teachers?"

Indeed they are Dear one, Dear heart.

Question: "And they are still here in sponsorship of you, as you are of the rest of us?"

It is so. For you see, they exist beyond a body. They exist beyond a form. They exist beyond the dual expression of time. However, if necessary, they put on a form at will, to provide whatever service may be needed.

A HIDDEN, GUIDING PLANET

Question: "I understand. So, this planet which is hidden is still inhabited by them but not at the dimension we can perceive?"

It is true Dear one. It appears now only as an abandoned, dark planet, with no life contained at all; however, as you move through the annals of time, that which I speak of as Dvapara Yuga, you will know and understand this with greater perception.

Question: "So, you are saying that we have to be in a different time period, where there is more luminosity for us, to be able to perceive their existence?"

It is true Dear one, Dear heart. However, at times, you do sense the presence of this greater force. This was the intention of the one who asked this question. The one who is aligned to ask this question feels a greater harmony and alignment to this greater force, feels this presence, greater and divine, guiding their life. That is why this question was asked.

Question: "So, this planet is still in existence. All of the alien visitors who have come to our planet are really overseen by this great civilization."

It is true Dear one, Dear heart. However, you must understand that all works upon these principles of frequency and vibration, of like attracting like, opposites repelling one another. Of course, I speak in such simple terms. In time, this understanding will grant enlightenment.

Question: "So those who are perceived, for example, in the so-called secret government, affecting and controlling the destiny of humanity, are they part of that Divine Plan and are overseen and guided by your teachers?"

It is obvious that they are, for they are here, are they not?

Answer: "Yes they are."

And we have had several discussions, have we not, regarding the Laws of Cause and Effect?

Answer: "Yes, we have."

Proceed with your questions.

Question: "We have another question by a person who asks, 'Is the hidden planet Nibiru?'"

THE NON-DUAL CHRIST FORCE

No. It is as I have spoken. However, this planet exists as well. I spoke of the hidden planet, so one could gain a greater insight into the timing of light and sound, to begin to master choice. But there is indeed this planet that is spoken of and these beings have played a role in the present condition on planet Earth. That is why it was sent out long ago for the Lords of Venus to come and build Shamballa. There are those present upon this planet who have worked in cooperation with the Lords of Venus. For you see Dear ones, Dear hearts, when we enter into higher consciousness, we all work from a greater energy force, that which is known beyond the limitations of duality. This energy force, as you well know and understand, is sometimes known as Unana, sometimes called the Christ Force, but it is presently also known as a Meissner Field. This is contained individually and yet collectively. It is important to understand that at this level of understanding, adversity does not exist. A greater harmony moves in a greater spectrum of light and sound. Questions?

Response: "What you are saying then is, in the dualistic world, where these visitors have come and played a part in the alteration of our genetics, at the higher levels, their presence is not discord."

It is true, for contained even within yourself are thoughts and feelings that are discordant and yet also contained within yourself are thoughts and feelings that have been brought into complete balance, are there not?

Answer: "This is all true, yes."

LOVE, CONSCIOUSNESS, AND PROPHECY

This is indeed the human condition, working to bring all within balance, working to bring that reconciliation to that neutral point of which I speak. At this neutral point comes the opportunity to experience the Law of Love, to move into greater arenas of understanding, to experience beyond dual understanding. It is true that Nibiru contains a comet trail, or shall we say, an asteroid or meteor that trails towards Earth. As described in the Earth Changes Prophecies, this is very possible. However, as you well know, prophecy is brought forward to bring about change. It is the change within the heart, you see Dear ones, Dear hearts, that affects all at an electromagnetic level. It brings one into greater healing.

Now, imagine if you will, three people activating this greater change within the heart and moving it towards a collective understanding, into a greater global arena. Imagine then, one hundred people, one thousand people, ten thousand people. This I know Dear ones, Dear hearts, has always been your focus and your goal. It is important then to understand that consciousness contains the key to prophecy, contains the key to circumventing all disasters and moving into that fresh perspective. Do you understand?

Answer: "Yes."

Questions?

POSSIBILITY AND PROBABILITY

Question: "Yes. This person also asked, 'Is Nibiru the planet that will pass close by our own planet and if so, around what year would this occur?'"

It is impossible to place a date upon such an event; for you see Dear ones, Dear hearts, time is a dual expression and the information and source of this instruction moves beyond the dual. However, as we have always stated, there will come a time where this will be a possibility. We state this as prophecy. We state this so there will be those who will move forward in their spiritual growth and understanding and be able to take these teachings and apply them into greater actions. As I have always stated before, there will be warnings that will come from the scientific community before such an event. There will be a minimum of seven years warning time given before such an event. Remember when we spoke of possibility versus probability?

Answer: "Yes."

This is still a great possibility. Probability lies within the wills of humanity. Proceed.

Question: "Are we as a planet acting out of character within the harmony of the solar system and this is how these types of events are attracted to us?"

"A CHANGE OF HEART"

It is one way of understanding. However, I would prefer to say that this is a planet that is moving, learning to move in greater light and sound frequencies. The Earth is not set upon a destructive path. It is set upon a path of construction and growth. Yes, there have been times upon the planet where destruction was necessary and indeed, these times may possibly come again. As I have always stated, that choice is left to each individual heart. Proceed.

Response and Question: "So, it literally is as you have said before, "A change of heart can change the world." It is one heart at a time, coming together in the unification of love that transitions all of us to that greater light. Is this not so?"

Sacred Fire 95

It is true Dear heart.

Response: "Then at this point, I have no further questions."

I shall take my leave and return at our next appointed session. Hitaka.

Response: "Hitaka."

CHAPTER EIGHT

The Master Within
Saint Germain awakens the Master within.

Greetings Beloved chelas, students of mine, in that mighty Violet Ray. I AM Saint Germain and I stream forth on that Violet Ray of Mercy, Compassion, and Forgiveness. As usual Dear hearts, I request your permission to come forth.

Response: "Please Saint Germain you are most welcome. Come forth."

THE METAPHYSICAL LAW OF RECIPROCITY

Dear ones, it is still important to note, for those who do not understand this, that I always ask permission to come forth. For you see Dear ones, we work together in this capacity through what is known as "Agreement." It is this reciprocal energy, you see Dear ones, Dear hearts, that allows this consciousness to stream forth. You see, you have said, "Yes, I am ready to receive" and I have also said, "Yes I am ready to give." In that same measure, you give back to what you know as me, the teacher, and I receive that energy back. You see, it works in a reciprocal approach. One often would think that they are always just giving their energy away to someone, but you see that is impossible, for all things work within a balance. Energy flows within; energy flows without. This is a Law Eternal of how this energy comes forth . . . of how this teaching comes forth . . . of how healing comes forth for all of humanity. Energy flows within; energy flows without.

Dear ones, Dear hearts, today I would like to give further insight into the relationship of the student and the teacher. For you see Dear ones, I have spoken before of this relationship. But it is important to understand this relationship, so one may gain deeper insight into the process. It is true that you and I have worked through many different lifetimes and have built an energy that was accessed in this lifetime with great ease. I have spoken of this in several past discourses to you. So it is no wonder Dear one, Dear heart, as you proceed in your own, shall we say, Mastership of taking on students to bring their learning to a greater level, that you too have had a past life relationship with those that you work with. That is why energy does flow within and it flows without.

Let us address another aspect, an element of this relationship. As this energy is built through lifetime after lifetime, it builds a reciprocity of the mental energies. That energy body that you call thought comes into a greater alignment. There is a sympathetic harmony and a sympathetic resonance that occurs within the teaching process. The teacher and the student also then receive this energy in a greater harmony and alignment to the Plan Divine. But it is also important to understand, in this sympathetic harmony or sympathetic resonance of energies, that there also exists an alignment to the emotional fields, the emotional bodies.

A TEACHER LIFTS EMOTIONAL BURDEN

As you have always understood, it is thought and then feeling that comes into this greater alignment. There is a resonance of feeling that is the emotion. Within this emotion, that comes forward for greater healing and greater release into the spiritual life, the teacher takes on any emotional fluctuations in a greater resonance. You well know, when you take a student on and begin to work with them, it requires a greater, shall we say, uplifting of burdens. In the same way, when the Master teacher takes on the student, you feel a great upliftment. In that moment, you feel a great joy, a great peace, a great inner harmony. For in that moment, all emotional burdens have been lifted from you, so the mental body can work with its greater clarity, in its greater capacity. Now, you with your own students, have you not noticed this? You lift their emotional burdens so that their thought processes can be freed to see with greater clarity?

Answer: "Yes and it is the path to do so."

GENTLE LEADERSHIP

It is indeed Dear one, Dear heart. It is the way that this time-honored tradition moves forward. From there, the Master teacher then withdraws the support of the emotional energy, gently, gracefully, with ease. This allows for that greater integration of thought and feeling to marry into a greater alignment of clarity; then, actions move forward. This is the way that we work, so that you may understand, in an energetic level. But it is also important to understand that, at all times, no expectation is held from the teacher to the student. No expectation is ever held at all. For you see, it is true that the Master teacher never truly tells the student what to do. Indeed, it is a gentle guidance or shall we say, leadership unto the natural laws, so the student may experience and experiment with the laboratory of the self. This you have come to know Dear ones, Dear hearts, that experimentation of the laboratory of the self.

WITHIN THE SILENCE

As I have often said, "To do, to dare, and to be silent." Sometimes it is within that Great Silence of the self that one finds the greater challenge that lies within, that one finds the greater mountains of emotional upheaval or painful emotional wounds that are yet to be healed. In that Great Silence is where we find a greater alignment; an alignment, yes, to the greater Plan Divine, but also an alignment to the self, choosing to gain that element of self-Mastery. Self-Mastery requires a honed focus, for the honed focus then understands and realizes that one is working with a greater harmony of these energy bodies of thought, feeling, and action.

It is true that the emotional burdens of the past sometimes limit or, shall we say, set askew the perceptual sight. But it is important, Dear one, to spend time within the deep silence, to ask of the self, within that one clear honest moment, "Is this truly within the intention of myself?" "Is this truly in the alignment with the heart of my desires?" "Am I truly moving beyond desire and into my spiritual liberation and freedom?"

OUT-PICTURING PERFECTION

Now, we know that all chelas, all students, that come unto this work are at different levels. Everyone, as you well know Dear one, Dear heart, moves and grows with a timing and intent. We cannot force a student to grow at a certain time. We cannot say at this moment, you will forget all that has happened, at this moment, you will transmute and purify and move to a new level of clarity. No Dear one, it does not happen that way. But that pure crystal out-picturing is always there, the out-picturing of perfection. Say unto yourself:

> Beloved mighty I AM Presence,
> I out-picture pure perfection in this moment of my Divine Self moving towards the Ascension and light in the Divine Plan, almighty I AM.

INTEGRATION, COMPASSION, AND ENLIGHTENMENT

Such a statement brings a clarity and focus to the consciousness, does it not? It brings, in that moment, a greater knowing of the true self. This knowing brings an understanding of the mental body, using the mental body as a tool. Now Dear ones, Dear hearts, begin to understand thought and feeling and how they work within the human body in duality. The emotional body was brought forward from the animal consciousness. The emotional body contains within it, the instinct and intellect for survival. But as this body becomes more integrated with the heart, through the path of compassion, one then is ready to begin to understand the tutelage of knowledge. Greater understanding brings within it an enlightenment. This enlightenment brings the understanding that one may hold in their perception, or shall I say, point of perception, an understanding of creation.

ABSOLUTE SELF-KNOWLEDGE

Of course, this point of perception is indeed, as you well know, a point of the Co-creation process. Co-creation moves one beyond animal behavior, moves one beyond the instincts and into pure knowledge. One does not have the gut feeling, but one has the absolute knowledge, for they are integrated as ONE with the point of perception. This is a choice indeed Dear ones, Dear hearts. It is a choice to gain such self-knowledge. But one is continually held back, shall we say, by the feelings of emotions. These emotions indeed are important, for they lead one into greater understanding of the human experience. Therefore Dear ones, Dear hearts, nothing is lost and all is gained.

OPENING THE HEART

But it takes time, does it not? It takes time to bring a greater understanding. It takes time to have the experiences, to know the difference. All of this leads, at the emotional level, to the opening of the heart and the greater plan of perfection. For in the opening of the heart, then one is able to understand the intention behind Alchemy, the intention behind transmutation, the intention behind a purification process that leads one then to a greater honing of the choice of thought.

Now I'll introduce this concept to you Dear one, Dear heart: the choice of thoughts.

CHOOSING THE THOUGHT

There are many thoughts to choose from in this world of Co-creation, many that come with their sets of beliefs, their sets of values, their sets of circumstances, situations, and experiences. These thoughts are played out in greater strata of harmony, in greater strata of understanding, in greater strata of feeling. These thoughts bring with them that greater experience of Co-creation, leading one then to the true perfection that exists within the Oneship. Now, as I explain these two bodies to you today, as we have talked about so many times before, it is my hope that you have gained greater insight, a greater insight in assisting your students, and a greater insight in understanding how energy flows within and energy flows without. Questions?

Response and question: "It is really choosing the thought that has a specific purpose, so that then the feeling aids the specific focus. We can choose many thoughts and yet, not all thoughts and feelings serve the great desire that we might have, whether it is to accomplish something or whether it is to be free, is this not so?"

As always Dear one, Dear heart, for Mastery understands all choices that are available, but it also accepts the circumstances that follow such choice, without expectation. The expectations show self-desires that are more designed to keep one trapped within illusion. There is only but one desire that shall free you and that is the desire to know God . . . that is the desire to know perfection . . . that is the desire of the heart, the true energy of the Source. Dear one, Dear heart, I would also like to remind you that I am always with you, that I am always here for your help and assistance. I am but your call away.

BE READY TO RECEIVE

In your weekly program that you are bringing forward, know this Dear one, that I will always be available to bring discourse to your students. I am always there at a moment's call, at a moment's notice. I offer this, as you see, for energy flows within; energy flows without. Those students who have now come forward are prepared and ready to receive a greater energy. They are prepared and readied now to receive this greater influx of energy, preparing them for that alignment to the Divine Plan. I bring this energy forward, not as a crutch; for as you see Dear one, Dear heart, even throughout your week, you too must take all into thought, feeling, and action.

AWAKEN THE MASTER WITHIN

In this moment, yes, while your heart leaps with joy to know such union with God, there comes that moment too where the Master Teacher steps back and allows you to have your own experience. This comes with its variety of human emotions: frustrations, joys, expectations, love, hate, fear, all of these, as part of the human condition. But know this Dear one, within that desire to know God is the most refreshing drink. Know, that in that desire to be as ONE, is your true Divine Heritage. As you well know, this great divinity that lies within is indeed a sleeping Master within. It is awakened and enlivened through the knowledge of the Great IAM.

> Beloved mighty I AM Presence,
> come forth and awaken the Master within.
> May the voice that I speak align in thought, feeling, and action
> to the truth of God, eternal I AM.

As you see Beloved, as you see Dear heart, when you call this decree into action, this, shall we say, scientific formula that I have given to you, you call upon the Master within. There indeed, the eyes open, the ears open, and a greater alignment comes forth. It is there to give you the support. It is there to give you the strength throughout your week. It is there to help you in your journey. Though small, yet baby steps, know this Dear one, Dear heart, that they are larger steps for you. For as you well know, as you travel this spiritual journey, the path does indeed seem narrow at times, the climb is arduous, but each step forward is monumental in gaining your freedom. For you see Dear ones, Dear hearts, you are working these days within yourself, using these laws eternal. This is how you do indeed gain your freedom. Questions?

Response: "Yes. My freedom is my greatest desire and to be with all of you as my family. In all honesty, this world many, many times does not offer me a great interest, except to bring forward what you have entrusted with us."

THE SPIRITUAL PATHS

There are several paths through which this is gained. You are familiar with these I am certain, but I will remind you. There is the Path of Love. There is the Path of Knowledge. There is the Path of Service, which is the strongest. Also, there is none at all. Sometimes a chela applies all three; sometimes the chela applies one that they feel a greater alignment towards. In your case, it has always been the Path of Service first. But it is important to understand, that all of these as a choice are just as important as any one individual. These paths come forward to give to the chela a broad spectrum of experience. They allow a greater alignment for their own Divine Plan.

It is true that some feel the harmony working day-by-day, helping another to rise above their own situation. It is true that some feel a greater harmony by understanding the mysteries of life, the laws eternal, and how they exist and work to bring mankind into greater healing and development. And there are those who simply love, love, love, and then, love more. For this is also a path of ultimate surrender to God. These unions bring a greater understanding of the quality of the Christ. They bring a greater understanding of the dimension that lies beyond duality, the dimension of Unana, the Oneship.

One path is not more important than the other, not one more pure or more innocent. But all of them work to bring the human, the one who desires perfection, to rise above the sorrows of the human condition . . . to see the joy that lies within . . . to express it on a daily basis. Is this not then the basis of immortality? Is this not then the basis of the true Oneship, of moving beyond the restraints of time, of left, right, good, bad, light, dark, or evil. Then one can clearly see with open eyes and open ears. Then one is ready to speak in the presence of the Master. This is indeed the heart that has been opened through compassion. Questions?

Response and question: "Love has brought me here to this place and instigated that service. Each of these paths is truly about feeling and in action, it is love. But there is much work we still have to do in the fulfillment of this path and it will be, in our time frame, a while before we are completely together. The question that I ask, is it only through the love for humanity and the world that all of this is brought forward?"

WE ARE ALWAYS ONE

There is a perception of separation Dear one, Dear heart, I realize, as you travel in the journey of duality. But know this, I am always with you. The Master resides within, but you must awaken the Master to bring it forward into its greater knowledge, its greater Work Divine. Know that I am always with you. Know that there are those who have gone before you and they too are with you Dear one, Dear heart. Know, as in that Law Eternal, energy flows within, energy flows without and this life force connects us all as ONE. For indeed, you must understand, in this context of knowledge, we are as ONE. In this moment of this transmission, the consciousness, or point of perception, is uniting our energy field. That is our thought force as ONE. Know this, that in that moment, at your request, we are always as ONE.

Question: "So Be It. It looks as though the decree you have given me is the next step?"

It is indeed Dear one. And know that I am always with you. Know that I am here for your assistance. Also, know this Dear heart, Dear chela, that there is no such thing as failure, only moving on the path, one sure step at a time. So Be It.

Response: "So Be It. I have no further questions."

I shall return for our next meeting. Hitaka.

Response: "Hitaka."

CHAPTER NINE

The Mighty Violet Flame
*Saint Germain shares teachings
on the Violet Flame.*

Greetings Beloveds, in that mighty Violet Ray. I AM Saint Germain and I request permission to come forward.

Response: "Please Saint Germain, come forward. You are most welcome."

CALL THE FLAME INTO ACTIVITY

Welcome Dear students, chelas, aspirants on the path of light and self-Mastery. I AM Saint Germain. Dear ones, Dear hearts, it is always important to address that mighty Violet Flame, its purpose, its intention, and why I always place such great emphasis upon the Violet Flame. As you well know, the Violet Flame has been brought forward at this time to lessen the karmic burdens of humanity. When it is used and brought into its proper application, it has the effect to eliminate karmas that happen at very subtle levels. When you use the Violet Flame, call it forth into its immeasurable activity:

> Violet Flame I AM, come forth from the ethers of the
> Great Divine.
> May the Violet Flame blaze in, through, and around me,
> transmuting the cause and effect, record and memory, forever,
> of karmas of the past, where I may be inhibited from my spiritual
> growth divine.

This statement has the power to bring the Violet Flame surrounding you. Yes, just one statement will bring this Violet Flame and magnetize your electromagnetic fields. Throughout that day, the Violet Flame then will be carried in all interactions. That Violet

Flame is also brought forth in the most trying of circumstance and situation.

> Mighty Violet Flame come forward
> and bring your Divine Intervention of comfort and peace
> to this situation.
> May all stream forward from the heart of the
> Great Central Divine Plan.
> So Be It.

Again, when you make such a statement and call that flame into its activity, into any situation and circumstance, one is lifted from all karmic inhibition and, there and then, its alchemizing fires bring a sense of purification ... bring a sense of Alchemy ... bring a sense of balance into any situation that is trying. It allows, at that time, for agreement to stream forth between any two individuals who may be in discord or disharmony. It allows for a harmony then to pursue an agreement which then can be enacted. In this Time of great Change, it is important that harmony reign supreme between those of humanity. It is important also to understand the Laws of Harmony and how they work at a much higher level to raise your consciousness and to bring you into a greater spiritual evolution.

THE GREAT CHANGE

The spiritual evolution is always important, Dear ones, Dear hearts. We have been discussing how human consciousness evolves and when I explained the Hidden Planet, I brought this discourse forward for you to begin to understand that there are those who have been engendered or entrusted with the Divine Plan of humanity. It is I, as a willing servant, who carry this Plan forward. Of course, I am also enjoined by my many Brothers and Sisters on the path of Mastery. There are also those among humanity who lift their hands and hearts in complete and total willingness, to bring this plan forward in a greater alignment to harmony, in a greater alignment to the great transitional change.

It was decided some time ago, that during the Time of the great Transition of Mother Earth, that this would give the greatest potential and the greatest possibility to also bring about a transformation in the collective heart of humanity. It has always been known that during these Times of great Transition, great Purification, and great Change, that the greatest possibility then awaits. Of course, we also must understand the Laws of Light and Sound and how the Ray Forces interact with the Great Central Sun, or the Great Galactic Center. It is important to see, in this timing and intention, how humanity is ordered and show how the universes, existing within the Solar System Divine, are all ordered in timing and intention.

JUSTICE AND THE VIOLET FLAME

But it is also important to understand the Violet Flame. The Violet Flame, you see Dear ones, Dear hearts, is that Law, yes, of Justice. Beyond that, it brings not only an equalizing effect but it opens up the potential for mercy and compassion in all situations. Of the highest of these two paths, it is always better to serve the heart, is it not Dear ones? It is always important to consider that compassion and mercy lift one into a higher vibration and order and prepare one for the consciousness of true Unana. Yes, it is good to feel that things are balanced. Yes, it is good to feel that things are in their right place and in their right order. But of all things Dear ones, Dear hearts, what have I taught you? But the path of the heart . . . the path of the Oneship . . . the path of compassion. This too is brought about through the understanding of the alchemizing fires of the Violet Flame.

> Mighty Violet Flame, blaze in, through, and around this situation.
> May the Heart of Compassion now open and bring me peace.

This decree is to be said in any situation where you feel there has been an injustice or a miscarriage of events. This also brings balance into situations that you may not understand. The human condition is one where, at times, one is constantly asking the question, "Why has this happened? What can I do? How can this be?" Such questions often are never answered, are they Dear ones? But questions bring an evolutionary leap in consciousness, lead one onward to seek the true nature of the self, to enter into that true

Sacred Fire

heart of desire. Within the heart itself and that great Eight-sided Cell of Perfection lies the true intention of the soul . . . lies that true connection to universal Oneship and the Brotherhoods and Sisterhoods of Breath, Sound, and Light.

YOUR DIVINITY

When I speak of the Master within, I also address this mighty Temple of the ONE, for this perfection is the divinity that lies within. This perfection is your great inheritance. You see Dear ones, Dear hearts, you were not brought here to just bring balance to actions. You were also brought here with great purpose and intention to move forward and to realize great potential and possibility. But this great potential and possibility lies only in the knowledge that you are as the God I AM. This I AM blazes in, through, and around you and you can command the I AM into action when you say unto yourself:

I AM the resurrection and the life.

You encode, in that moment within that Perfect Cell, the vibration and the energy of life effervescent when you command unto yourself:

I AM eternal life. Down with death.
Conscious immortality arise through I AM.

In that moment, you affirm that life eternal is the essence over death and that the life eternal, the immortality, the true essence of the soul, is within your being. This perfection, you see Dear ones, Dear hearts, is commanded and demanded into its being. Why is this so? For you see again, as I have stated, you did not just come here to bring balance to situations. And why balance is, at times, demanded through that mighty Law of Nature, it is also important that you realize and understand your Divine Godship that lies within.

USE OF THE I AM AND THE VIOLET FLAME

In the last three discourses, we have been addressing elementary steps to self-Mastery. Today, we talk about the Great IAM and its integration with the Violet Flame, to bring one into a heightened area of realization of self. In the realization of the true self, one understands in that moment, their Co-creatorship. One understands in that moment, that in any given situation, through quiet and careful recollection, through quiet and careful silencing of the self, one can call forth that perfect source of the I AM. Yes indeed, I speak of the I AM as the great Eight-sided Cell of Perfection, but I also speak of the science of the Rays and how they work so masterfully together. As I have stated before, it is through the use of the I AM and the Violet Flame, that these two elements scientifically come together and bring comfort to the Ray Forces, melding them in one group effort, raising them to another level of understanding, and vibrating them to another Cause Divine.

Yes indeed, Dear ones, Dear hearts, the Violet Flame is a Divine Intervention. It is an intervention that has been brought at this specific time for a specific purpose. Use it daily in your applications and I promise you Dear ones, Dear hearts, that you shall have and imbibe that most refreshing drink. And now I ask, do you have any questions?

Question: "Yes I do. The Violet Flame, as I understand it, is here in its transformative ability for our growth and development, so that we may move on in our own evolution. Is this the most direct way to do this evolutionary process?"

It is true Dear one, for not only does it bring balance and justification to the karmic Law of Nature, to cause and effect, and to justice, as one would say, it also opens the heart to that ever evolutionary step of compassion and love.

Response: "So, at the simplest level, the Violet Flame is the calling forth the Ray into action and it is our Divine Right to be able to do this."

It is calling forth not only the Ray but a higher force, a higher vibration that is enjoined by many of those who have gone before you. For you see Dear ones, Dear hearts, the Violet Flame, while yes, identifies with certain Ray Forces, it is also a motion that has been set into the creation by a conscious force, to bring forward a greater evolution in humanity at this important time.

Question: "There is a difference though between the Violet Ray and the Violet Flame, isn't there?"

HIGHER VIBRATION

It is so Dear one, Dear heart. The Violet Ray is the Ray Force as it energizes and imbibes, shall we say, upon the Earth Plane and Planet. The Violet Flame is Mercy and Compassion in action. It is indeed a spiritual force that one may access on a much more subtle level. The Violet Flame is carried throughout that Tube of Light and indeed, it crosses, shall we say, for lack of better understanding, with the Ray Forces and can be detected as a visible light force and as an audible sound. The Violet Flame is indeed a spiritual teaching that brings one to a higher order or vibration of consciousness. Do you understand?

Answer: "Yes."

THE NEW CONSCIOUSNESS

This is not to state that it is only a spiritual teaching, for it is not. It contains so much more. It contains within it, an awakening to another way of being. It contains the ability to adjust perception. It contains the ability to change circumstances and situations. Proceed.

Question: "So, the Violet Flame interacts with the Earth Plane and Planet?"

It brings a lightening of consciousness. When I speak of this lightening, I speak again of Rays of Light and Sound. But it also enters one into the threshold of the beginning stages of the new consciousness, that which I have always spoken of as Unana. This consciousness of the ONE is where all functions through the ONE and understands the ONE. Now I know in this moment, to introduce such an idea, especially for those who are still struggling even with the concept of dual consciousness, it is important to understand that as we move into this new understanding, the heart of love erupts with the most joy.

It is also important to understand that the Violet Flame comes at a time of great and intense suffering of humanity to uplift, to give hope. It also brings an evolutionary opportunity to move beyond the current situation. It allows the light bodies to integrate and adjust. It allows the creation of new light bodies to appear. It allows, shall we say, that burst of the new wine skin. Therefore indeed, it is a consciousness akin to the birth of the Christ, the new child within. It contains all hopes and possibilities . . . it contains all potentials to bring about self-Mastery. Questions?

THE EARTH PLANE AND PLANET

Question: "Would you specifically define the difference between the Earth Plane and the Earth Planet?"

The Earth Plane is the realms of consciousness that exist. For instance Dear ones, there are many levels or forms of consciousness that exist at one given time. There are those, who in the most simplistic approach, have much fear. There are those who have much doubt. There are those who have education. There are those who have love. There are those who have compassion. Now, each of these are at varying degrees. There are states or levels of consciousness. There are indeed, as one would also begin to understand, points of perception. The Earth Plane is filled with many levels, many dimensions that exist of consciousness and the creations that ensue thereof. However, know this Dear ones, Dear hearts, that the Earth Plane, in its own evolution, is an illusion. Now, when I state this, it is an illusion brought with purpose, brought with intention. It is an illusion that is the balance of karma and purpose.

But now, let us move on to the Earth Planet. The Earth Planet is also a consciousness. In the same way that the Earth Plane contains many levels of consciousness, the Earth Planet is comprised of the Mineral, Vegetable, and Animal Kingdoms, and the humans. It also contains a greater comprised consciousness, the systems of Beloved Babajeran. The Earth Planet, Babajeran, exists in her own timing and intention, for she serves at this time as a great schoolroom, to assist and help mankind, to assist and help humanity, as we all well know. Babajeran serves the many rounds of incarnation that one may take into the Earth Plane and Planet.

The Earth Planet contains the physical body that must give to the Laws of Nature. And in Babajeran, the Mother Earth, exists the many Laws of Nature, the Deva Kingdoms, and the Elemental Kingdoms. Within the Elemental Kingdom are the sylphs, as the wind spirits; the undines, as the water spirits; the mighty salamanders, as the spirits of the fires; the little ones of the gnomes and the fairies; and all of the kingdoms that some have had the opportunity to contact and give information about. The Earth Planet serves in the mighty evolution of its own solar system. It serves for the arcing of Ray Forces to other planetary streams. It serves in its greater condition in this way, arcing vibrations of light and sound to other planets and getting, at will, a greater understanding of higher life forces.

THE HEAVENLY LORDS

The Earth Plane and Planet, when stated together, contain this higher frequency or vibration as a higher consciousness that knows and understands the two as they work simultaneously together. This higher consciousness is where many of those, who have obtained liberation from the physical body, then move into these greater dimensional vibrations. These are known as the Heavenly Lords where they preside. At times, we speak of these as entering into the Fourth or the Fifth Dimension. These other dimensions indeed do exist and these are also comprised of the Earth Plane and Planet.

A PLANE OF CONSCIOUSNESS

   The human knows and understands very much of the Earth Plane, for there it comes to test, shall we say, the score of consciousness. There it comes to make choices, to learn about the will, thought, feeling, and action. As it travels in its many sojourns, learning through many situations and circumstances, it is awakened to the idea of the planet itself and its connection to a more vital life force. In that moment, it is awakened to the ONE process, understanding the common ground, or the universal consciousness, that affects all things. This universal consciousness is of course very important in all spiritual development, for then, one begins to understand the true meaning of the Earth Planet. What is the Earth Planet? How does the Earth Planet move and evolve? What is the science of the Earth Planet? You see, science then serves in its greater movement and understanding and brings the consciousness, or shall we say, active intelligence, to another level. Now this may also be perceived as a plane again of consciousness but it is a plane of consciousness that begins to integrate and move one into a greater understanding. Questions?

Response: "Yes. That was a very thorough explanation, thank you. And now, I ask permission to ask questions from those who have sent us emails."

   Proceed.

Question: "One person states, 'This week I saw a program on tech TV. A physicist was explaining the String Theory, something that some think is the next step to combine relativity and Quantum Theory into a Unified Field Theory. He said, "The mind of God is music resonating through ten dimensional strings." Can you share insights?'"

BEYOND IMAGINATION

   This is indeed related to Unified Field Theory. However, it is suggested that this individual begin to study Hermetic Law. There they will find the complete teaching in its totality. It is true that all things within the universe are interrelated, in the same sense that the Earth Plane and the Earth Planet are as ONE. However, they exist simultaneously as two. It is important to understand cycles and rhythms, then one can more easily understand the idea of a Unified Field Theory.

Dear ones, Dear hearts, it is also important to understand this time, for this time is of great import to humanity. While this is stated over and over again in many discourses that I have brought forward to you, it is a wonderful opportunity that is being presented at this time. This too, is related to Unified Field Theory. You see, it has to do with the idea that consciousness can grow beyond what can be imagined. Now that may seem unusual for one who is commanding and demanding with intention and in purpose, but there are also laws that exist within the field of rhythm, as I have suggested, that allow the concept of momentum to overtake. This shall give this Dear one some solution.

Response: "Thank you. I have another question."

Proceed.

AWAKENING FROM DARKNESS

Question: "Regarding Kali Yuga, I heard that in India, in January, many sages gathered for a week long celebration of the end of Kali Yuga. If you have seen a book called the 'Lemurian Scrolls,' it seems that Kali Yuga began to finish in around 1849, when the first light bulb was made. Is it an overlapping process, as you have mentioned?"

Not only is it an overlapping process, it is also stated as a level of defining consciousness. Often times, when I speak of Kali Yuga in teachings, I speak of the broad based percentage of population. Now, at this time, it would seem that most of the population is still within the darkness of Kali Yuga, the time of iron, the time of lesser light that humanity has recently experienced. However, this is a great time of opportunity, awakening, and opening to greater light and consciousness.

SILICON-BASED CONSCIOUSNESS

The next stage of conscious growth is that of Dvapara Yuga, where we will see the opening of the mind to greater possibilities and potential. We will see the development, not only of the mind, in terms of its ability to receive new information, but growth within the Third Eye. We will see the use of telepathy to integrate with new technologies as they are developed within the next 200 years. We will see also this, as I have always stated, the silicon-based consciousness that is erupting within humanity. We will see many great changes in the medical field. In this, in particular, you will see in the next 150 years, great changes in terms of longevity. This is also one of the newer opportunities presented through the greater light spectrum of Dvapara Yuga.

It is true that in the Time of Kali, the consciousness fell and the teachings that were guarded needed to be kept from those who would misuse them and bring even greater suffering upon the ignorant masses. But it is time now for these spiritual teachings to come forward for the greater understanding of the Oneship, of Unana, to be present and applied. Dvapara Yuga now rules for those who have the eyes to see and the ears to hear. In this same respect, so does Kali Yuga. But a Golden Age, Dear ones, Dear hearts, also can exist, if you but have the eyes to see and the ears to hear. Now, this would also indicate that, at any time, consciousness can be raised to its fullest potential. That I cannot deny, for I AM THAT I AM. Questions?

THE GIFT

Question: "Are you saying that the energy that flows from within and from without, as things transition, can overlap, but that the focus the individual carries allows them to interact with either the Kali Yuga cycle, the Dvapara Yuga cycle, or the Golden Age cycle, depending on the choice of focus?"

Perception always creates reality, as I have always stated in many of the teachings. It depends on how you wish to see it. Is the glass half filled or half empty? Does the rose have thorns or a sweet smelling petal? Again Dear one, it is up to the perceiver of experience. But realistically too, in timing and intention, this is also a time where things can vastly open up for those who choose for them to open. Dear ones, Dear hearts, the awakening is at hand. As Dear Sananda has said, "The time has come for man to receive the gift." Questions?

TRUST THE PROCESS

Question: "Another asks, 'We have received extensive information about the possibility of the dual Sun in our solar system and the race of people that have influenced our planet for hundreds of thousands of years. Is the theory possible, that a brown dwarf star is generating heat and light for a string of orbs, where at least one of these orbs is habitable?'"

It is possible indeed Dear ones, Dear hearts, and as we move into greater consciousness and light, more will be understood with this. In the next seventy-five years, there will be massive discoveries that will be made on such a theory. Now it is important to understand, indeed, as you are the progeny of perfection, your purpose is guided and directed by those elder Brothers and Sisters who have been entrusted with the Greater Plan Divine. Now we know at times, it is impossible to understand this greater consciousness and its existence. It is hard to understand that a science of predestination also fits like a glove with that of the science of the will and the development of the Master. But trust in the process, Dear ones, Dear hearts. This is my message to the one who has asked this question.

Question: "Thank you. Another asks Saint Germain about a Vortex that is in Oklahoma City, Oklahoma. 'I am inclined to think that we have an area that has developed by the events that have taken place there. It feels like a holding area, where those who have passed from this life and need to make their transition wait.' Would you comment?"

INTERACTION OF THE ELEMENTAL AND DEVA KINGDOMS

What is being addressed is a great emotional energy that has had an effect on the collective astral body of the Earth. Now, we all well know how these paranormal types of situations can sometimes exist but it is important to understand the Law of Nature, the Deva and Elemental Kingdoms, and the service that they provide. Very often, when an event of this nature has taken place with a great emotional sorrow, with great anguish, that at that moment in time, the Elemental and Deva Kingdoms come in and begin to adjust the energy fields that surround such an area. This is what this person has been sensing. It is also important for this person to begin to study this interaction, to begin to understand the Earth Planet and how it works in its own interaction in assisting and helping mankind.

This is bringing about a great healing effect, not only for those who have crossed over, for know this Dear ones, that they have gone on in the greater evolution and purpose. But the suffering and anguish, as we all well know, on the Earth Plane is for those who have been left behind. That is why the Elementals and the Devas come in and bring, shall we say, a great comfort to the suffering of the many. They come forward and remind us, that again the Sun will shine . . . that again the soft rains will fall . . . and the seasons will progress in their order and majesty. Questions?

OPENING THE GATE

Question: "Thank you. This one also asks, 'I have been working in the dream state and I need to inquire about it. At night, I have been doing work with the souls that are trapped and not able to go into the light and go home. My job has been to usher them to the light and to somehow keep the gate open. I feel rushed when doing this work, as I have trouble sustaining the opening of the light gate. How can I hone my skills, so that I can be more effective, stay longer, and reach the ones that are confused?'"

Before entering into the sleep at night repeat this:

> I AM surrounded with the Light of God that Never Fails.
> Mighy Violet Flame be with me
> through my travels and journeys into the other side of life.
> Assist and guide me Great Master within,
> so that I can help in the Plan Divine, I AM.

This will bring about a sense of protection and purpose, for it is only a matter of focus. I would also suggest that during the waking hours that this Beloved one take up the meditation with a candle, as I have instructed you. It is important now that you give her this instruction to hone her focus. This will give her great assistance.

IMMERSION INTO THE DIVINE

Question: "Thank you. Another asks, 'I discovered the Saint Germain teachings via the I AM Foundation a little over ten years ago and was turned away at a few of the I AM centers because I used illicit drugs, including LSD and other psychedelics, for a spiritual purpose. This was the foundation's strict policy. Presently, I am in my early thirties and not using drugs anymore but I would like advice from the Ascended Masters on the subject and some clarification. It was interesting to me why indigenous peoples have used these psychoactive drugs in ceremonial events, as a jump-start for their consciousness. Is this tradition one that probably continues to some degree in the present day, in even our youth festivals, with designer drugs and such? Has using mind altering substances been a sort of unwholesome shortcut or a necessary bridge between spirit and matter on the path of Ascension?'"

> May light stream forth into the hearts and minds
> of those who serve the Plan Divine, I AM.

This is a decree that you call forth at any time that you wish to use a mind-altering drug to take you into the other realms of consciousness. You see Dear ones, Dear hearts, the use of such mind-altering substances was brought forward in the time of Kali Yuga, where humanity had lost touch with the true teachings. However, at any time through the Violet Flame, one can bring about purification and alchemization within the body. This is indeed a teaching I bring forward. Now, it also important to understand the power of belief and how belief will inhibit groups, churches, individuals, and societies. Is this not true, Dear ones, Dear hearts? It is as simple as understanding that point of perception. But as we know, here upon the Earth Plane and Planet, many situations and circumstances are brought forward for our education, are they not? There are situations and circumstances that one may learn through these activities. One may simply shrug and say "a karmic path," but another one may say, "experience without judgment." Of course, to obtain these higher unions with God, which is what indeed the soul is seeking to obtain, is immersion into the divine. One simply calls upon the Violet Flame:

> Violet Flame I AM,
> come forth in the name of the God I AM.

VIOLET FLAME MANTRA

In the force of that one statement, the Violet Flame then surrounds you and brings you into a higher vibration, a higher understanding. If you are having trouble reaching the true spirit of the God source . . . if you are feeling disconnected or discontented . . . if you feel conflict in your spiritual path, it is important to spend time in meditation and silence. Work at the silence of the mind. Then repeat silently within your mind, the mantras of the Violet Flame.

> Violet Flame I AM,
> God I AM Violet Flame.

JUDGMENT IS A TRAP

This begins to soothe the mind. Repeat it, seven times seven. Now, it is important to understand the Laws of Surrender and Nonjudgment. These I have spoken of in many past discourses. Judgment is indeed a rare trap, for one says, "I am but discerning, I am but choosing." But understand this, that one discerns and chooses for self and does not inflict or enforce what one chooses upon the other. Again, as you well know, when one asks me, "What shall I do?" I never tell another what to do, but I only reinforce the Law and to take it unto the self; then one finds, in that grand experiment, their own result. To this Dear one, I bring this suggestion again. Try this yourself. I will not tell you what to do. You must take this into your own experience. Test the waters for yourself. Have your experience. So Be It.

Response: "Thank you. I have no further questions."

Then I shall take my leave and come forward again at the next Divine Appointment. Hitaka

Response: "Hitaka."

CHAPTER TEN

The Heart of Peace
With Saint Germain and Sananda.

Greetings beloved chelas in that mighty Violet Flame. I AM Saint Germain and I stream forth on that mighty Violet Flame of Mercy, Transmutation, and ultimate Forgiveness. I ask permission to come forward Dear ones, Dear hearts.

Response: "Please Saint Germain come forward. You are most welcome."

ALL EVENTS ARE IN THE DIVINE PLAN

This day I stream forth on that mighty Violet Ray. But today, that Mighty Blue Flame also assists this discourse. The Blue Flame of the Will of God, that streams forth through the heart of the Mighty Logos, the heart of the Great Central Sun. Dear ones, Dear heart, there is much more still for us to continue with our work, much teaching still to impart.

But I know Dear one, with the current events upon the world scene, there are many whose hearts are very heavy, who wonder at this time how can we make much sense from these situations? But know Dear ones, Dear hearts of mine, those who follow these teachings, that all streams forth in accordance to the Divine Plan and the Divine Will. At times it is impossible to understand the meaning of such events. Sometimes, one may wonder, "How could this serve the Greater Will? How could this be in alignment to any Divine Plan?" Those who are faced with such sorrow ... those who are faced with the rebuilding ... those who are faced with such fears of the unknown, know this Dear one, Dear heart, that there is no mistake ever, ever, ever. And I repeat this lesson again to you, that all streams forth in a Divine Plan and in a Divine Will.

THE TIME OF TESTING

What I am speaking of is not only that law that exists in all of duality but also that law that is understood as balance. All comes forward seeking a balance. This you have always known. This I have always taught to you. It comes forward, as you would know, in Hermetic Law, in that Law of Rhythm. One side swings to the next; all extremes find their other complement; all seek to find balance in any given situation. You know Dear one, Dear heart, you can only attract unto yourself that which would seek the same vibration. Understand and know this higher law and you will then begin to know and understand the forces that are at work. In this moment, at this moment, you can only attract unto yourself, that which is a like vibration. That is why Dear ones, we have given you the work of the Violet Flame. Call upon that mighty law, that will in action.

> Violet Flame come forth. Stream forth into my will.
> Align my will to the Divine Plan. Bring balance to this situation.

THE VIOLET FLAME AND THE TUBE OF LIGHT

In that moment you call that Violet Flame to bring forth its mighty will in action, the Violet Flame comes forth transmuting and alchemizing any given situation. Yes indeed, as I have stated before, the Violet Flame brings karma, or shall we say, those actions to be understood at a new level, to be understood in a new context. It is important at this time to continue your vigilant use of the Violet Flame, along with the Tube of Light. For you see, I stated some time ago that this would be indeed a Time of Testing. We, at that time, also talked about the end of the Time of Transition. This, of course, was given in accordance to an understanding of the Laws of Prophecy and how prophecy can be used to reach a greater Co-creation alongside the Divine Plan and the Divine Will.

EVALUATE YOUR CHOICES

You have well known that prophecy is always given to bring forth a greater change that aligns to a greater harmony. In this context, know and understand that a test is only given to a student when the student is ready. It is not given as a punishment; it is not given to see "Is this person right? Is this person wrong?" A test is given Dear ones, Dear heart, so that one can reevaluate their choices. They can then reevaluate their perspective and they can move on in their own spiritual evolution.

Have you not noticed with major events, that many feel polarized. This polarization can bring great fears for those who hold peace within their heart. But also, in that polarization, there is also a shift in perception, in perspective, allowing the soul to be able to see again from a different viewpoint. This allows a plethora of lessons to come forward for the soul in its growth and evolution. Now there are those who will say this is just duality. Duality bringing forth its many, many travels but it is also, Dear ones, Dear hearts, a place to gain experience without judgment. There are many experiences that come forward in this life on the Earth Plane and Planet; experiences of being the victim; experiences of being the oppressor; experiences of being the leader; experiences of being led; experiences of feeling passion within the heart; experiences of being led blindly; so many experiences Dear ones, Dear hearts, that come forward in these situations.

Now, as you well know, it is never up to the Ascended Master to tell you what to do. It is never up to the Master Teacher to tell a student what will happen. It is only up to the Master to guide and lead through the universal laws. This you understand Dear ones, Dear heart, that the application of the universal laws will lead you truly beyond duality ... will lead you to the solace ... will lead you to that effervescent drink. The Cup of Balance is always there Dear ones, Dear hearts. Neutrality always exists for those who have the eyes to see and the ears to hear.

At this time, this test brings about a great search for inner peace. Inner peace is always what man is truly seeking, for in that inner peace comes the silence. It is in this Great Silence that all acceptance becomes as ONE, all experiences become as ONE. In this moment, search for the inner peace. Find the Master within, as I have stated before. There you will find that inner garden that we have traveled to so many times before. There you will be refreshed. There you will find solace. Now travel with me Dear one, Dear heart. Let us find the calm there in that center of balance, there in that center of true knowing.

REST IN THE CHRIST CONSCIOUSNESS

Choice becomes not a quandary, but is seen as an alignment to your Divine Will. This Divine Will that flows through you, flows through all of the universe. This interconnectedness of this will is in all things, flowing and letting life produce its glory. The Divine Will works out this Divine Plan, flowing in a harmony and a rhythm. The Divine Plan and the Divine Will flow beyond duality, as you well know, Dear one, Dear heart. Beyond duality lies what you have always known as the Christ Plane. Here, in the Christ Consciousness, we urge you to bring yourselves and rest. In this Christ Consciousness is where all beauty lies, where cooperation, harmony, and true Brotherhood and Sisterhood await.

KEEP THE FLAME OF LOVE IN YOUR HEART

The prophecies that we have brought of the Earth Plane and Planet, the Prophecies of Earth Change, have all been a backdrop for you to understand the need for peace and bringing this inner peace into a collective Oneship. This Plane of Christ Consciousness is indeed Unana. Unana exists for you to partake of. It brings with it an effervescent energy, an immortality of consciousness, that aggregate body of light of ONE. Light the aggregate body of light among humanity. Light and keep this light burning throughout you, throughout the day. If you are feeling fear, if you are feeling vengeance, if you are feeling anger towards your Brother, it is important to keep the Flame of Love within your heart.

It is important to keep the Light of the Christ Consciousness burning within your rational mind. Remember Dear ones, Dear hearts, those who have the eyes to see and the ears to hear, also have the heart that is open. This open heart is the Heart of Compassion. It understands the suffering that happens in the plane of duality. It understands the pain of those who have suffered loss. It is important to understand also, that in this situation where pain and loss has happened, indeed in both sides involved, is again the Law of Attraction. There is no solution to bring forward to the Earth Plane and Planet. Understand, it is a place that you have been brought to, to learn, to perfect, and to move in your evolution. But when one knows and applies the higher laws, one then knows to call forth that Violet Flame into its mighty activity.

THE ACTION OF THE MIGHTY FLAME

As I have stated so many times before, the Violet Flame brings the consciousness to a higher level of understanding. It transmutes any given situation into a higher understanding. At this time, it is important for all chelas to bring forth, to call forth, that mighty flame in action into any circumstance in their lives that they do not find to be in balance, do not find to be in harmony.

> Mighty Violet Flame blaze forth from the heart
> of the Central Sun.
> Leap into my heart and light the Flame of Compassion within me.

As you well know Dear ones, Dear hearts, when the Violet Flame is brought into its mighty activity, situations of the severest are softened. An opening of light then occurs. One then sees at the end of the dark tunnel and hope. Know in the darkest of hours that the Violet Flame has been brought to bring hope, to instigate a rational mind to move forward into activity. Questions?

Question: "Yes. When a group or a nation feels sorrow and pain, a rational mind may not be easily accessible. A rational mind can elude, not only the population, but also the leaders of the world. Is there anything to help these leaders?"

Each chela can call forth from their own authority, from their own God I AM, that embraces the world within the Violet Flame:

> Mighty Violet Flame, in the name of God that I AM,
> embrace this entire planet and flood it with the light supreme of
> the Violet Ray.
> May the Violet Flame enfold all leadership of this world
> and align the harmony of the spheres through the
> Great Law I AM.
> So Be It.

Response: "So Be It."

FROM THE INNER TO THE OUTER

You see again, when this law is called into its eternal activity, all is brought again to a higher frequency, a higher vibration. Then that Law of Attraction is called in again, is it not? And only a like vibration can attract a like vibration. Do you understand?

Question: "Are you saying that what occurred at our World Trade Center and at the Pentagon are only like attracting like?"

As is in everyone's daily world, those who are learning through the dual experience, all is always seeking balance, is it not?

Answer: "Yes, all is always seeking balance. It is."

When one understands these higher laws, they begin also to understand that the answer is not simplistic, even though it would appear to be. But do not, Dear ones, Dear hearts, be trapped by illusion. Realize that you too must move forward now in your own spiritual evolution. Peace is that which you hold within. Inner peace is that which you call upon. Peace among Brothers is again, that manifestation of the Law Eternal. Now you know, as you visualize a thing, as you see it and hold it in the out-picturing, you can bring that into the outer activity. First, it is known within the inner activity; then, it is manifested into the outer; is it not?

Answer: "Yes, that is the process."

It is true, Dear ones, in all manifestation processes but there are also those beliefs that are co-creating. Very often, we have no idea where these beliefs come from. They have come through activities of shame, guilt, processes not related to true Co-creatorship. But yet, experiences become empowering teachers, do they not?

Answer: "Yes, experiences are empowering teachers."

PERCEPTION AND REALITY

From this Dear one, Dear heart, there is no mistake ever, ever, ever. As we begin to examine the universal laws eternal, we also then begin to understand their application. This is the higher knowledge of the rational mind. Sometimes it is better to stand into the Great Silence, to take your time and to wait, to observe, watch, and listen with open ears; then, you truly can see with open eyes. It is true Dear ones, Dear hearts, that there are always conspiracies that await. There are always the evil and the dark recesses that exist in all situations. But as you well know, as I have trained you so well, is a glass half full or is a glass half empty? It is up for you to see and point out where you choose to be in your own perception of reality.

Question: "So, if the glass holds universal water and whether it is seen as half-full or the half-empty is a dualistic perception, the true perception is that it is part of the universal water?"

It is true Dear one, Dear heart. Those who understand that this is only experience then are led to that greater understanding. They are here to move beyond experience and into their true Mastery of the God I AM. Now are there any further questions?

Question: "Is there a decree for the individuals who are feeling unsettled in their own hearts and cannot find peace that may be shared?"

Sacred Fire 129

In this moment, I shall step down and allow Dear Sananda to bring forth instruction.

THE LOVING CHRIST

Sananda steps forward.

Greetings beloveds. It is important at this time for those who seek the Christ within to find it through inner meditation. First, it is important to silence the mind. This may be done with several decrees, one that the individual may choose. But bring within, an inner silence. Sit in contemplation. Gently close the eyes. Focus all energy upon the heart. In that moment of the focus of energy upon the heart, feel within the connection to all of life. Feel, as this heart is connected to all of life, the radiating pulse that is in all living creatures, that is in all living consciousness. This consciousness that permeates all living things is the consciousness of the ONE, Unana. Meditate upon this pulse. Work to hear this pulse within the inner ear. In this inner hearing comes a radiation. This radiation is the growth of a new energy body. This energy source is carried with you throughout the day. Bless all that you come in contact with throughout the day. Carry the radiance of this loving Christ throughout your day. This I encourage all to do. Questions?

Question: "Yes. In this meditation and visualization, is there a symbol that we can focus upon that would universally unite us to this ONE?"

There are symbols for all cultures and each of them mean different things to different cultures. But focus upon white and gold. This will bring about a calming and a healing effect upon the consciousness. It also brings about unification of the self. So Be It.

So Be It.

Sananda is now backing away and Saint Germain is coming forward.

THE LOWER FREQUENCY OF FEAR

Beloveds, Dear hearts, there of course has been much talk among the Great White Brotherhood and Sisterhood of Light, of how to approach humanity at this time. For we realize the great fear that is traveling among many. It is important to understand the work that is in front of you at this time. It is also important to understand the great God I AM that resides in each and every one of you. We have spent much time, have we not Dear one, Dear heart, speaking about the God I AM, the Master within, the Eight-sided Cell of Perfection? It is now time to reflect upon all of those teachings and bring them forward into their greater understanding. Use the meditation technique that Dear Sananda has brought forward to calm the mind.

It is also important to call upon the alchemizing, Violet Flame into all situations that you feel are being hindered by fear. Fear, you see Dear ones, Dear hearts, is a vibration that lowers frequency; that lowers energy fields; that brings about these lower animalistic qualities; that brings about a more emotional response. It is also important to stay focused upon the work at hand, to not allow the disruptions of life to come in and interrupt the greater Focus Divine. Beloved El Morya stands by my side at this moment as a reminder that the Will of God does move forward in the most mysterious of ways. Now if there are not further questions, I should like to continue.

Response: "Please continue then."

EARTH, OUR DIVINE MOTHER

Our work shall now continue upon dispensing information on the grid of the Earth. You see Dear ones, Dear hearts, we have spoken before of those grand intersections of lei-lines and how they do indeed create at this time a new energy or force upon the Earth Plane and Planet. It is true Dear ones, Dear hearts, that the Awakening is at hand. The time has come for man to receive the gift. Mother Earth, Beloved Babajeran, in her own evolution, is coming forward at this time to offer herself of service. This service is bringing forward a higher frequency and a higher vibration. As you well know, the Ascended Masters have also come forward to bring their service along with Beloved Mother Earth, Babajeran.

What does this mean, when we speak of Mother Earth? Yes, we speak of her as a higher consciousness. We also speak of her as our Mother, as our Divine Mother. Yet, we also acknowledge her presence as a system, a system that we have spoken of before in our definitions of the Earth Plane and the Earth Planet. Mother Earth comes forward in her own evolution, in accordance to a Divine Plan and a Divine Will, as you well know. This science of timing is predetermined by the Ray Forces and that Great Galactic Center, or Great Central Sun, the Mighty Logos. Mother Earth, in her own evolution, has offered to sponsor those who are now coming forward to bring a higher frequency and vibration to this planet. At this time, many Ascended Beings are coming to the Earth to offer their service. But there are also the vibrations and the frequencies of new incoming souls, which have never incarnated upon the Earth before but yet, are brought here to bring a higher service. This is allowing for greater like frequencies to imbue the Earth, to bring it out of darkness and into light.

It is still possible that there will be many Earth Changes upon the Earth Plane. It is very possible that there will be changes of the Earth Planet. These changes come, shall we say, to usher in a new vibration, for like can only understand like; sameness only understands sameness; balance seeks to give balance. This is an important teaching to know and to understand; for in this time, Mother Earth will come forward, working at will, in accordance with all Ray Forces, to bring forward this higher frequency, a Golden Age, a Golden Time.

A GENTLE BIRTH OF CONSCIOUSNESS

We have spoken about Kali Yuga. We have spoken of the consciousness of Dvapara Yuga. We now know and understand that it is a matter of your own personal, individualized consciousness, whether you are presently within one or the other. Yet, there is the potential and the possibility, through desire, to raise all in consciousness. This group consciousness could bring forth even a higher vibration, a higher quality. It is true Dear ones, Dear hearts, that Mother Earth at this time may go through many rumblings in this massive change but, if assisted by those who have the eyes to see and the ears to hear, this too could be a much gentler birth of consciousness. That is why we have given the instructions on the Golden City Vortices. That is why we have given instructions of the many lei-lines in their intersections, so you can bring this into a greater understanding.

STARS OF GOLDEN CITY VORTICES

We have outlined and given the teachings of the Doorways of the Golden Cities, but it is important too that we understand the work and the functions of the Stars. For you see Dear ones, Dear hearts, the Stars are indeed the most powerful areas of influx in any Golden City. They work as a radiating nucleus of the original intention of the Ray Force. From there, the Ray Force enters; from there, the Ray Force permeates; from there, the Ray Force influences. That is why we have asked for those who wish to bring their own personal, individual alignment into a greater harmony, to go to the Stars to seek in solace and prayer and to find, in their own inner meditation, the contact with their own Master within. Finding their own answers, they can then work in harmony with the influence of that particular focus.

This is also why Stars of Golden City Vortices have been earmarked as places for ceremonial work, as well as spiritual understanding. In times of great turmoil, they are places to go to pray for peace. They are places to go to meditate upon peace. For you see Dear ones, Dear hearts, it could only stand to reason that these vibrations then would continue to flow throughout the grid of the Earth and create a new energy, a new focus, a new vibration.

THE GATEWAY POINT MASTERS

The Golden City Vortices have been brought forward to bring a greater understanding to humanity of the process of Co-creation. In each of the Golden City Vortices, a Master Teacher stands at each of the points on the gateways. Some Master Teachers are well known.

Some are silent, always guiding, but yet in their own quality of service, they come forward leading and guiding humanity into greater evolution, into greater hope, into greater light. Know that the work is unfinished but yet within you is perfection. This perfection is and always will be, but that perfection too is waiting to be released, to express its highest potential. Dear ones, Dear hearts, questions?

TEMPLES OF CONSCIOUSNESS

Question: "In these Stars are the Ray Forces that you may be attracted to, to work with for your own transformation and the transformation of the Earth Plane, is this true?"

This is true Dear one, Dear heart. Each individual, at any given moment, is a little different. For instance, one person who may have a dominance with the Green Ray is suddenly feeling the influx of the Ruby and Gold Ray; therefore, they travel to Malton to continue their work. Another who is has always felt an alignment to the Violet Ray, suddenly feels in harmony with the work of the Blue Ray and an alignment to the Divine Plan. You see, the Ray Forces and the Golden Cities indeed are Temples of great Consciousness, that have been brought forward as a grand Divine Intervention. The assistance is there Dear ones, Dear hearts. We stand in guard of these Temples. We stand in eternal protection.

Question: "The points that you are referring to are the points that form a Maltese Cross on the surface of our planet?"

In one Doorway, for instance, there are up to six different points total but seven is the aggregate of each of these combined. So seven points exist within each Doorway. Do you understand?

GOLDEN CITY GATEWAY POINT RETREATS

Question: "Yes. And so you are saying that there is an Ascended Being, an immortal, if you will, in each of these points?"

It is true Dear one, Dear heart and they stand guard over their own individualized retreat that exists over that point. That is why, in the Golden City Vortices, there is so much potential and possibility for spiritual growth, for spiritual evolution. As we move into this Time of greater Light, these cities will grow in greater and greater appearance. For those whose eyes are clearly opened, they will see them at times as if they were resting gently in the heavens. But it is true Dear ones, Dear hearts, even for those who yet do not see, but know the truth in their heart, they do exist. Proceed.

Question: "So, as a spiritual journey, as a personal path, any individual who feels called to take a map and go to these areas to search is being called to their own transformation?"

WHEN THE STUDENT IS READY

It is true. But know this, within the Law Eternal, there is no mistake ever, ever, ever. Dear ones of humanity know this: Let your hearts unite as ONE . . . follow that Law of Love supreme . . . and there is healing grace. So Be It.

Response: "So Be It."

Questions?

Question: "So, we are to encourage those aware of the I AM America Material of prophecy to travel to these Points and Stars as they feel so guided?"

When the student is ready, the Master indeed appears.

Response: "This is true. It appears to give the student the discipline that is necessary for their growth. There is not much that I can say about that other than it is an individual choice. And it is truly in my heart that all those who will hear this or see this in print, will be called and will go and follow that calling."

For those who have the eyes to see and the ears to hear, know that I AM.

Response: "So Be It. I have no further questions."

CHAPTER ELEVEN

Unified Plane of Understanding
Saint Germain on duality and the Golden Cities.

Greetings Beloved chelas in that mighty Violet Flame. I AM Saint Germain and I request permission to come forward.

Response: "Please Saint Germain, you are most welcome. Please come forward."

WE ARE BY YOUR SIDE

Greetings Beloved Dear ones, Dear hearts, chelas of mine. Yes indeed, during times like this, there is much turmoil upon the Earth Plane and Planet. Many still feel great sorrow and fear but let me assure you Dear ones, Dear hearts, that peace reigns supreme. Carry always peace within your heart. Call upon that mighty Violet Flame to transmute any discord, any disharmony you may be feeling in the current situation. Always know Dear ones, Dear hearts, that we are always there, stalwart Brothers and Sisters by your side. Know that we are always there to lift you through any situation, any circumstance that leads you into great fear, that leads you into any situation where it may be hard for you to make a choice for peace.

Know Dear ones, Dear hearts, that we have traveled this path before. Know, in our embodiments upon the Earth Plane and Planet, that we too knew of these times of war upon the Earth Plane, knew of these times of great fear and experienced great fear ourselves. Know that through the transmutation process and keeping our focus upon the ever-present ONE, seeking harmony first within the heart, that we were always then able to overcome situations. Know Dear ones, that we are always there standing by your side, ready to help and give you assistance in your path leading to the Ascension and spiritual liberation.

Sacred Fire 137

A SIMPLE CHOICE

Dear ones, Dear hearts, life is filled with many experiences . . . experiences of joy . . . experiences of life. Also know that life holds experiences of pain and experiences of death. This is duality Dear ones, Dear hearts. It is how the soul learns. It is how the soul chooses. You see at this time you are being presented with a choice. It is that simple. Do I choose fear or do I choose love? It is always that simple. Even in the Teachings of Prophecy, it always comes down to a simple choice. You know the difference between the vibrations of fear and when you experience the vibration of peace and love. It is that simple in understanding that Law of Attraction.

When you call upon that mighty Violet Flame, not only does it bring your heart to that feeling of peace, to that location mathematically of neutrality, it also charges all of your energy fields electromagnetically. And in that moment, you come to a different understanding. Through this charge within the electromagnetic field, comes forward a different attraction, does it not? All is based in duality upon that Law of Attraction. You are constantly attracting unto yourself that focus of your desire. It is true at all times, Dear ones, Dear hearts, that you are Co-creating the experience one moment at a time. Now it is important to hold that focus throughout your whole day, to constantly reassure yourself in making that choice for what you wish to create. Do I wish to create fear? Do I wish to create love? These are the simple questions sometimes presented in duality but often they are not seen.

THE MIRROR OF DUALITY

Often within the travels of illusion, we see fear disguised as love, love disguised as fear. It is important always to question the self. Is this appearance only, or is there more that lies behind this? We have taught you Dear ones, Dear hearts, that in creation, intentions are very important. For you see intention also helps to determine the outcome. What is the intention here? Why am I doing this? What is the purpose of this creation I am now sending forward? Sometimes this takes a brutal honesty of the self, examining intention, examining the how and whys of the self. Sometimes the self-examination turns one so inward, they no longer relate to the outside world. But yet, the outside world is there to mirror back and show you how powerful you are Dear ones, in the use of the God I AM.

UNITE THE DUAL FORCES

You know that you are here to gain a Mastery of the forces, to begin to understand the dual reality and how it exists. Look at your body. Contained within your body is a masculine side and a feminine side. You have left and you have right; two arms and two legs. You also have two ears and two nostrils through which you breathe. When you look at the body, you see duality mirrored throughout. There is the inner expression; there is the outer expression. In this Time of great Change, we have come forward to bring you assistance in leading you onward into understanding the uniting of these two forces within the self and how they can create a balance and a harmony within. To bring the dual forces into greater balance, call upon the mighty I AM. Call upon the Violet Flame to bring yourself into this greater harmony, into this greater balance.

> Mighty Violet Flame, come forth through the dual expression and raise all energies to the Plane of the Christ I AM.

When you call upon this force, you are uniting the energies within the body. You are bringing them to that neutral point where they come not only to a balance, but to a harmony and an expression that allows entry into the Plane of the Christ energy. The Christ energy, you see Dear ones, Dear hearts, accepts all sides as even. It accepts and judges with complete tolerance. It comes forward with complete acceptance. It allows all creation to exist, as it is in its complete perfection.

A UNIFIED PLANE

In the experience of the perception of duality, it feels like things are not balanced. It feels like things are not just, that things have not been righted and must be brought to balance. Please understand Dear ones, Dear hearts, that when one rises in consciousness to this unified plane of understanding, everything then becomes right. Everything becomes balanced. Everything is in the right place, as it should be. This contains a great power, a great power to promote harmony, and a great power to promote abundance for all peoples of the Earth. It contains within it a perpetual energy, for lack of a greater understanding, an energy that moves beyond the solar light. This energy is timeless. This energy is breathless.

Dear ones, moving into this energy of unified knowledge, that Plane of Unana, brings one to the gentle peace that the heart requires; brings one to this greater understanding of the I AM and the force of the I AM. It brings its healing solace to those who seek ease . . . to those who seek release from pain, not only of the physical, but pain that is contained within emotional fields and mental fields. It releases the power of the rational mind and then one is able to see, with clear understanding and concrete knowledge, how all works together for the greater whole. At times, it is difficult to see in duality just how things do work together but know and trust Dear one, the Divine Plan is always working. It is difficult to understand sometimes why a thing must be the way it is but know and understand this, from the perspective of the Christ Plane, all is in balance; all actions or karma are coming together for their complete purpose.

Now let us move on. Before I proceed with more information on the Golden City Vortices, are there questions?

Question: "Yes, those who have lost loved ones, who have lost at financial levels, who face the loss of a job, and can only sense suffering, loss, and doubt, how do these people sense that everything is right with creation or call God I AM into action and the Violet Flame to bring balance?"

FROM THE CENTER POINT

What we are speaking of are levels of consciousness and the experience of perception. Let me explain. In the simplistic understanding of the Monad, of the ONE, of the one consciousness, there is no perception per se of separation. There is no perception but that one perception of life. All life exists for the purpose of life. When life is no longer, there is even no perception of death. All exists for the one plane of understanding, which is life itself. When one moves into duality, one begins to understand that there is life and death. One begins to understand that there is fear and love. But there are two sides to every coin; two sides to an argument; two sexes involved; left and right; up and down; forward and backwards. The pairs of opposites come forward in their multiple mirrors to give a greater understanding of life itself, the function and the purpose of evolution.

When moving to a different perception, a different understanding beyond duality, one then sees another plane of understanding, where perhaps all are existing simultaneously. And indeed, it is true. For from man and woman a child is born. This plane of understanding is brought together, this uniting of forces of negative and positive produces another plane that is called a plane of neutrality. From this comes the development of the will, a development known as choice. Choices can lead one back into polarization, into left or right, forward or backward, up or down. But choices can also lead one into a greater understanding through the spiritual evolution and knowledge, a perception comes that is known as the Christ.

There can indeed be a choice for benevolence. There can indeed be a choice for peace. But not all choices are left or right, up or down. Choices can all be seen from this center point that is developed in the human too as the heart. There are those who would state that the heart and the mind are at constant war within the human but there is a development of the heart and a development of the mind that leads one then into this greater union of understanding, that produces a higher quality of consciousness. This higher quality of consciousness is known

Sacred Fire

as the Christ Plane. It is there, where all comes together in reconciliation, that one is able to see that it is as it is. Questions?

FOR THOSE WHO SUFFER

Response: "You are addressing individuals whose perception is developed to a certain level to even consider what you say. But for the masses who are suffering, these concepts are very far from their perception."

But yet so many times, I remind you Dear chela, (this) knowledge is not for the uninitiate.

Response: "I would never disagree with that, but it is my desire to build a bridge to those suffering masses, to help them understand the sense of balance that does exist. "

> Mighty Violet Flame blaze in, through, and around
> this situation and circumstance.
> Raise all vibration into the balance
> and harmony of the Christ Plane.
> So Be It.

Let their perception be adjusted, so that suffering will be lessened. So Be It.

Questions?

Response: "I do have a group of questions but I would like those to be asked at your completion of the discourse. Please continue."

QUIETING MIND AND HEART

Now let us continue with the work at hand. In our last session, Dear Sananda came forward and gave you information regarding a meditation of the heart. Of course, all meditation is good at this time Dear ones, Dear hearts, any meditation which can lead you into the access of a new perception, a new understanding which leads you into access of this Christ Plane. It is important, in such times where there is such turmoil within duality, where the extremes are meeting with such viciousness on a daily basis, to quiet your mind and heart and lead it into this greater understanding.

GROUPS OF SEVEN

As you well know, the use of the Violet Flame is always brought forward prior to meditation, for it brings a purification of the electromagnetic fields. It also brings a purification of the room in which you are bringing forth such a statement or decree. It allows a rhythmic harmony to bring forward a higher vibration, a focus of the will into the activity. As I have often stated before, when two or more are joined in the decree, a greater focus, a higher energy is achieved. When three, four, or five are added, again there is even a greater strength that is added to that focus. But it is always ideal to gather in groups of seven. For you see Dear ones, Dear hearts, then a complete resonation occurs, not only with the Chakra System, but also with the energy fields.

You well understand how the septenary order is related to creation and Co-creation activity on the Earth Plane and Planet. When these groups gather in groups of seven and then move into a group or collective meditation, again a greater force is then acquired. As Dear Sananda taught in the last discourse, this meditation technique does indeed begin to build a larger energy field individually, but yet, this energy field is also built collectively within that group. So it is suggested that these decrees and meditations, particularly at this Time of great Testing, are used with greater efficiency in groups of seven. Also, it is important to understand that when these decrees and meditations are done in the Stars of Golden City Vortices for the focus of creating world peace and bringing more into this greater perception, knowledge, and understanding of Unana, that this creates a great and grand momentum.

FORCEFIELDS AND MOMENTUM

Each time that a group gathers for such an intention or purpose, it is magnified by seven. That is, it is sent with a frequency and a vibration into the Earth but also into the outer layers of the field of the Earth. So you can begin to understand it, it is felt throughout the radius of the Star as high as 300 to 400 feet in vibration, just those seven gathering together. It creates a force field that is felt throughout the Star. Now remember, this force field is forty miles in diameter. Depending upon the force of the group in its decree and prayer work, it is felt for approximately three to four days afterwards. That is why decree work and meditation work that is used on a daily basis then builds a momentum that protects for years and time to come. That is why there have been monasteries and retreats that have been set up by the Great White Brotherhood and Sisterhood that are intact and in use year after year after year.

STARS OF PROTECTION

You must now begin to see the Stars as your new retreats, as your new monasteries; for indeed, these are the locations that have been set up and given assistance by Mother Earth and the Great White Brotherhood and Sisterhood, to build a greater Protective Grid about the Earth. In the Earth Changes Prophecies, you well understand the teachings that were given for the work that was to be completed in the Stars, bringing forward a protection from these types of changes. Understand Dear ones, Dear hearts, change is duality and so even in a situation where the safety of a country is threatened through acts of war and violence, that this too brings about a healing effect.

It is important to understand that the work we give to you is indeed incremental. We understand that it happens one step at a time but for those who have the eyes to see and the ears to hear, the daily calls do indeed help. It is important too, to understand that if you are not in the Star of a Golden City that, yes, you still continue with your daily decrees, with your daily meditation, for indeed this helps. But it is also important to direct, through a focus of the mind, energies towards the Stars. This can be done through simply placing the left hand over the heart and the right hand out in projection towards a visualization of the Star. I have taught you this technique in all out-picturing lessons, have I not?

Answer: "Yes, you have."

This is also an instruction that can be given to those groups that gather and would wish to project such energies, to begin to create this new grid for the Golden Age. You see Dear ones, Dear hearts, when things are brought into this structure and into this type of order, a different harmony then is created. Instead of ideas and thoughts brought into the dualistic qualities, one then begins to understand the importance of creating this New Time, the importance of living in the Golden Age. It is true that what a man thinks, he brings into creation to himself. Know and understand, as all thoughts are brought of peace, what then would you bring unto yourself but peace?

FOCUS AND DISCIPLINE

This mighty Law of Attraction is always working its great wonder at all times. It is true that if a man thinks of violence and death, he attracts violence and death unto himself. But if one then becomes focused upon these higher vibrations, upon the higher laws eternal, one then can create harmony, one then can create peace. It is a matter of focus. It is a matter of disciplining the will. Yes, this is true, but it is also a matter of just simply taking the time to do so Dear ones, Dear hearts. Now I shall continue on with instruction, unless of course you have questions.

Response: "Not at this time, please continue."

DOORWAYS OF THE GOLDEN CITIES

Each of the Doorways has their own intention, as I have given in other past discourses. We all know that Northern Doors bring about great manifestations. Southern Doors bring forward great physical regeneration and healing. Eastern Doors bring about harmony in groups and collective movements of families and one-on-one situations. And Western Doors always bring about a greater consolidation of the mind. You can use the same premise Dear ones, Dear hearts, within the Golden Cities. We have chosen of course the center points, the Stars, because all energies coalesce throughout and there is a greater disbursement of these energies. They come forward in their greater intention and understanding. But to do decree work and to come forward in meditation also upon these Doorways will also bring a greater intention and quality to your Co-creations.

If you wish to bring about global healing for the planet, move your energies into Southern Doors. If you wish to bring about a greater manifestation for the world economies, move your manifestations, your decrees, your meditations into Northern Doors. If you wish to bring harmony among Brother and Sister, between all of the nations, so there is a greater understanding of the collective humanity that we share, move these meditations, move these decrees, your work together into Eastern Doors. If you wish to bring enlightenment, knowledge that will serve the greater heart of humanity, this of course includes scientific discovery as well as greater knowledge of the unified field, move your work into the Western Doors.

MANY MASTERS OF SERVICE

Now, I have given you, in the past discourses, the points also that you can work. In these different points and locations that I have disclosed to you Dear ones, Dear hearts, are also focuses of Master Teachers. Again, as I told you in our last discourse, there are many more Masters now that are coming, for they have heard the clarion call of your prayers. It is known and understood at this time, that humanity has the opportunity to take a great leap into a new focus for peace. Those who have tread this path before you are here, Dear ones. They offer their hearts in service. They are those Master Teachers who came forward in the earliest part of this effort, to offer their focus in the center part of each Golden City, in the Star itself, to anchor that Ray Force firmly into its action and activity.

ACTIVATION

Now all five Golden Cities of the United States are in action, working that Ray Force, bringing it forward for its higher intention and purpose and Service Divine. These points now in each of the gateways, the Doorways of the Golden Cities, are now being activated, to bring forward their greater service and understanding of Unana, the ONE, the Christ Force. This will bring about a collective force in energy across the entire planet. Now it is true that there are those Golden Cities that have not yet been activated in their full service, but yet those throughout the world can travel to them and begin to feel these energies and integrate them into their being. They can still move with that greater intention where the template is in place.

A NEW ENERGY

Five is a very important number Dear ones; for you see, it is that work of Alchemy in nature that guides the energy of the five. There are four doorways and one center point. There are five Golden Cities that exist within the United States. Five is the mystic Divine Alchemy of Nature coming into its fuller manifestation. Five also represents that from the Christ Plane. We can rise into a new energy of light and sound through the understanding of the Fourth and the Fifth Dimension. Dear ones, Dear hearts, everything has moved with great timing and intention. This is the Divine Plan in its greater motion.

For those who have the eyes to see and the ears to hear, that is, they have developed the Seven Chakras and opened that Seventh Seal, are readied now to perceive at will, those Master Teachers who have come to bring their great service. There is great teaching and healing to occur among humanity. And even though it is a time where duality also plays its role, there are those who are readied who come forward now into this greater evolution. Questions?

THE GREAT WHITE BROTHERHOOD AND SISTERHOOD

Question: "In referring to these other Master Teachers coming forward at this particular time, you are referring to your own teachers and their teachers and so on, are you not?"

These are all members of the Great White Brotherhood and Sisterhood. For you see Dear ones, this organization moves beyond the Earth Plane and Planet. It moves beyond your own solar system. It is a group of likeness, of like vibration and consciousness. It contains within itself, yes, those teachers of the Earth, but it also contains those who understand, in a greater harmony, the working of peace. It also contains those who understand, in a greater harmony, the Great I AM. It also contains those souls who understand that freedom must be held and protected.

The Earth schoolroom is not the highest in terms of vibration and it is not the lowest. It is indeed, shall we say, a midrange frequency. Now you must understand too that like attracts unto like. And only so much can be bourn by one planet, one schoolroom at a time. The light work that has occurred during the Time of Transition is now allowing this greater frequency to come forward and greater opportunity now awaits humanity. But again, as you well know Dear one, Dear heart, it is only through choice. Questions?

THE DIVINE TEMPLE

Question: "Yes. Then a suggestion for the masses of humanity is to choose peace, to choose love, to choose abundance, to choose harmony, to choose alignment to the Divine Plan and the Divine Will and then it becomes so, is this not true?"

It is true. Mankind is indeed awaiting the Temple Divine. It is here but it must be realized. It must be activated. It must be put into its Divine Motion. Questions?

Question: "And that Divine Motion comes specifically through individual choice, the development of the will, is this not true?"

It is true.

Question: "And so for an action to come into reality or manifestation in the duality, the first step is choice, is it not?"

CHOICE AND CO-CREATION

As I have often reminded chelas, choice is divine. Beloved El Morya often says choose, choose, and then choose again. For in choice, the soul then gains education, gains that experience that is ever so important. But in these teachings, one begins to understand the power of choice, the nature of choice; not blind and random choice, but they begin to understand their own God I AM, that source within that brings forward a greater Co-creation. Dear ones, Dear hearts, it is important to focus upon your self-Mastery at this time. It is important to focus upon the lessons that you have been given and bring them now into greater action. As I have often stated, when a test is in front of a student, that means that the student is ready. As you have always understood, this again is vibration; this again is the Law of Attraction. Questions?

Response and question: "Yes. And so as we all face these tests, all of us here in this plane of duality of the Earth, we are facing tests in the Divine Plan that we are prepared for and we can choose in such a manner to bring forth our great desires of harmony, abundance, prosperity, peace, love, and joy. We can bring these forward through our choices and our actions, is this absolutely so?"

So Be It.

Response: "So Be It. I have no further questions with regard to this part of the discourse but I do have some questions that have been sent in to us, if you can stay."

Proceed, for this is the service that I offer.

BELIEFS

Question: "A person asks, 'It is my understanding that there are only two anointed messengers for the Great White Brotherhood, is this true?'"

An anointed messenger? Dear ones, Dear hearts, we must speak now of vibration again, for there are those who, through their belief systems, must have things in a structure and in such a manner that they can relate to it, so that they can grow through it and understand. This is no different than any other type of organized religion. This is not to say that organized religion does not have its place, does not have its meaning, does not have its particular structure that helps a person to grow and to learn. But beliefs are indeed beliefs. We move through them all the time. We choose our beliefs. Through these beliefs, we create. In these creations and also Co-creations, we come to a greater understanding of self and move forward in our own soul's evolution. There are those who have been brought forward to bring such a purpose, to bring that movement of energy forward, to bring that teaching forward. As you well know, as I have spoken to you Dear one, Dear heart, there is a particular focus and energy to this work. Very often, I do not bring you information from what others are learning and in this case, these particular anointed messengers are working for their particular focus, for their particular energy of that which they are learning in helping others.

THE MASTER WITHIN

We must move beyond judgment. We must move beyond critical analysis. Is this person the one? Is this person the one? We are always waiting for the one who has the greater knowledge, the greater insight. It is important to understand that the Master lies within. That is why an Ascended Being will never tell another what to do. We will only make a suggestion and give assistance, to bring that one into higher vibration, into higher understanding. To see the universal laws and how they are applied can help to bring one into greater understanding of the Ascension process.

TOLERANCE

This is not to say that one path is better than another; for indeed, we all have the individual will. One may not understand the individual karma that one is dealing with; one may not understand the individual's dharma or purpose that one must now bring forward. I ask that we judge not, that we allow with complete tolerance. These messages do exist. But again, it does require choice and that choice is based upon your heart. It is also based upon the vibration and energy that you have achieved at that given moment. Look back but just a few years Dear ones, Dear hearts and you will see the growth that you have made during these Great Times. Know this in this work that I bring forward from the great heart of I AM THAT I AM. I AM Saint Germain and I blaze forth on that Violet Flame of Mercy, Transmutation, and Forgiveness. So Be It.

Question: "So Be It. It would seem to me that it would be more a matter of choice, what particular resonation or vibration of teaching a person decides to embrace, is this not so?"

If this individual is drawn to this vibration, to this energy, and is growing and learning through it, then one must never interfere with another's path. For you see, sometimes what is poison for one is bread for another. It is important to move forward and to exercise the will, to bring it into greater understanding. There is no mistake, know this Dear ones, Dear hearts, ever, ever, ever.

Response: "Thank you. I understand that."

CHAPTER TWELVE

Science of Solutions
Saint Germain on solving crisis and problems.

Greetings Beloved chelas, in that mighty Violet Flame. I AM Saint Germain and I request permission to come forward.

Response: "Please Saint Germain, you are most welcome. Come forward."

PREPARING THE MIND

Greetings Beloveds, Dear hearts, chelas, and students of mine. There is much work for us still to discover, much more information that I must impart. Dear ones, Dear hearts, the work upon the Earth Plane and Planet that we bring forward streams, yes, upon that Green Ray of Healing and Ministration to humanity, but also streams forth on that mighty Violet Ray of Mercy, Compassion, and Forgiveness. This Violet Ray comes forward at this time in humanity's history to open the Heart of Compassion, but also to transmute karmas of the past, to bring the soul into greater balance, so that the mind is ready to receive the information that is about to be given.

BUILDING CONSCIOUSNESS

Higher teaching, higher awareness comes forward to lead the soul into a new evolution. This evolution of consciousness leads the soul into beginning to understand how, like one building block after another, each state of consciousness is built upon the other. When one begins to move out of fear, one then recognizes and sees that they are no longer a victim of the past, that everything has happened for a reason, and everything fits together one step at a time. That is why I always say to you "move in small incremental steps and you will not miss one bit along the way." For it is important Dear ones, Dear hearts, that you understand each stage of consciousness as you move along in your own awakening, in your own evolution. When one moves beyond fear, one begins to recognize that they have touched the Master within. The Master within always has the courage to heal.

THE I AM PRESENCE

It is important always to touch the Master within, the mighty I AM Presence, this higher power that exists for all of humanity. It is the power that moves all into a greater awakening, into a greater understanding. Indeed, it is likened to the consciousness of Unana, but it is a power that moves freely. It is a power that is there to always give you help, to always give you refreshment. When I say refreshment, I always speak of the Cup, for this Cup represents the Cup of Balance. It is a Cup of Neutrality. It is filled with this effervescent energy of the I AM, the higher power, the Master within The I AM Presence is the individualized Presence of God that exists within you. It is there for you to call upon at any time. The I AM Presence is your perfected state. It is how you are seen throughout the Eyes of God. At any time, it is the most perfect state of consciousness that you, as an individualized consciousness, can access. The I AM Presence is indeed the pathway of how you shall be set free. Accessing and utilizing the I AM Presence brings you into a greater and greater harmony with the ONE, with the consciousness of Unana. As you access the I AM Presence, it grows too in its own energy states.

As you have noticed in every teaching as I come forward, the energy begins at a slower rate and as we get to the midstream of each teaching, the energy is growing and growing in its release and transference of energy. It is the same too with the I AM Presence. As it is accessed by you through your conscious will, this activity releases more and more of the energy of the Great I AM. The I AM exists as a universal substance, exists as an Omnipotent or Omniessence energy that is permeating all things at all times. But in the same way that the wind exists in the air that you cannot see as an unseen force, you at times cannot see but feel the Presence of the Great I AM.

The I AM Presence is your individualized experience of the I AM. The I AM Presence, as you begin to access it, more and more grows in energy. Each time you access the I AM Presence and call it into activity, it comes closer and closer to your daily experience of consciousness. It brings you into a greater level of awareness, a greater states of consciousness. There, you are able to accept with great willingness its ability to bring harmony into your life, to bring balance into situations, and lead you onward to the state of consciousness, the path of the heart known as love.

Love, you see Dear ones, Dear hearts, through the I AM Presence, opens the door to Unana, a state of consciousness where many Brothers and Sisters of like mind reside. That is why, at this state of consciousness, one feels an overall connection to the All That Is, to all of life. At the state of love, one begins to hear the voice within and the Master within becomes individualized, the mighty Master that exists within you as the individualized Presence of God. Your divinity becomes alive. It is true in lower states of frequencies of consciousness, the God Presence is always present, but it is not as activated. It is not being used to its fullest potential. But again, as I say there is no mistake, ever, ever, ever and one step at a time, Dear ones.

CAMARADERIE ON THE PATH

Let us move Brother to Brother, Sister to Sister, heart to heart, in these incremental steps that allow us not to miss one thing along the way. Sometimes the student says, "Oh, but if only I could reach these higher states of consciousness, each problem of mine will then be removed." This is true to some degree Dear ones, Dear hearts, but it is important not to miss anything in the path of Mastery. For you see Dear ones, as you proceed through each state or level of consciousness, there is the little "aha," the little awakening that comes at each level or state, that brings such delight, such joy. It is this joy, as it opens the heart, that is so ever important. You see, this joy is the laughter of the soul. This joy brings true camaraderie for those who share along the path. This camaraderie is so important. Even in this moment, as I give this information to you, as we sit teacher to student, Master to chela, we too have grown along the way, along the path. We too, in our own experience, have developed this relationship of sharing, of laughing, of learning. Yes, it is true Dear ones, Dear hearts, we too share sorrows and we also share misgivings, but we also share joy and open the heart of love.

CRISIS AND PROBLEMS

It is said that crisis often is unifying, that it brings many together for a point of problem solving. It is true. Crisis comes forward to bring a unification of the self. In the Time of Testing, many will be tested at the ability that they are performing. But at the time when they are called to this test, when they are called to bring forward their understanding, they will wonder, "How can I proceed? How can I move forward?"

Know this Dear ones, Dear hearts, that a test is always given at the level for which one has achieved, for which one is fully capable of delivering a solution. Know this, as duality exists still for you in the present state of consciousness, there is no problem without its other side, the solution. It is important in the Time of Testing to focus always upon solutions, for in the solution is the answer that will move you to the next level, the next "aha," to the next burst of joy that will bring you into a greater evolution of consciousness. Questions?

PROBLEM AND SOLUTION ARE ONE

Question: "Yes. Problem and solution, is that not duality?"

Indeed, when they are viewed as polar opposites, when they are seen in a dual perspective, but the answer exists as well. Problem-answer-solution; problem-solution-answer; answer-problem-solution; when you see them all linked together as ONE, they work from a whole new paradigm of consciousness. This leads the consciousness into functioning (away) from dual perspectives, knowing and understanding that the solution always exists, that the answer always exists, and that the problem and answer-solution function together as one greater collective. This greater collective is the Christ Consciousness. It is a state of perfection known as Unana. Whenever there is a problem, immediately you know there is a solution. Proceed.

JUXTAPOSITION OF PERCEPTION

Question: "The question then is how does one perceive the answer or the solution, when all that can be seen is the problem?"

It is important to understand that all is a state or level of consciousness. At times, there are those who are blocked only (stuck) within problems. All they see are problems. It is important when this happens, to move in the juxtaposition. Again, it is perspective. Is that glass half full? Is that glass half empty? How can I make lemonade from a lemon? How can I move forward in this, one step at a time? Of course, the immediate solution is to move from a negative position into a positive position. But let us take this even one step forward. In that positive position is the solution, is the answer. They exist simultaneously as answer-solution, solution-answer; these two exist side by side in the positive aspect. The problem exists through the negative aspect. This juxtaposition of perspective, within positive levels of consciousness, creates an even higher understanding, which brings the consciousness into again a new juxtaposition.

CONSCIOUS RECOGNITION

Energy flows where attention goes, as I have always told you Dear ones, Dear hearts. But one does not understand this until they have that clear experience. When attention is placed always upon problem, problem, problem, problem, one stays blocked within this perception. It is as if they are always facing a northerly wind, blowing directly upon them, but they have not yet learned how to turn their back to the wind, so that the wind will no longer force them into one position. It is that simple, of turning around, first from negative to positive. Then, from positive, one begins to understand this

Sacred Fire

plane of neutrality, where one may enter into even higher states of consciousness, where one can see through juxtaposition that all is encompassing as ONE.

To even visualize, to even ask the question, brings it into the mind that there is a problem. To have conscious recognition that there is a problem in the state of duality would immediately force the consciousness to understand and know that there is indeed an answer; there is indeed a solution. These are the dual forces at work. But beyond that is the Christ energy. The three are always married as ONE. Proceed.

REMOVING BLOCKS WITH THE VIOLET FLAME

Question: "So, are you saying that when the problem is perceived, that moving from this negative to the positive, of knowing there is a solution, all the possibilities to solve the problem will come?"

It is true. It is the marriage of negative and positive, coming together to create yet another field of conscious awareness. When a problem is perceived, know this, the answer indeed exists. The solution then leads one into higher states of awareness and consciousness. But if one is always focused upon problems, one cannot clearly see answers. If one cannot see an answer, how could one see a solution? Perhaps the work of the Violet Flame is one of the best, to begin to remove these types of blocks.

> Mighty Violet Flame, blaze within this problem.
> (You can then address the problem directly.)
> Remove all discords. Remove all disharmonies
> and allow me to see the solution to this problem immediately.

SOLUTION COMES WITH MANY CHOICES

When you call this forward, it activates your own individualized Presence of God. You then begin to see through that new juxtaposition. You then begin to see through a new conscious awareness that there is an answer. Once the answer is given, this leads the consciousness naturally to the next level of solution. From this position, energy is then placed within the solution. From solution comes again many choices. The will then moves in greater development. The will moves forward in greater understanding. But it is as simple as growing that energy.

EMPOWERMENT THROUGH THE I AM

Have you not noticed, there are those sad-sack human beings who are always placing energy upon problems, problems, problems, problems? They grow and escalate an energy force. They seem to walk with a cloud of grim energy surrounding them at all times. It is because their focus has been built upon the creation of one problem after another. Then, there are those who understand that a problem is merely a means to find an answer and from that answer comes even a greater opportunity, the solution. Or, shall I say, solutions, for often there are many solutions, many ways of seeing how a problem can be solved. From this comes the creative process. The will then is placed into a greater exercise, choice.

Then one begins to see how the great God I AM and choice move one forward into understanding and applying their own will in any given situation. This allows the soul to move forward, to move into greater understandings and levels of consciousness. It is a state and a level called empowerment, where one is in touch with the Great I AM. This energy then grows with greater depths, with greater clarity. A harmonizing effect begins to take hold over the individual. This harmony then creates an energy force which becomes the growth and the fostering of positive thoughts, positive thinking. These types of individuals, when you encounter them, are as if a breath of fresh air has blown right in the door. You can note it in their voice, in their demeanor, in their posture, for they carry within them an infectious optimism. It is important Dear ones, Dear hearts, to understand this process, to call upon the mighty I AM Presence, to activate the Master within. Questions?

SHIFTING NEGATIVE INTO POSITIVE

Question: "Yes. So for every possible scenario, prophecy, or event in an individual's life, or on the world stage, are you saying that there is always a solution, or groups of solutions?"

Prophecy is one of the greatest spiritual teachings, showing how positive energy can change the most negative of all situations. Prophecy, as you well know, Dear ones, Dear hearts, speaks to the heart of humanity, to bring about a shift in perception, a shift in consciousness. It is true, that at any time, the most negative situation can change through the work of the Violet Flame, through working with perception and consciousness, as a shift in attitude and perception. This can change the most trying of all circumstance and event. Questions?

AWAKENING DIVINITY

Response and question: "So, it is truly our point of perception. We can perceive the problems, but without that balance, everything comes to a halt. Consciousness does not move on because it is that creative interaction that stretches the consciousness beyond the boundaries of its perception, is it not?"

It is true Dear ones, Dear hearts. But it is important also to exercise the consciousness. It is nothing to be taken lightly. That is why we have encouraged all students and chelas to engage in meditation at least for ten to fifteen minutes per day when they are beginning. For you see, this too builds an energy field, an energy force. It allows contact with the true self, with the Master within. The student or chela gains that contact and begins to trust that within this process, the solution always is within them. Sometimes students, chelas, when encountering a problem, perceive that the answer is out there; that the answer awaits in another individual; that the answer to all problems, to all their discomfort, lies in something that is outside of them. But know this Dear one, Dear heart, all solutions, all answers, lie within. They are contained within you as states of consciousness, points of perception, readied and willing to reveal themselves to you. This is the awakening of divinity within. It comes through the openness and the receptivity, the trust and acceptance, that the Master is truly within.

THE WORK

You see Dear ones, Dear hearts, it does indeed take work to reveal this Master. There is no quick fix. There is no artificial means to find this Master. You must do this work yourself. That is why meditation becomes of increasing import for those who wish to proceed to these levels of consciousness. The Heart of Love awaits you at all times Dear ones, Dear hearts. Silence yourself and receive. Questions?

INFECTIOUS OPTIMISM

Question: "Yes. When one actually finds solutions and has stepped onto that path of self- empowerment, would this not help many others to catch that wave of solving problems from within and help the world to move on in a collective?"

It is true Dear one, Dear heart. As I have said, "infectious optimism," for it is important to understand that as a chela or student moves and experiences within the higher states of consciousness, that they have a great affect on those who may be at lower states of consciousness. They become a magnet that draws this lower consciousness into a higher energy field. You well know, that when you bring disease into a higher vibration, it comes to a point of healing. But healing is a choice, as you well know. As one, who is filled with this higher state of consciousness, begins to help and assist many around them, these too are brought to a place where the will is brought into greater development. So you see, in the same way that I come forward this day and give my assistance, you move forward throughout your day and give your assistance and on and on and on. From this level of perception, we are all connected as ONE. This is indeed the state of Unana, although there will be those who do not perceive or understand this state. But yet again, as I have said before, that wind does exist; you cannot see it, but yet you feel it. It is so. Proceed.

Question: "With your permission, may I now go to questions that have been posed to us?"

I am always here for service. I AM Saint Germain.

PARADIGM OF TWELVE

Question: "A person asks, 'Is it not a fact that there are twelve planets in our solar system, thirteen including our sun. Is the hidden planet one of these planets?'"

It is true. We have spoken of this before. This paradigm of twelve, you will see throughout many schoolroom situations. For you see, it is divided equally, six plus six; six to one negative side, six to one positive side. And yet, from other points of perception, it is seen as three multiplied by four, or four by three. The potential to move from the Third Dimension to the Fourth Dimension also exists within this paradigm. But it is true that there are twelve, in the same way that there are always twelve adepts or avatars that exist at any one time on each of these twelve planets. Each exists in their own frequency, as you would understand dimensional activity. Questions?

LEARNING THROUGH LEVELS OF CONSCIOUSNESS

Question: "Yes. And so that brings us to the number twelve. Is this number considered a sacred number of creation?"

For a schoolroom activity, that is why Twelve Jurisdictions have been given, for they are Laws of Jurisprudence. Based upon levels of consciousness, each one of them achieve their own level, purpose, and intention for the new creation, the Golden Age, the New Times. It is based upon an expansion of consciousness. For you see Dear ones, when one moves to another field of experience, beyond the schoolroom, one's consciousness then reaches new experiences, moving into systems that exist beyond this. However, very often they make the choice to return and to help, to give, and to be of service. This is so.

PLUTO, AN ANCIENT MOON

Question: "It has been thought that the planet Pluto is not really a planet, but possibly an asteroid or a moon. What is it?

It is an ancient moon that was thrown off from a completely different solar system. However, it is now a planet that is part of this system. In the future, another planet will be identified and Pluto will, at that time, through this process of higher consciousness and greater light to the system, be identified more as this ancient moon.

LIGHT OF THE GREAT CENTRAL SUN

Question: "I see, but for the time being in our system, it does function as one of the twelve planets?"

At this time, indeed it does. But as you see, as light from the Great Central Sun emanates more and more, bringing consciousness to a higher peak, so to speak, this light of consciousness then allows for greater discovery, for greater embracing of ideas, thoughts, and consciousness. Do you understand?

THE TWO SUNS

Question: "Yes, I do. In this continuous expansion, as more light comes from our Central Sun, does this mean that the secondary solar Sun for our solar system will also be illuminated at some point?"

At the time that the two Suns begin to illuminate, it is true there will be greater and greater light. At that time, as you well suspect, then twelve more planets will be added to the system. But that will not be for many more years to come.

Sacred Fire

SUNDAY PEACE MEDITATION

Response and question: "I see. That is very interesting. The energies on our planet have been fluctuating, not necessarily stable. Is there something that we are to expect in the not too distant future that would be along the lines of a change in the Earth's grid or a tectonic plate movement? It almost feels as though there is a buildup for a shift."

There is a great buildup at this present moment upon the Earth Plane, of emotional energy that is building at a low vibration. This is the low vibration of anger, hate, and violence. It is important to continue with the Sunday Peace Meditation. This was instigated, not only to bring peace among humanity, but also to instigate a calming effect to the Earth Planet. For you see, as this buildup of emotional energy proceeds, there could be great and violent storms, which will bring adjustments then to the energetic lei-lines of Mother Earth. You see Dear ones, Dear hearts, even though humanity very often views itself as a very separate entity to Mother Earth, all are interconnected in one great system. [Editor's Note: For more information regarding the Sunday Peace Meditation, see Appendix I.]

GOLDEN STAR MUDRA

In the same way that I have introduced to you this principle of negative plus positive equals neutrality, the same is true with humanity and Mother Earth. When I speak of the Earth Plane and the Earth Planet, I am always addressing this as one system. The recent events among humanity, among the governments of the world, are bringing about a great emotional turmoil. This tumultuous energy must be balanced upon Mother Earth. That is why it is important to use, as I have taught you specifically and directly, the mudra which will direct energy to the Stars of the Golden Cities. This is very important.

Response: "I see. So, it is important that in our Sunday meditation for global peace, that we use an *I AM America Map* or a world *Free-*

dom Star Map and with our left hand over our heart, we open our right hand toward the Star of a Golden City that is close to us."

Let me demonstrate for you. In this moment, you now see how this energy is being directed from the center of my palm. It is as if a laser focus is now directing. Now direct it through the breath, drawing up from the lower chakras and projecting the energy from the heart. Do you see? Do you feel this energy source?

Answer and question: "Yes. This now connects you with the planet, doesn't it?"

Indeed it does. And it brings forth a balancing effect that is very important at this time. For you see Dear ones, Dear hearts, as I have given and directed this to you, you will give and direct this to many others. We are all connected as ONE in this great energetic movement. Do you understand?

Response: "Yes I do. To reiterate, so that it is clear for everyone, when we meditate, we breathe up through the bottom chakras, connecting to the Earth core, and bring this energy into our heart. We then focus it through our right hand into the Golden City hologram that is on the maps. That will enhance the actions of peace in our world."

EARTH HEALING THROUGH THE GOLDEN CITIES

It is true. It brings about an energetic adjustment, directed at the lei-lines of Mother Earth. At this present moment, there are great solar storms that are beginning to erupt upon your Sun. With the electromagnetic fields as they are upon the Earth, a great attraction of these storms could then also cause many severe problems upon the Earth. This brings about another energetic adjustment of Earth's energy fields. You are well aware of this, for you see Dear ones, Dear hearts, the Golden City Vortices function very much like chakras do upon the human body. In this way, humanity serves as a greater part of the system of Earth and serves to bring about a healing effect, not only for peace in the collective mind, but peace in the collective system. Proceed.

Response: "I see. So, the individual and collective focus of groups doing this meditation sets forth this new paradigm for world peace. And this expansion, or a wave of consciousness, then will take hold with all."

For all is based upon that mighty Law of Attraction. Again, it is as simple as problem to answer to solution.

Response: "Yes, I see this. This is a very interesting way to perceive things. All problems have answers and solutions. It is the way things are structured here. I understand that very clearly now. I have no further questions at this point with regard to this specific topic."

Then I shall take my leave from you and come forward at the appointed hour. I AM Saint Germain.

Response: "Thank you."

CHAPTER THIRTEEN

I AM Awareness

*Saint Germain gives instruction on the
I AM Awareness.*

Greetings Beloved chelas. Shall we resume our work together?

Response: "Yes, we shall."

I request permission to come forward?

Answer: "Please identify yourself and come forward."

VIBRATION AND CONSCIOUSNESS

This is Saint Germain and I stream forth on that Violet Ray of Mercy, Compassion, and ultimate Forgiveness. Dear ones, Dear hearts, what you are experiencing is the work of vibration. Did you not notice a difference in the room as I entered? Did you not notice a difference before? Vibration is very important Dear ones, Dear hearts. That is why we have given you specific guidelines regarding diet and specific guidelines regarding the use of the Violet Flame. It is very important Dear ones, for you see, vibration will determine the quality of the consciousness that you are experiencing at any given time. It is also important to understand that vibration has a predictability that is related to consciousness. The predictability of consciousness often times is misinterpreted in a dualistic manner; that is, it is judged from a point of perception.

It is important to understand that it is always, always important to know where one is, to know oneself, and to understand the state of consciousness that one is experiencing. But it is also important, as we have stated so many times before, to judge not, lest you be judged yourself. In judging, this is where one enters into a dualistic state of consciousness. We realize Dear ones, Dear hearts, that it is often very difficult upon the Earth Plane and Planet, very difficult indeed, for one is always judging. One is always measuring left from right, right from wrong, up from down, or asking, "Is this the right move for me? Is this the wrong move for me?" Such is the state in nature of the human condition. This indeed becomes a predictable state of consciousness. But as you well know, it is very important to see consciousness in the great out-picturing. The out-picturing of consciousness is then used to create a vibrational state. This is often used through the Violet Flame, which indeed brings your consciousness resonating to a certain vibration.

> Mighty Violet Flame stream in, through, and around
> all circumstances at this moment.
> Raise my vibration to the level of the Violet Flame.
> Release all judgments.
> So Be It.

Response: "So Be It."

As you see Dear ones, Dear hearts, in that moment, your own consciousness is then raised to a level that vibrates with the Violet Flame. You have called it forth into your consciousness. Do you understand?

YOU CREATE YOUR VIBRATION

Response: "Yes, I do. At that moment, it is your focus."

It is also a vibration within the focus. Yes it is true, the focus helps in the creation process but it is also important to understand vibration. We have given you many, many teachings on vibrations, but you know Dear ones, Dear hearts, it is not until you have the experience that you begin to understand that all important difference. Vibration is all around you at all times. There are different frequencies all around you at all times. But it is important for you to choose the vibrations that you will create your own point of perception from. Now, it is important to understand; for you see, when you begin to create your own vibration, it is almost as if you are dealing with a blank slate and you are able then to call out the qualities that you wish to use for the level and the state of consciousness. One may choose from a point of perception, the quality of love, along side the attributes of devotion and the qualities of cooperation. Now these come forward in that greater Co-creation, love sending its vibration, streaming forth from the heart of great intention. This vibration comes forward almost with a prophetic consequence, creating its own energy, its own vibration.

WHEN LIFE "HAPPENS"

But in that which is the human condition, there are predictable consequences. Not choosing a level of vibration, one is always living in a vibration and accepting a vibration. Often this comes through a dualistic quality, as I have all ready explained. Life and its circumstances just seem to happen. Life and circumstances just seem to pile up, do they not, one on top of the other? And one feels as if they are chained to the predictable state of consciousness. Yes it is true, that if a person engages in anger, that there is too, a vibration then of hate. This vibration of hate leads only to more and more self doubt of the mighty I AM and the God within. One can no longer then call upon the vibrations of the Great I AM, for one doubts that even such a Source would exist within oneself.

BALANCE

Now we have just described for you two states of consciousness. One has a prophetic consequence, imaged as a Co-creator, and one has a predictable consequence. How does the state of consciousness then move beyond such duality? As we have always said, Dear ones, Dear hearts, it is through balance. It is through that state of neutrality of non-judgment. This requires surrendering of the will to the Divine Will and accepting all situations and circumstances as being in their correct place, timing, intention, and order. That is why, so often we have said to you, there is no mistake, ever, ever, and ever. This statement alone is a great affirmation of the vibration of neutrality. All states of consciousness exist, do they not? Accepting one another and allowing, with complete tolerance, without judgment, aligns to that Mighty Will in action.

RELATIONSHIP OF CONSCIOUSNESS TO SPIRITUAL GROWTH

States and levels of consciousness do indeed affect then, a point of perception. The way that you see things can be so changed, just by that shift in juxtaposition. This is always so important in the growth and evolution at a spiritual level. That is why the prophecies of I AM America were sent forward to humanity, not only to teach about the relationship between consciousness and Beloved Babajeran, but also to show a relationship between states and levels of human consciousness and spiritual evolution and (to) growth. This is not to say that it is bad to hate, or that it is good to love; it is rather to understand that all states of consciousness do exist simultaneously as an experience. Once aligning to that Greater Will within the experience, one begins to see that quality of choice.

THE POWER OF THE GREAT I AM

Choice is one of the greatest teachings of the Great I AM. For would you not say, Dear ones, Dear hearts, that when you call upon the Great I AM, you begin to see all things in a different rhythm and in a different order. Through the Great I AM, one is calling forth, not only the power of the God Omni-essence, they are calling forth the energies of all of those who have gone before them. When one calls forth the power of the Great I AM, they are calling forth the energy, not only of this hierarchy of consciousness, they are also commanding and demanding the substance of universal force to cooperate in willingness with the great Eight-sided Cell of Perfection. This of course leads the consciousness to understanding that all dual states of consciousness, existing simultaneously, side by side, merge as if into ONE. All states of consciousness merge into the great consciousness of Unana.

It is true Dear ones, that the I AM is related to this state of consciousness of Unana. The I AM is the great entry point into understanding that God is indeed within. As I have always told you Dear ones, Dear hearts, believe not a word I say, but take it unto your own greater counsel. Call upon the I AM and test the law for yourself. Experience is always the key in understanding. Experience is always the key in awareness.

Mighty I AM Presence come forth
in the awareness of the Great I AM THAT I AM.

Even in this moment, as I call forth the awareness of the Great I AM, do you feel another shift now in vibration and energy?

Response: "Yes, there is a change in the room."

HARMONY'S BLESSING

It is important always to understand how any situation, at any time, can be adjusted, shifted, altered, and changed to bring about greater understanding. This of course is an elementary teaching to what I have given you before as the Principles of Harmony. When all is functioning in that greater alignment to the Divine Plan, this harmony comes forward and gives its bountiful blessings. It is the hallmark of a greater level of consciousness. For you see Dear ones, Dear hearts, as I have taught you so many times and has been brought forth in the Jurisdictions, harmony streams forth from the Heart of the Central Sun. This harmony is the bond through which the septenary qualities come forward, orchestrating at will, the Divine Plan. Do not think for one minute whether or not these Rays, streaming forth from the Great Central Sun, are resonating or vibrating at the proper level. They come forward from that point of neutrality, streaming forth from that Great Heart, in their essence of All That Is, the Great I AM.

I AM AWARENESS

Now this is illustrative of the fact that Omni-essence is always existing. It always is as it is. Within you, the Great I AM can carry forth its great lesson within your life. The Great I AM also can help any situation, any circumstance that you wish to bring a greater solution towards, a greater understanding and increased awareness. Calling upon the I AM Awareness at all times leads you then to be able to perceive a situation from that different point of perception. Questions?

Question: "The I AM Presence is the presence of our consciousness or our awareness of the I AM, is it not?"

It is true Dear ones, Dear hearts. When I speak of the I AM Awareness, I speak of a joint consciousness. That is the awareness of the I AM, as I teach in this moment, and your experience of the I AM Presence. The I AM Awareness exists between all who have activated the I AM, to bring it into its greater creative ability. The I AM Awareness, while it streams forth from the I AM Presence, is a quality of the Presence of God. Now, the I AM is the individualized presence of God that resides within every person. We have spoken about this on many occasions, spoken about the I AM Presence as it has been implanted in the great Eight-sided Cell of Perfection. But the I AM Awareness is that now which we share; for you see Dear ones, Dear hearts, the I AM Awareness leads one into a greater quality of understanding, a greater unity of states or levels of consciousness, and prepares one for the path into Unana. When you call upon the I AM Awareness, it is as if a universal consciousness is then released for you to utilize. Do you understand?

Answer: "Yes, I do."

Proceed.

Question: "In calling upon the I AM Presence to come forward into a situation, that is an acknowledgement of your personal surrender of your will to the Presence of God, is it not?"

THE INTERCONNECTIVITY OF THE I AM

To the Presence of God and also the surrender of your will to the Greater Will, that is, the Will that recognizes the I AM Awareness, the I AM that exists in all individuals. It is as if the I AM Awareness is the energy or the interconnectivity between two individuals. Now it is always important to understand, for in the individualized Presence of God, one may think that is a separate version of God from an overall version of God. This is not so. That thought would indeed be in error, for the I AM Presence and the I AM Awareness are interconnected as if as ONE. The I AM Presence indeed is always with you Dear ones, Dear hearts, ready to serve and acknowledge the I AM Awareness. The Great I AM exists in all circumstances and situations. Have you not noticed that when you are in a trying circumstance or situation and you call upon the mighty I AM, instantly an opportunity or a solution to your problem then appears? Is this not so?

Response: "Yes, it is so."

That is the essence and the energy of the I AM in its awareness. Now, it is almost as if it is of a prophetic consequence, is it not? For you know in that instance, that even a greater solution can come forward when the proper focus is placed upon the right state, level of consciousness, or as in the earlier part of this discourse, on vibration. Predictable levels of consciousness are those that are not tuned into, do not understand this state of higher consciousness, this state of the I AM Awareness. It is true that even animals, although they do not contain the individualized Presence of God, are also tuned in to the I AM Awareness. All that is upon the Earth Plane and Planet are all interconnected through the Great I AM Awareness. But human beings are indeed individualized through the I AM.

CULTIVATE TOLERANCE AND PATIENCE

Souls that are perfecting on their sojourn, perfecting thought, feeling, and action in this great evolution of energy, are led to understand that there are these vibrational differences that do exist. But often, the predictable human consciousness judges things through dual experience; is this good or is this bad? The I AM Awareness accepts it all, in its perfect place and in its perfect order. Very often, the perfect order is not pleasant for one. Very often, one is disappointed for one reason or another. But the cultivation of tolerance and patience, one then begins to see the harmony that truly exists in all things. Proceed.

CALL FORTH THE I AM AWARENESS

Question: "It is true that divinity is in all things and this divinity is the source of creation or God?"

This divinity could be very much compared to the I AM Awareness. But remember, as one may have the consciousness that all things have and contain God within them, divinity within, until you command and demand the I AM Awareness to come forward and work for you, this awareness may not be able to give you the results that you require. That is why, so often when we call upon that mighty I AM Presence, a shift of quality and vibration immediately ensues. This is collecting and calling the I AM Awareness into its greater activity. For instance, you may call upon the I AM Awareness through the I AM Presence. You do not notice that anything has immediately happened, but you notice a calming effect over circumstances, over situations. And yet, three weeks later, upon that circumstance, there is the answer. Someone else appears at the front the door, presenting to you a solution to a problem that seemed unanswered at the time. Now again, I speak in metaphors and symbols but also Dear ones, Dear hearts, there are those instances where the I AM Awareness brings complete and total balance to a situation.

> Mighty I AM THAT I AM,
> I call forth the Awareness of the Great I AM,
> to bring balance and harmony to this situation.
> So Mote It Be.

Response: "So Mote It Be."

In that instance, you will notice a quality, a calming, a vibration. Tuning into this frequency, one then begins to have a different experience. Immediately, the clouds begin to part; the Sun begins to shine; things are seen from a new perception again. This awareness is the gift of God. It comes forward only to serve. Questions?

DIVINITY EXISTS IN ALL THINGS

Question: "Yes. So, if divinity is in all and the I AM Awareness, why isn't it simply within its nature to call or command the I AM Presence into action?"

The difference, Dear one, as I have always stated, is experience. It is important again, to not believe a word that I say to you. It is important only to review this lesson and to bring that mighty law into your own experience. But for simplistic matters, divinity indeed exists in all things. It exists in the air in this room. It exists in the chair that you sit upon. It exists in the candle that you light. It exists in the food that you eat. The Awareness is that divinity called into motion, to put forward that Great Plan of the Divine Will, bringing forward a greater alignment to circumstances and situations. Do you understand?

Question: "Yes, I do. And so, in calling upon the I AM Presence, an individual can call God action into a circumstance or situation, into a thought of healing or personal action, so that it is completely aligned with the Divine Plan and Divine Will? And this will happen in a way that the individual will understand and comprehend, is this not so?"

It is so Dear one, Dear heart. But for the chela, the student, who wishes to understand how such a situation can exist, how such a situation even would exist in the qualification of experience, this is why I give this instruction. Now Dear one, it has been some time since we have last had discourse. Are there any questions?

Response and question: "Yes. It is my experience, in the ability to manifest something, if the picture is envisioned in a very clear manner in the mind, without the use of words, and one can see it occurring and then create a model of it in an out-pictured manner, that it comes to fruition, comes into existence in this reality. And so, is the simplest method for this Co-creative process to envision without words or thoughts, just pictures?"

Sacred Fire

OUT-PICTURING, FOCUS, AND THE UNIVERSAL FLOW

Out-picturing, you know Dear one, Dear heart, is also connected, as another way of understanding the I AM Awareness. Out-picturing also Dear ones, as I have taught you, brings into a great understanding the visualization process. Now this sometimes is easier for a chela or student to begin with; for you see, the object of their desire is instantly in front of them. They are able then to see, in this manner, a materialization in their mind's eye of the result that they seek. Now there are those who are able to work with the out-picturing process in a more abstract form and manner, but it is important to understand each level within this Co-creative process and understanding that these are all keys to self-Mastery.

Out-picturing is given for the chela, so that they can begin to understand the incremental steps that are involved in the honing of the focus. As the focus becomes more and more exercised, not through belief but through experience, one begins to see the results that do occur through this process. Then one is ready to understand and activate the I AM Awareness. For in that moment, Dear ones, Dear hearts, the chela understands that there is no mistake, ever, ever, ever. All is working with a Divine Intention, in a Divine Plan, in accordance to the Divine Will. But this does not say that one just accepts conditions the way they are; no, that is not what I imply when I state this law. Beyond acceptance is tolerance and the energy of tolerance is a vibration. In this vibration, there is a greater understanding; there is a greater knowledge. This is the I AM Awareness. One then releases expectation and begins to flow into a greater vibration or energy, for lack of better word, of the universe. Does this explain?

PAIN, THE EQUALIZER

Question: "Yes. If one is experiencing a situation that is completely uncomfortable, is that existing discomfort the Divine Plan and the choice to change it, the ability to change it, and the laws that can change it, are also within the Divine Plan?"

It is Dear one. As you well know, pain is often the greatest teacher. Pain often shows you where not to travel again. Pain often will immediately stop you from traveling down the wrong path. Pain, you see Dear ones, when it is not resisted but understood, also becomes a great equalizer. It places you with tolerance upon this path of neutrality, for one then is able to understand this higher frequency of which I speak.

Question: "So here, in our experience in this schoolhouse, the ability to choose and to continue to choose to alter circumstances and situations, is our birthright?"

It is true, Dear ones, Dear hearts, in as much as the I AM Presence is connected (to you).

CHAPTER FOURTEEN

Eternal Balance

Saint Germain discusses spiritual growth.

Greetings Beloved chelas, in that mighty Violet Flame. I AM Saint Germain and I request permission to come forward.

Response: "Please Saint Germain, you are most welcome. Come forward."

LAW OF CORRESPONDENCE

There is still Dear ones, Dear hearts, much work for us to complete. Many changes indeed are happening upon the Earth Plane and Planet. And there are changes yet to come; these changes, known as prophecies, are also designed to shift the perception in consciousness of the Earth Plane. In the Law of Correspondence, the changes upon the Earth Plane are destined to happen. For you see Dear ones, Dear hearts, humanity and her people are sponsored by Beloved Earth, Beloved Babajeran. The Earth, in her sojourn and travels, is also going through a great change and it is no mistake, almost by Divine Appointment, that all are here.

You are here as well, experiencing this great change, for you see Dear ones, Dear hearts, this too is an evolution of your own consciousness. As the planet moves forward in her consciousness, in her vibratory rate, you too move forward in your own evolution, in your own spiritual growth. Dear ones, Dear hearts, this too is happening by Divine Order. As you so well know, there is no mistake, ever, ever, ever. Both of you have been brought together in this instance through that mighty Law of Attraction, this law always attracting like unto itself. This electromagnetic pulse, you see, cannot be denied. It is indeed a law of pushing and pulling, of attracting onto itself and repulsing onto itself. You see Dear ones, this too is another Law of Correspondence, of like seeking like, the same vibration seeking same vibration. These are laws eternal. Laws that must be paid attention to. For you see Dear ones, Dear hearts, when you pay attention to the laws eternal, then you are able to focus upon the true God-like qualities that exist in all things. That mighty I AM Presence that is within you is also focused upon the eternal laws.

THE CLARITY OF THE TEACHING

The temporal illusion gives many tests indeed to the soul and gives many tests to the soul in its sojourn within the Earth Plane and Planet. This indeed is a Time of Testing and we know at times that you wonder "how much more must I endure?" But as I have stated so many times Dear ones, Dear hearts, one is never tested beyond the ability that they are capable to perform. Again, this is based upon that mighty Law of Correspondence and the Law of Attraction, in the same essence, that when the student is ready, the Master appears. When the student is ready, also the test comes forward at the level that they are perfectly capable of performing. In this moment, so many lessons are being learned. And as lessons are being learned, one must then come forward in that lesson and declare the clarity of its teaching.

This clarity of its teaching comes forward when one is tested upon the content of the material of the lesson. Indeed, there are many changes that are happening now upon the Earth Plane and Planet, many of these changes orchestrating great changes within yourself but also orchestrating great testing for all levels of humanity, at many different levels of spiritual growth and evolution. At times, it may appear that things are so chaotic, that things do not make sense, that all is working with such chaos and disorder. But know Dear ones, Dear hearts, trust within that the plan assuredly shows that all is happening in a great Divine Orchestration. All is happening in a great Divine Order.

"THE DIFFERENCE IS EXPERIENCE"

At times, one may see or think such an insidious thought, such an insidious plan, that they would wonder how such darkness could be upon this Earth Plane and Planet at this time? But know this Dear ones, Dear hearts, all play their role. All play a part in letting the true role of light supreme reign. Know this Dear ones, Dear hearts, that the Earth is a blessing brought to you, to be your schoolroom, a place where you are brought to learn many experiences. As you well know Dear ones, Dear hearts, it is not belief that moves you forward in your evolution but experience is the guide. These experiences move you forward in your own evolution. They move you forward, one step at a time. That is why Dear Sananda has always said to you, "What is the difference?" Indeed Dear ones, Dear hearts, it is the experience. For you see, only through experience are you able to grow and understand.

COMPASSION AND THE OPEN HEART

One level to recognize growth is first the opening of the heart. Through the opening of the heart, one then is able to walk into greater levels, or shall we say, experiences of compassion. As you well know Dear ones, mercy, love, and forgiveness are always earmarks of compassion working at this level. This is one way to always gauge spiritual growth, for the chela who has grown in their own evolution, exhibits these qualities of compassion. Never is there a rush to judgment over any situation but there is the ability to discern through the Heart of Compassion, knowing that all is moving in its own timing and its own intention. All is moving forward, expressing that great and mighty love eternal. Dear ones, Dear hearts, this is always one of the first earmarks of a chela when they have experienced a level of growth.

BEYOND "RIGHT" OR "WRONG"

Another level of growth is the development of detachment, that one does not have to have something one way or the other. That is, they are able to move beyond the dualistic perception of their own experience. They are able then to accept that both sides, of left or right, can exist simultaneously. These Laws of Detachment leave one to an understanding of the truer Laws of Neutrality. When one sees that something is neither right nor wrong, but that all sides are existing, bringing forth the great eternal balance of the ONE, growth then is achieved.

LOVE FOR ALL

Another earmark of spiritual growth is that of love, love for all things; not only love of the fellow man but also love of nature; love of the Animal Kingdom; love of the Flower Kingdom; love of the Mineral Kingdom; love of the Elemental Kingdom. This love is always expressed and given without any expectation. Love is brought forward in this essence at an unconditional level.

THE LAW OF FORGIVENESS

Of all of these, the most important earmark to note within spiritual growth is that of forgiveness. Forgiveness, Dear ones, Dear hearts, right now for humanity, is one of the greatest stumbling blocks that exists for all. Often we hold as humans, little injustices. These little injustices keep the Heart of Compassion from growing. These little injustices keep a level of detachment from ever forming. These little injustices limit and restrict the release of the Law of Love. Forgiving oneself first is a matter of understanding how to shift your perception. Forgiveness, at all times, is a matter of being able to see something from a whole new viewpoint, a different standing point, so to speak.

It is important always to utilize that mighty Law of Forgiveness, the Violet Flame. That is why Dear ones, Dear hearts, the Violet Flame has been brought to you. For this mighty Violet Flame is indeed a Divine Intervention, a great gift that has been brought for humanity at this time. You see, it is used almost as a fertilizer for the soul, so it can have something to feed upon to attain the next levels of growth that are essential for evolution. Now, we know these earmarks of growth always lead one to another level of understanding. That level is the level of ONE, which is the Christ. Plane. We have spoken of this in many other discourses as Unana.

SPIRITUAL STAGNATION

But not to distract us away today from this discourse, we will stay focused upon the work at hand. At times in the Times of Testing, the student, chela, or aspirant, feels as if they are moving nowhere, that they are stagnating in a pool of their own diseased thoughts, feelings, or actions. I have given these levels of understanding in this discourse today so the student may cultivate those areas which they may feel need more practice. Have we not often spoken that practice, practice, practice, always brings about a more permanent experience? This permanent experience imbeds itself within the consciousness. Then compassion, love, detachment, forgiveness, all come about with such ease and grace. The chela, the student, has practiced this so often that it becomes a simple state of consciousness. It fits as easily as a glove.

WAHANEE AND THE VIOLET FLAME

Dear ones, Dear hearts, the Golden City of Wahanee is indeed one of the greatest Golden Cities to travel to and experience the energies of Beloved Babajeran, assisting the processes of the growth of the soul. For you see, that is where the Violet Flame is anchored firmly into the center of the Star of Wahanee. It was carried forward at a much, much earlier time and held within the spiritual grid of Mother Earth for this time. It is of no mistake that this time has come forward, Dear ones, Dear hearts, coming forward now to bring you into another level of growth, another level of experience. Wahanee, you see Dear ones, Dear hearts, is brought forward in a more cosmic sense, that is, for all at a level of Brotherhood and Sisterhood.

For those who wish to travel to Wahanee, they can receive great personal growth, great personal support, great personal instruction upon the levels of which I speak. Yes, it is true that Wahanee holds an energy to bring about a United Brotherhood and Sisterhood of the World. Now when I speak of this, do not confuse this with a one-world government of control, but it is rather, a one-world experience of love, complete Brotherhood, and peace. This that I speak of is the energy of Unana and Wahanee is very important, as it plays a continued role throughout the millennium of peace and grace, holding in continuous motion, an energy for the Dove of Peace to land upon the planet.

The ethereal schools of Wahanee are accessed, Dear ones, Dear hearts, when one travels to this Golden City Vortex and can also be experienced through meditation or the dream state, where the great instruction comes forward. Sometimes these energies are integrated just through the presence of traveling to the area, but often it is of great assistance if one is able to access the more subtler planes of energy. Know Dear ones, Dear hearts, that I am always there helping and guiding. Under my focus and direction, the energies bring about this process of compassion, the process of detachment, the process of all encompassing love eternal. Dear ones, Dear hearts, if you cannot travel to Wahanee, you can also travel in your meditation. I have given some instruction on this but before entering into the state of meditation, often it is good to meditate upon the Violet Flame. Before meditation, state this decree:

> In the name of that mighty Christ I AM,
> may the Violet Flame flow in, through, and around me.
> I AM now ONE with the Star of Wahanee.
> I AM love. I AM complete detachment.
> I AM Mercy and Forgiveness. I AM Compassion.
> So Be It.

Response: "So Be It."

THE SCHOOLS OF LIGHT

This statement comes forward, Dear ones, to prepare the consciousness to enter into that mighty Ray Force of the Violet Flame. The Violet Flame, as you well know, transmutes the consciousness and prepares it, in this sense, as an initiation to enter into the greater Temples of Light Supreme. These temples of consciousness, or shall we say, schools of light, lead one into a greater instruction. This is the purpose for all fifty-one Vortices upon the Earth Plane. They are brought forward at this time as a great intervention, for those who have the eyes to see and the ears to hear. It is true Dear ones, Dear heart, that when entering in to these higher schools of light, one begins to feel very differently. The first thing that they will notice is that their diet no longer works for them. They will notice that animal products seem to limit their ability to sustain the time that they enter into these schools of light. They will also notice that there is a high-pitched ring that is often vibrating within an audible sound Ray. This high vibration is indeed a shift in your consciousness.

Sometimes throughout the day, the mind begins to wander and an instant telepathic vision comes forward. One is able to see images that, at the time, may not make much sense, but when understood in the context of contact at another level, which is often known as a simultaneous reality, they are given a clearer and more lucid knowledge. For you see Dear one, when one begins to contact the School of Light, one then begins to understand that all is existing simultaneously; all is within you at once. Until these states or levels of consciousness are anchored more firmly within that permanent experience, one will feel at times a type of shaky motion, for lack of a better description, in terms of understanding their experience within these schools.

One also then begins to sustain contact, not only with the I AM, but with the I AM Awareness. As in our last discourse, the I AM Awareness is of all-importance; for you see, it is a higher consciousness frequency of relating to life eternal. That is why, when I explain relating to love, love in terms of all kingdoms of life, one is then relating through the I AM Awareness. One will also feel the presence of the Master Teacher. In this instance, if you are attending the Golden City Light Schools of Wahanee, one will feel an immediate contact or familiarity with my teachings and my tutelage.

THE FIRST SEVEN GOLDEN CITIES

Now know Dear ones, Dear hearts, if you identify with other Golden City Vortices and the teachings that they bring forward, you can use the techniques as I have described in the same manner. But I bring this teaching forward today, so you may begin to understand the importance of the Wahanee Vortex and the Golden City energies that have been placed there to serve humanity at this most important time. It is true that each Golden City Vortex is aligned to a certain continent upon the Earth. We have given some of this information in the beginning material. But now, it is important to understand that each of the Golden City Vortices, that is the first seven of them that are activated upon the Earth Plane and Planet, stabilize and help a certain continent during the great Earth Changes.

Of course, Gobean is affiliated with Gobi. It is there to stabilize the energies of Asia. Malton, you see Dear ones, is there to stabilize the energies of Europe. Wahanee is to stabilize the energies of Africa. Shalahah is there to stabilize the energies of India, even though there are those who would say that this is part of the Asian continent. At one time, this whole area was a separate continent and was related also to ancient Lemuria. Australia is also stabilized through this to some extent. It is also important to note that Klehma is there to balance North America and also South America together. The Golden Cities within Canada, Pashacino, to be exact, is there to stabilize Antarctica. [Editor's Note: The Golden City of Shalahah, (United States) is metaphysically connected to the Golden City of Sheahah, (Australia).]

The seventh Golden City, in its activation to come forward, holds an energy for the entire world. [Editor's Note: The seventh Golden City activated is Eabra in the Yukon Territory. The Master Teacher is Portia, Twin Flame to Saint Germain, holding the Violet Flame and the purpose of bringing forth joy, balance, and equality.]

So you see Dear ones, Dear hearts, this gives even a more added dimension to understanding the work of the Golden Cities and how this grid is interconnected at many, many levels. Dear ones, Dear hearts, there is much, much, more teaching that will be given upon the Golden Cities. But now, I sense your questions and open the floor.

FORGIVENESS AND PERCEPTION

Question: "Thank you. So that this is clarified, in the area of forgiveness, are you forgiving the person you sense is transgressing you or are you forgiving yourself for even perceiving a transgression and not just accepting it as an experience?"

Perhaps it is important to understand that all works simultaneously. When one has moved their perception to forgive self, one instantaneously then releases attachment to the one that they perceive a transgression has occurred with. It is most important always Dear one, to forgive the self first, for in the forgiveness of self, one then is able to see things from a whole new point of view. This indeed is that point of perception which is always so important.

Response: "I see. So in essence, there really isn't a transgression, you're just having an experience and if you forgive yourself for perceiving the experience as a transgression, then you will not have that sense of contention or disagreement with the other person."

It is as simple as shifting your perception. When one moves to understand a situation or circumstance from as many perceptions as possible, then one is able to easily forgive the self. This cannot occur when one righteously assumes one level of perception and insists that is the only way that a certain situation or circumstance can be viewed. This is most important.

Question: "I understand what you're saying. The Golden Cities are activated in the planet but are they also activated through the individuals who are present there?"

They are activated through the agreement of Beloved Babajeran and the Ascended Masters. Dear ones, Dear hearts, this is a work of cooperation, that is why we have stated this to be an Age of Cooperation, a New Time for peace and prosperity for the Earth and humanity.

GOLDEN CITY ACTIVATIONS

Question: "I understand. So as more Golden Cities are activated, they will increasingly stabilize the planet. Is this at a geophysical level or is this at a spiritual level?"

Of course, it is at a spiritual level but, as you well know, it is that template of thought and intention that creates the physical manifestation, does it not?

Answer: "Yes, I would agree with that."

So, as you see Dear ones, Dear hearts, this is of vast importance.

DIVINE INTERVENTION OF THE GOLDEN CITIES

Question: "Yes, I understand what you're saying. The Golden Cities, in their sponsorship from the Ascended Masters and the planet, are they here to transmute the planet and to also transmute all of humanity?"

It is true Dear ones, it is true Dear heart. The Golden Cities have been brought forward as a great Divine Intervention, not only to bring a stabilization to the Earth at this most wondrous time, but also to bring forward the Schools of Light, so many may have access to them. This is why there were many that were given within the Earth grid, that is, in terms of their locations, so those who had the eyes to see and the ears to hear could travel to them in physical proximity. If this was not something that could be achieved, then they could also travel through working with the finer light bodies. Do you understand?

Answer and question: "Yes, I do. And so these Schools of Light are specific for each of the Rays?"

It is true Dear one. But as you so well know, it is always better to have choice, is it not?

Question: "Yes, it is. That truly helps to expand our experiences on our path of upliftment. In understanding these Schools of Light and the Masters being present, is it important that actual buildings are built in the future for these schools to exist here?"

These schools exist without physical buildings. But again Dear ones, certain buildings formed with certain sacred geometrical shapes, as you well know, have the ability to intensify the result. This I have given to you in previous discourses.

Question: "Yes, you have. Just to clarify, are there specific buildings for specific Rays?"

Dear one, Dear heart, the Rays of Light and Sound exist without the formation of a building. However, if you are referring to intensifiers, that is, buildings that serve as Step-down Transformers of Ray Forces, this too can be achieved. However, this is an advanced knowledge and will be released at a later date, if you so require.

Response: "Yes, I would think these intensifiers would be very helpful to the individuals or groups who are drawn to each of these schools."

As you well know Dear one, certain Rays of Light and Sound vibrate better to certain minerals. Substances also vibrate better to certain colors and vibrate to certain types of building materials. It is a little more detailed and a little more complicated, however, totally achievable, as it has been in past civilizations.

Question: "Yes, so in the future, if I do request, you will come forward with this detailed information for each of the Rays?"

So Be It.

Spiritual Lineage of the Violet Flame

The teachings of the Violet Flame, as taught in the work of I AM America, come through the Goddess of Compassion and Mercy Kuan Yin. She holds the feminine aspects of the flame, which are Compassion, Mercy, Forgiveness, and Peace. Her work with the Violet Flame is well documented in the history of Ascended Master teachings, and it is said that the altar of the etheric Temple of Mercy holds the flame in a Lotus Cup. She became Saint Germain's teacher of the Sacred Fire in the inner realms, and he carried the masculine aspect of the flame into human activity through Purification, Alchemy, and Transmutation. One of the best means to attract the beneficent activities of the Violet Flame is through the use of decrees and invocation. However, you can meditate on the flame, visualize the flame, and receive its transmuting energies like "the light of a thousand Suns," radiant and vibrant as the first day that the Elohim Arcturus and Diana drew it forth from our solar Sun at the creation of the Earth. Whatever form, each time you use the Violet Flame, these two Master Teachers hold you in the loving arms of its action and power.

The following is an invocation for the Violet Flame to be used at sunrise or sunset. It is utilized while experiencing the visible change of night to day, and day to night. In fact, if you observe the horizon at these times, you will witness light transitioning from pinks to blues, and then a subtle violet strip adorning the sky. We have used this invocation for years in varying scenes and circumstances, overlooking lakes, rivers, mountaintops, deserts, and prairies; in huddled traffic and busy streets; with groups of students or sitting with a friend; but more commonly alone in our home or office, with a glint of soft light streaming from a window. The result is always the same: a calm, centering force of stillness. We call it *the Space*.

Invocation of the Violet Flame for Sunrise and Sunset
I invoke the Violet Flame to come forth in the name of I AM that I AM,
To the Creative Force of all the realms of all the Universes, the Alpha, the Omega, the Beginning, and the End,
To the Great Cosmic Beings and Torch Bearers of all the realms of all the Universes,
And the Brotherhoods and Sisterhoods of Breath, Sound, and Light, who honor this Violet Flame that comes forth from the Ray of Divine Love—the Pink Ray, and the Ray of Divine Will—the Blue Ray of all Eternal Truths.

I invoke the Violet Flame to come forth in the name of I AM that I AM!
Mighty Violet Flame, stream forth from the Heart of the Central Logos, the Mighty Great Central Sun! Stream in, through, and around me.

(Then insert other prayers and/or decrees for the Violet Flame.)

Glossary

Age of Cooperation: The age humanity is currently being prepared to enter; it occurs simultaneously with the "Time of Change."

Age of Information: The Information Age is characterized as the time of the computer, or Digital Age; however, according to the Master Teachers, the Age of Information is a tenuous time in Earth's history when threshold decisions regarding the Earth and her natural environments will be made. The crux is the physical and psychic pollution that remains from the once expansive vision of the Industrial Revolution, and the new growth of spiritual consciousness beyond corruption, exploitation, and corporate greed.

Akashic Records: The recorded history of all created things from time immemorial, and constructed with the fifth cosmic element: ether.

Alchemy: A hidden yet transformative and sacred science which bridges the world of chemistry and metallurgy with the spiritual worlds of Mastery and Ascension Process.

Alignment: Balance

All-seeing Eye of God: Divine protection, Divine Intervention, and Divine Guidance in the affairs of humanity by the Spiritual Hierarchy. Esoteric researchers claim that the *Eye of Horus* and the *Eye of Providence* are other historical names associated with the All-seeing Eye of God and metaphorically represent the human pineal gland, the source of telepathy and clairvoyant sight. In Ascended Master Teachings, this is known as an important point in the Eight-sided Cell of Perfection, the Evolutionary Point, "Faith."

Ascended Master: Once an ordinary human, an Ascended Master has undergone a spiritual transformation over many lifetimes. He or she has Mastered the lower planes—mental, emotional, and physical—to unite with his or her God-Self or I AM Presence. An Ascended Master is freed from the Wheel of Karma. He or she moves forward in spiritual evolution beyond this planet; however, an Ascended Master remains attentive to the spiritual well-being of humanity, inspiring and serving the Earth's spiritual growth and evolution.

Ascension: A process of Mastering thoughts, feelings, and actions that balance positive and negative karmas. It allows entry to a higher state of consciousness and frees a person from the need to reincarnate on the lower earthly planes or lokas of experience. Ascension is the process of spiritual liberation, also known as moksha.

Ascension Process: The Ascension Process, according to Saint Germain, gathers the energies of the individual chakras and expands their energy through the heart. The Law of Love calibrates the energy fields (aura) to Zero Point—a physical and philosophical viewpoint of neutrality. From there, the subtle and fine tuning of the light bodies is effectuated through the higher chakras, sequentially including the Throat Chakra, the Third Eye Chakra, and finally the Crown Chakra. Zero Point is key in this process and it is here that the energies of all past lives are brought to psychological and physical (karmic) balance. Then the initiate is able to withdraw their light bodies from the physical plane into the Astral Light of the Fourth Dimension. The Ascension Process may take several lifetimes to complete and the beginning stages are defined through the arduous process of obtaining self-knowledge, the acceptance of the conscious immortality of the soul, and the use of Alchemy through the Violet Flame. Intermediate stages may manifest the anomalies of Dimensional Acceleration, Vibrational Shifting, Cellular Awakening and Acceleration, and contact with the Fourth Dimension. Use of the Gold Ray at this level accelerates the liberation process and unites the individual with soul mates and their beloved Twin Ray. Later stages of Ascension include the transfiguration of light bodies and Fifth Dimensional contact through the super-senses as the magnificent Seamless Garment manifests its light. It is claimed that the Golden Cities assist the Ascension Process at every stage of development. According to the Master Teachers diet and fasting will also aid the Ascension Process at various phases.

Astral Body: This subtle light body contains our feelings, desires, and emotions and exists as an intermediate light body between the physical body and the Causal Body (Mental Body). According to the Master Teachers we enter the Astral Plane through our Astral Body when we sleep, and many dreams and visions are experiences in this Plane of vibrant color and sensation. Through spiritual development the Astral Body strengthens, and the luminosity of its light is often detected in the physical plane. A spiritual adept may have the ability to consciously leave their physical body while traveling in their Astral Body. The Astral Body or Astral Plane has various levels of evolution, and is the heavenly abode where the soul resides after the disintegration of the physical body. The Astral Body is also known to esoteric scholars as the Body Double, the Desire Body, and the Emotional Body.

At-One-Ment: The spiritual practice and state of Unity. This spiritual ideal is philosophically affirmed through the recognition of humanity's innate divinity, equality, and human connection to ONE source of creation. This results in the At-ONE-ment, and the advanced practitioner morphs into a Step-down Transformer of the Seven Rays of Light and Sound as an expression of beauty and creation. The At-ONE-ment facilitates the consciousness of Unana.

Aura: The subtle energy field of luminous light that surrounds the human body.

Babajeran: A name for the Earth Mother that means, "grandmother rejoicing."

Belief: A conviction or opinion of trust based on insufficient evidence or reality. This confidence may be based on alleged facts without positive knowledge, direct experience, or proof. According to the Master Teachers, beliefs may be negative, positive, or both. Often the unchallenged nature of beliefs form the nucleus of Co-creative activity. The spectrum of individual and collective beliefs can vary from innocent gullibility to unwavering religious faith and conviction.

Blue Flame: The activity of the Blue Ray, based upon the activation of the individual will, manifests the qualities of truth, power, determination, and diligence in human endeavors. The Blue Flame is associated with the transformation of our individual choices, and its inherent processes align the individual will to the Divine Will through the HU-man qualities of detachment, steadiness, calm, harmony, and God-protection.

Blue Ray: A Ray is a perceptible light and sound frequency, and the Blue Ray not only resonates with the color blue, but is identified with the qualities of steadiness, calm, perseverance, transformation, harmony, diligence, determination, austerity, protection, humility, truthfulness, and self-negation. It forms one-third of the Unfed Flame within the heart—the Blue Ray of God Power, which nourishes the spiritual unfoldment of the human into the HU-man. Use of the Violet Flame evokes the Blue Ray into action throughout the light bodies, where the Blue Ray clarifies intentions and assists the alignment of the Will. In Ascended Master teachings the Blue Ray is alleged to have played a major role in the physical manifestation of the Earth's first Golden City—Shamballa and six of fifty-one Golden Cities emanate the Blue Ray's peaceful, yet piercing frequencies. The Blue Ray is esoterically linked to the planet Saturn, the development of the Will, the ancient Lemurian Civilization, the Archangel Michael, the Elohim Hercules, the Master Teacher El Morya, and the Eastern Doors of all Golden Cities.

Cause and effect: Every action causes an event, which is the consequence or result of the first. This law is often referred to as Karma—or the sixth Hermetic Law.

Cellular Awakening: A spiritual initiation activated by the Master Teachers Saint Germain and Kuthumi. Through this process the physical body is accelerated at the cellular level, preparing consciousness to recognize and receive instruction from the Fourth Dimension. Supplemental teachings on the Cellular Awakening claim this process assists the spiritual student to assimilate the higher frequencies and energies now available on Earth. Realizing the Cellular Awakening can ameliorate catastrophic Earth Change and initiate consciousness into the ONE through the realization of devotion, compassion, Brotherhood and the Universal Heart.

Chakra: Sanskrit for wheel. Seven spinning wheels of human-bioenergy centers stacked from the base of the spine to the top of the head.

Chela: Disciple

Chohan: Another word for Lord.

Christ Consciousness: A level of consciousness that unites both feminine and masculine energies and produces the innocence and purity of the I AM. Its energies heal, enlighten, and transform every negative human condition and pave the way for the realization of the divine HU-man.

Co-creation: Creating with the God Source.

Compassion: An attribute of the Violet Flame is the sympathetic understanding of the suffering of another.

Conscience: The internal recognition of right and wrong in regard to one's actions and motives.

Consciousness: Awakening to one's own existence, sensations and cognitions.

Conscious Immortality: Awareness, acceptance, and knowledge of the immortal, spiritual soul.

Cup: A symbol of neutrality and grace. The Ascended Masters often refer to our human body as a Cup filled with our thoughts and feelings.

Cycle of the Yugas: Vedic Rishis claim the evolutionary status of humanity is contingent upon the quality of Ray Forces streaming to Earth as a non-visible quasar light from the Galactic Center—the Great Central Sun. While the Rays are invisible to the naked eye, their presence contains subtle electromagnetic energy and psychics may detect their luminous astral light. Ancient astrologers visually observed and experienced the Seven Rays of Light and Sound. Their astronomy, advanced beyond today's science, maintained that our solar Sun was in reality a double star. Our Sun rotates with a companion—a dwarf star which contains no luminosity of its own. This theory suggests that as our Solar System orbits the Great Central Sun, Earth experiences long periods of time when the dwarf star impedes the flow of the Rays from the Galactic Center; likewise, there are times when this important stream of light is unhampered. Since the light energy from the Central Sun nourishes spiritual and intellectual knowledge on the Earth, the Vedic Rishis expertly tracked Earth's movement in and out of the flow and reception of this cosmic light. This cycle is known as the Cycle of the Yugas, or the World Ages whose constant change instigates the advances and deterioration of cultures and civilizations. There are four Yugas: the Golden Age (Satya or Krita-Yuga); the Silver Age, (Treta-Yuga); the Bronze Age, (Dvapara-Yuga); the Iron Age, (Kali-Yuga).

Desire: Of the source; the ninth of Twelve Jurisdictions and states the heart's desire is the source of creation.

Deva: Shining one or being of light.

Dharma: Purpose.

Divine Mother: The Mother Goddess or feminine aspect of God.

Dvapara Yuga: The Bronze Period of the cycle of the yugas when fifty to twenty-five per cent light from the Galactic Center is available on Earth. During the last Puranic Dvapara Yuga it is alleged that the fabled continent and culture of Atlantis existed.
Dwarf Sun: A companion Sun that orbits with our Solar Sun and has no luminosity of its own. Astrologers speculate its juxtaposition between the Earth and our Sun obstructs, and therefore controls, the flow of this important galactic energy to Earth.

Eight-sided Cell of Perfection: An atomic cell located in the human heart. It is associated with all aspects of perfection, and contains and maintains a visceral connection with the Godhead.

Elemental Kingdom: A kingdom comprising an invisible, subhuman group of creatures who act as counterparts to visible nature on Earth.

El Morya: Ascended Master of the Blue Ray, associated with the development of the will.

Energy for energy: To understand this spiritual principle, one must remember Isaac Newton's Third Law of Motion: for every action there is an equal and opposite reaction. However, while energies may be equal, their forms often vary. The Ascended Masters often use this phrase to remind chelas to properly compensate others to avoid karmic retribution; and repayment may take many different forms.

Ever Present Now: Time as a continuous, unencumbered flow without past or future.

Fifth Dimension: A spiritual dimension of cause, associated with thoughts, visions, and aspirations. This is the dimension of the Ascended Masters and the Archetypes of Evolution, the city of Shamballa, and the templates of all Golden Cities.

Fourth Dimension: A dimension of vibration associated with telepathy, psychic ability, and the dream world. This is the dimension of the Elemental Kingdom and the development of the super senses.

Freedom Star: The Earth's future prophesied name.

Galactic Center: The great Sun of our galaxy, of which all of its solar systems rotate. The Galactic Center Sun is also known in Ascended Master Teachings as the Great Central Sun, which is the origin of the Seven Rays of Light and Sound on Earth. In Vedic tradition it is known as Brahma, which is the creative force or navel of Vishnu. This great Sun emanates spiritual light that determines life and intelligence on Earth and distributes karma.

Galactic Web: A large, planet-encircling grid created by the consciousness of all things on Earth—humans, animals, plants, and minerals. Magnetic Vortices, namely the Golden Cities, appear at certain intersections. The Ascended Masters often refer to any type of energy point (i.e. Chakra, lei-line, Golden City Vortex, etc.) to be included in the Galactic Web. Since the Angelic Host protects this Web of Creation, the protective web of the Angelic Host is often interchanged with the Galactic Web.

Gateway or Gateway Adjutant Points: Two Golden City power points that are located on either side of each directional gateway of a Golden City Vortex and are situated to the outer perimeter of the Vortex. These points are also the locations of ethereal retreats where a Master Teacher oversees and protects the Golden City.

Gobean: The first United States Golden City located in the states of Arizona and New Mexico. Its qualities are cooperation, harmony, and peace. Its Ray Force is blue, and its Master Teacher is El Morya.

Gobi: A Golden City named for the Great Desert of China, Gobi in Mongolian means "the waterless place." Ascended Masters claim the Golden City of Gobi is a Step-down Transformer for the energies of the Earth's first Golden City—Shamballa. Gobi's esoteric definition comes from the Chinese translation of "go—across," and bi in Indonesian (Abun, A Nden, and Yimbun dialects) means "star." The Golden City of Gobi means "Across the Star," or "Across the Freedom Star." "Freedom Star" is a reference to Earth in her enlightened state.) Gobi aligns energies to the first Golden City of the New Times: Gobean.

Golden Age: A peaceful time on Earth prophesied to occur after the Time of Change. It is also prophesied that during this age, human life spans are increased and sacred knowledge is revered. During this time, the societies, cultures, and the governments of Earth reflect spiritual enlightenment through worldwide cooperation, compassion, charity, and love. Ascended Master teachings often refer to the Golden Age as the Golden-Crystal Age and the Age of Grace.

Golden Age of Kali Yuga: According to the classic Puranic timing of the Yugas, Earth is in a Kali-Yuga period that started around the year 3102 BCE the year that Krishna allegedly left the Earth. During this time period, which according to this Puranic timing lasts a total of 432,000 years—the ten-thousand year Golden Age period, also known as the Golden Age of Kali Yuga, is not in full force. Instead, it is a sub-cycle of higher light frequencies within an overall larger phase of less light energy.

    This Golden Age is prophesied to raise the energy of Earth as additional light from the Galactic Center streams to our planet. This type of light is a non-visible, quasar-type light that is said to expand life spans and memory function, and nourish human consciousness, especially spiritual development. There are many theories as to when this prescient light energy began to flow to our planet. Some say it started about a thousand years ago, and others claim it began at the end of the nineteenth century. No doubt its influence has changed life on Earth for the better, and according to the I AM America Teachings, its effect began to encourage and guide human spiritual evolution around the year 2000 CE.

The Spiritual Teachers say that living in Golden Cities can magnify Galactic Energies and at their height, the energies will light the Earth between 45 to 48 percent—nearly reaching the light energies of a full-spectrum Treta Yuga or Silver Age on Earth. The Spiritual Teachers state, "The Golden Age is the period of time where harmony and peace shall be sustained."

Golden City Doorway: The gateway to the Golden City, based on the Maltese Cross and the four cardinal directions: North, East, South, and West. There are four doorways to a Golden City and are based on the subtractive color wavelengths of: black, blue (cyan), red (magenta), and yellow. Each doorway has two Gateway Points, located on either side to the outer perimeter of the Vortex.

Golden City Vortex: A Golden City Vortex—based on the Ascended Masters' I AM America material—are prophesied areas of safety and spiritual energies during the Times of Changes. Covering an expanse of land and air space, these sacred energy sites span more than 400 kilometers (270 miles) in diameter, with a vertical height of 400 kilometers (250 miles). Golden City Vortices, more importantly, reach beyond terrestrial significance and into the ethereal realm. This system of safe harbors acts as a group or universal mind within our galaxy, connecting information seamlessly and instantly with other beings. Fifty-one Golden City Vortices are stationed throughout the world, and each carries a different meaning, a combination of Ray Forces, and a Divine Purpose. A Golden City Vortex works on the principles of electromagnetism and geology. Vortices tend to appear near fault lines, possibly serving as conduits of inner-earth movement to terra firma. Golden Cities are symbolized by a Maltese Cross, whose sacred geometry determine their doorways, lei-lines, adjutant points, and coalescing Star energies. Since their energies intensify experiences with both the Fourth and Fifth Dimensions, Golden City Vortices play a vital role with the Ascension Process.

Gold(en) Ray: The Ray of Brotherhood, Cooperation, and Peace. The Gold Ray produces the qualities of perception, honesty, confidence, courage, and responsibility. It is also associated with leadership, independence, authority, ministration, and justice. The Gold Ray is currently influencing the spiritual growth and evolution of the divine HU-man. It is also associated with karmic justice and will instigate many changes throughout our planet including Earth Changes and social and economic change.

Golden Thread Axis: Also known as the Vertical Power Current. The Golden Thread Axis is physically composed of the Medullar Shushumna, a life-giving nadi physically comprising one-third of the human Kundalini system. Two vital currents intertwine around the Golden Thread Axis: the lunar Ida Current, and the solar Pingala Current. According to the Master Teachers, the flow of the Golden Thread Axis begins with the I AM Presence, enters the Crown Chakra, and descends through the spinal system. It descends beyond the Base Chakra and travels to the core of the Earth. Esoteric scholars often refer to the axis as the Rod of Power, and it is symbolized by two spheres connected by an elongated rod. Ascended Master students and chelas frequently draw upon the energy of the Earth, through the Golden Thread Axis, for healing and renewal by using meditation, visualization, and breath techniques.

Great Central Sun: The great Sun of our galaxy, around which all of the galaxy's solar systems rotate. The Great Central Sun is also known as the Galactic Center, which is the origin of the Seven Rays of Light and Sound on Earth.

Great Silence: Periods of tranquil power are referred to as the Great Silence. This Ascended Master spiritual principle encourages contemplative periods of quiet and stillness, which create intense spiritual energies in certain circumstances and situations.

Great White Brotherhood (Lodge): A fraternity of ascended and unascended men and women who are dedicated to the universal uplifting of humanity. Its main objective includes the preservation of the lost spirit, and the teachings of the ancient religions and philosophies of the world. Its mission is to reawaken the dormant ethical and spiritual sparks among the masses. In addition to fulfilling spiritual aims, the Great White Lodge pledges to protect mankind against the systematic assaults – which inhibit self-knowledge and personal growth – on individual and group freedoms.

Green Ray: The Ray of Active Intelligence is associated with education, thoughtfulness, communication, organization, the intellect, science, objectivity, and discrimination. It is also adaptable, rational, healing, and awakened. The Green Ray is affiliated with the planet Mercury. In the I AM America teachings the Green Ray is served by the Archangel Raphael and Archeia Mother Mary; the Elohim of Truth, Vista—also known as Cyclopea, and Virginia; the Ascended Masters Hilarion, Lord Sananda, Lady Viseria, Soltec, and Lady Master Meta.

Guru: Teacher

Harmony of the Spheres: A superior form of music, founded on beauty and harmonious combination, heard by those who have developed the ears to hear—clairaudience. The Harmony of the Spheres is an esoteric term that refers to an exacting form of balance and synchronization often realized through the hidden geometric and mathematical perfection of all created forms. The movement of the heavenly bodies is said to be timed to such mathematical precision and perfection that the planets create a celestial music.

Heart Chakra: The location of this chakra is in the center of the chest and is known in Sanskrit as the Anahata. Its main aspect is Love and Relationships; our ability to feel compassion, forgiveness, and our own feeling of Divine Purpose.

Heavenly Lords: Ascended Masters who no longer serve Earth; instead, their work is associated with other aspects of creation including our solar system, and star systems located in various galaxies.

Hidden Planet: A planet that is located between our solar Sun and the non-luminous dwarf Sun.

HU-man: The integrated and spiritually evolved human; the God Man.

I AM: The presence of God.

I AM Awareness: A higher consciousness considered to be universal to all kingdoms of creation in nature, and is comprised of all conscious calls, decrees, fiats, prayers, and spiritual practice that has activated the use of the I AM.

I AM Presence: The individualized presence of God.

I AM THAT I AM: A term from Hebrew that translates to, "I Will Be What I Will Be." "I AM" is also derived from the Sanskrit Om (pronounced: A-U-M), whose three letters signify the three aspects of God as beginning, duration, and dissolution – Brahma, Vishnu, and Shiva. The AUM syllable is known as the omkara and translates to "I AM Existence," the name for God. "Soham," is yet another mystical Sanskrit name for God, which means "It is I," or "He is I." In Vedic philosophy, it is claimed that when a child cries, "Who am I?" the universe replies, "Soham – you are the same as I AM." The I AM teachings also use the name "Soham" in place of "I AM."

Immortality: Everlasting and deathless. Spiritual immortality embraces the idea of the eternal, unending existence of the soul. Physical immortality includes the notion of the timeless, deathless, and birthless body.

Initiation: Admission, especially into secret, advanced spiritual knowledge.

Inner Marriage: A process achieved through the spiritual integration of the masculine and feminine aspects of self, uniting dualistic qualities into greater balance and harmony for expression of self-Mastery.

Intention: Acts, thoughts, or conceptions earnestly fixed on something, or steadfastly directed. Intentions often reflect the state of an individual's mind which directs their specific actions towards an object or goal.

Jiva: The individual, immortal soul that survives death

Judgment: The act of forming negative assumptions and critical opinions, primarily of fellow human beings.

Kali Yuga: The Age of Iron, or Age of Quarrel, when Earth receives twenty-five percent or less galactic light from the Great Central Sun.

Karma: Laws of Cause and Effect.

Klehma: The fifth United States Golden City located primarily in the states of Colorado and Kansas. Its qualities are continuity, balance, and harmony; its Ray force is white; and its Master Teacher is Serapis Bey.

Kuan Yin: The Bodhisattva of Compassion and teacher of Saint Germain. She is associated with all the Rays and the principle of femininity.

Kundalini: In Sanskrit, Kundalini literally means coiled, and represents the coiled energy located at the base of the spine, often established in the lower Base and Sacral Chakras. Kundalini Shatki (shatki means energy) is claimed to initiate spiritual development, wisdom, knowledge, and enlightenment.

Law of Attraction and Repulsion: Physically, like charges repel; unlike charges attract. Through the Spiritual Law of Allowing, like attracts like.

Law of Correspondence: "As above, so below."

Law of Forgiveness: The transmutation of karma through the use of the Violet Flame.

Law of Love: Perhaps every religion on Earth is founded upon the Law of Love, as the notion to "treat others as you would like to be treated." The Law of Love, however, from the Ascended Master tradition is simply understood as consciously living without fear, or inflicting fear on others. The Fourth of the Twelve Jurisdictions instructs Love is the Law of Allowing, Maintaining, and Sustainability. All of these precepts distinguishes love from an emotion or feeling, and observes Love as action, will, or choice. The Ascended Masters affirm, "If you live love, you will create love." This premise is fundamental to understand the esoteric underpinnings of the Law of Love. The Master Teachers declare that through practicing the Law of Love one experiences acceptance and understanding; tolerance, alongside detachment. Metaphysically, the Law of Love allows different and varied perceptions of ONE experience, situation, or circumstance to exist simultaneously. From this viewpoint the Law of Love is the practice of tolerance.

Law of Rhythm: Everything ebbs and flows; rises and falls. The swing of the pendulum is universal. The measure of the momentum to the right is equal to the swing of the left.

Lei-line: Lines of energy that exist among geographical places, ancient monuments, megaliths, and strategic points. These energy lines contain electrical or magnetic points.

Light: "Love in action."

Lords of Venus: A group of Ascended Masters who came to serve humanity. They once resided on the planet Venus.

Love: "Light in action."

Maltese Cross: The Maltese Cross, a symbol often used by Saint Germain, represents the Eight-Sided Cell of Perfection, and the human virtues of honesty, faith, contrition, humility, justice, mercy, sincerity, and the endurance of persecution.

Malton: The second United States Golden City located in the states of Illinois and Indiana. Its qualities are fruition and attainment; its Ray force is ruby and Gold; and its Master Teacher is Kuthumi.

Mantra: Certain sounds, syllables, and sets of words are deemed sacred and often carry the power to transmute Karma, purify the spirit, and transform an individual. These are known as mantras. The mantra is a foundation of Vedic tradition and often treated as a devotional upaye—a remedial measure of difficult obstacles. Mantras, however, are not limited to Hinduism. Buddhists, Sikhs, and Jains also utilize mantras. The Ascended Masters occasionally provide mantras to chelas to improve resonation with certain Golden Cities.

Master Teacher: A spiritual teacher from a specific lineage of teachers—gurus. The teacher transmits and emits the energy from that collective lineage.

Mastery: Possessing the consummate skill of command and self-realization over thought, feeling, and action.

Master within: The fully realized God aspect of our spiritual being. The Master within is akin to the I AM.

Meditation: Quieting or silencing the mind in order to give focused attention or devotion to one thing.

Meissner Field: A magnetic energy field that does not contain polarity. It is produced during a transitory state of superconductivity. Ascended Master teaching associates this type of energy field with HU-man development, Unana, and Christ Consciousness.

Mental Body: A subtle light body of the Human Aura comprising thoughts.

Monad: From an Ascended Master viewpoint, the Monad is the spark or flame of life of spiritual consciousness and it is also the Awakened Flame that is growing, evolving, and ultimately on the path to Ascension. Because of its presence of self-awareness and purpose, the Monad represents our dynamic will and the individualized presence of the Divine Father. Ultimately, the Monad is the spark of consciousness that is self-determining, spiritually awake, and drives the growth of human consciousness. The Monad is the indivisible, whole, divine life center of an evolving soul that is immortal and contains the momentum within itself to drive consciousness to learn, grow, and perfect itself in its evolutionary journey.

Mudra: A symbolic ceremonial or spiritual gesture, mostly expressed by the hands and fingers. It is often used by evolved spiritual beings and Ascended Masters to signify or emit spiritual energies.

New Day: The process of seeing or perceiving a problem or an obstacle from a different point of view. This often involves a shift in consciousness.

ONE: Indivisible, whole, harmonious Unity.

Oneness: A combination of two or more, which creates the whole.

Oneship: A combination of many, which comprises the whole and, when divided, contains both feminine and masculine characteristics.

Outpicturing: To envision in the mind and project to the outer world.

Paradigm of Twelve: This metaphysical law relies on the notion of sacred numerology. It is comprised of six negative and six positive energies that creates a field of neutrality. This leads both individuals and groups beyond the Third Dimension and opens the Fourth Dimension.

Perception: Awareness through the senses, including the super-senses.

Pink Ray: The Pink Ray is the energy of the Divine Mother and associated with the Moon. It is affiliated with these qualities: loving, nurturing, hopeful, heartfelt, compassionate, considerate, communicative, intuitive, friendly, humane, tolerant, adoring.

Point of Perception: A Co-creation teaching of the Ascended Masters and its processes pivot on the fulcrum of choice. By carefully choosing certain actions, a Master of Choice opens the world of possibility through honing carefully cultivated perceptions, attitudes, beliefs, thoughts, and feelings. This allows the development of outcome through various scenarios and opens the multi-dimensional door to multiple realities and simultaneous experiences that dissolve linear timeframes into the Ever Present Now.

Prana: Vital, life-sustaining energy; also known as orgone or chi.

Prophecies of Change: Primarily prophecies of Earth Changes, but also include political, social, and cultural change alongside spiritual and biological changes to humanity.

Prophecies of Peace: Prophecies and spiritual teachings aimed towards humanity's spiritual growth, evolution, and entrance into the New Times and the Golden Age.

Prophecy: A spiritual teaching given simultaneously with a warning. It's designed to change, alter, lessen, or mitigate the prophesied warning. This caveat may be literal or metaphoric; the outcome of these events are contingent on the choices and the consciousness of those willing to apply the teachings.

Protective Grid: The world-wide network of Golden Cities. As the Protective Grid expands into space it is known as the Galactic Web.

Purification: A clearing process, especially in spiritual practice, which frees consciousness from encumbering or objectionable elements.

Ray: A force containing a purpose, which divides its efforts into two measurable and perceptible powers, light and sound.

Ruby Ray: The Ruby Ray is the energy of the Divine Masculine and Spiritual Warrior. It is associated with these qualities: energetic; passionate; devoted; determination; dutiful; dependable; direct; insightful; inventive; technical; skilled; forceful. This Ray Force is astrologically affiliated with the planet Mars and the Archangel Uriel, Lord Sananda, and Master Kuthumi. The Ruby Ray is often paired with the Gold Ray, which symbolizes Divine Father. The Ruby Ray is the evolutionary Ray Force of both the base and solar chakras of the HU-man; and the Gold and Ruby Rays step-down and radiate sublime energies into six Golden Cities.

Saint Germain: Ascended Master of the Seventh Ray, Saint Germain is known for his work with the Violet Flame of Mercy, Transmutation, Alchemy, and Forgiveness. He is the sponsor of the Americas and the I AM America material. Many other teachers and Masters affiliated with the Great White Brotherhood assist his endeavors.

Sananda: The name used by Master Jesus in his ascended state of consciousness. Sananda means joy and bliss, and his teachings focus on revealing the savior and heavenly kingdom within.

Seamless Garment: The idea of the Seamless Garment symbolizes perfection and immortality, or what's known as the Electronic Body. This is the regalia of the Ascended Masters; not woven by hand, but fashioned by the perfected thought and manifestation process. It is the essence of eternal youth and beauty; it is unbound by limitations; and it exists in a consciousness free of space, time, age, and place. The term also refers to the Ascension Process or a symbol of Oneness—unity.

Serapis Bey: An Ascended Master from Venus who works on the White Ray. He is the great disciplinarian—essential for Ascension; and works closely with all unascended humanity who remain focused for its attainment.

Seven Rays: The traditional Seven Rays of Light and Sound are: the Blue Ray of Truth; the Yellow Ray of Wisdom; the Pink Ray of Love; the White Ray of Purity; the Green Ray of Healing; the Gold and Ruby Ray of Ministration; and the Violet Ray of Transmutation.

Seventh Manu: Highly evolved lifestreams that embody on Earth between 1981 to 3650. Their goal is to anchor freedom and the qualities of the Seventh Ray to the conscious activity on this planet. They are prophesied as the generation of peace and grace for the Golden Age. South America is their forecasted home, though small groups will incarnate in other areas of the globe.

Shalahah: The fourth United States Golden City located primarily in the states of Montana and Idaho. Its qualities are abundance, prosperity, and healing; its Ray Force is Green; and its Master Teacher is Sananda.

Shamballa: Venusian volunteers, who arrived 900 years before their leader Sanat Kumara, built the Earth's first Golden City. Known as the City of White, located in the present-day Gobi Desert, its purpose was to hold conscious light for the Earth and to sustain her evolutionary place in the solar system.

Simultaneous Reality: A non-linear perspective of time. It prepares us for potential possibilities in all situations—past, present, and future—and retains the capacity for multiple encounters and outcomes. Each reality exists side by side, so humans can consciously open up to these events to gain insight and self-knowledge.

Spiritual Liberation: The process whereby the soul gains freedom from the Wheel of Karma, and the need to reincarnate in a physical body on Earth. In Ascended Master Teachings, spiritual liberation is known as Ascension. Depending on the spiritual level and evolution of each soul, after spiritual liberation from the Earth Plane the soul travels onward into higher levels of Astral or Causal Planes, where yet another liberation process ensues. This new level of consciousness and spiritual evolution may include Earth or other planets. In Hinduism, spiritual liberation is known as moksha, which is the release from suffering, and the cycle of death and rebirth. It is claimed that the soul is released from duality as the concept of self expands into the sublime realization of the I AM and the soul merges with the I AM Presence. This also includes the realization of the Christ Consciousness or birth of the Quetzalcoatl energies as the soul enters Fourth and Fifth Dimensional Awareness. This perfected state of consciousness realizes the Earthly Plane as illusion or Maya and exists without separation from the God Source, the spiritually free at-one-ment.

Spiritual Awakening: Conscious awareness of personal experiences and existence beyond the physical, material world. Consequently, an internalization of one's true nature and relationship to life is revealed, freeing one of the lesser self (ego) and engendering contact with the higher (Christ) self and the I AM.

Spiritual Preparedness: The practice and application of various spiritual techniques and disciplines that help to increase and leverage spiritual potential alongside the Ascension Process during the Time of Change.

Star (of a Golden City): The apex, or center of each Golden City.

Star seed: Souls and groups whose genetic origins are not from Earth. Many remain linked to one another from one lifetime to the next, as signified by the Atma Karaka, a Sanskrit term meaning "soul indicator." Star-seed consciousness is often referred to by the Spiritual Teachers as a family or soul group whose members have evolved to and share Fifth-Dimensional awareness. Star seeds can also contain members who have not yet evolved to this level, who are still incarnating on Earth.

Step-down Transformer: The processes instigated through the Cellular Awakening rapidly advance human light bodies. Synchronized with an Ascended Master's will, the awakened cells of light and love evolve the skills of a Step-down Transformer to efficiently transmit and distribute currents of Ascended Master energy—referred to as an Ascended Master Current (A.M. Current). This metaphysical form of intentional inductive coupling creates an ethereal power grid that can be used for all types of healing.

Third Dimension: Thought, feeling, and action.

Third Eye: Also known as the Ajna Chakra. This energy center is located above and between the eyebrows. The Third-eye Chakra blends thought and feeling into perception and projection for Co-creative activity.

Thousand Eyes: This term refers to the endless rounds of death and rebirth the soul encounters before entering the Ascension Process of spiritual liberation.

Time Compaction: An anomaly produced as we enter into the prophesied Time of Change. Our perception of time compresses; time seems to speed by. The unfolding of events accelerates, and situations are jammed into a short period of time. This experience of time will become more prevalent as we get closer to the period of cataclysmic Earth Changes.

Time of Change: The period of time currently underway. Tremendous changes in our society, cultures, and politics in tandem with individual and collective spiritual awakenings and transformations will abound. These events occur simultaneously with the possibilities of massive global warming, climactic changes, and seismic and volcanic activity—Earth Changes. The Time of Change guides Earth to a new time, the Golden Age.

Time of Testing: The Time of Testing is a period of seven to twenty years which began around the turn of the twenty-first century, following the time period known as the Time of Transition. According to Saint Germain and other Ascended Masters, the Time of Testing is perhaps one of the most turbulent periods mankind will experience and its first seven years is prophesied as a period of change and strife for many. As its title suggests, the Master Teachers claim this timeframe may challenge students by testing their spiritual acumen and inner strength.

True Memory: Memory, as defined by Ascended Master teachings is not seen as a function of the brain, or the soul's recall of past events. Instead, True Memory is achieved through cultivating our perceptions and adjusting our individual perspective of a situation to the multiple juxtapositions of opinion and experience. This depth of understanding gives clarity and illumination to every experience. Our skill and Mastery through True Memory moves our consciousness beyond common experiences to individualized experiences whose perceptive power hones honesty and accountability. The innate truth obtained from many experiences through the interplay of multiple roles creates True Memory, and opens the detached and unconditional Law of Love to the chela.

Twelve Jurisdictions: Twelve laws (virtues) for the New Times that guide consciousness to Co-create the Golden Age. They are Harmony, Abundance, Clarity, Love, Service, Illumination, Cooperation, Charity, Desire, Faith, Stillness, Creation/Creativity.

Unana: Unity Consciousness.

Unfed Flame: The three-fold flame of divinity that exists in the heart and becomes larger as it evolves. The three flames represent Love (pink); Wisdom (yellow); and Power (blue).

Vertical Power Current: *See Golden Thread Axis*

Violet Flame: The Violet Flame is the practice of balancing karmas of the past through Transmutation, Forgiveness, and Mercy. The result is an opening of the Spiritual Heart and the development of bhakti—unconditional love and compassion. It came into existence when the Lords of Venus first transmitted the Violet Flame, also knows as Violet Fire, at the end of Lemuria to clear the Earth's etheric and psychic realms, and the lower physical atmosphere of negative forces and energies. This paved the way for the Atlanteans, who used it during religious ceremonies and as a visible marker of temples. The Violet Flame also induces Alchemy. Violet light emits the shortest wavelength and the highest frequency in the spectrum, so it induces a point of transition to the next octave of light.

Wahanee: The third United States Golden City located primarily in the states of South Carolina and Georgia. Its qualities are justice, liberty, and freedom; its Ray Force is violet; and its Master Teacher is Saint Germain.

White Ray: The Ray of the Divine Feminine is primarily associated with the planet Venus. It is affiliated with beauty, balance, purity, and cooperation. In the I AM America teachings the White Ray is served by the Archangel Gabriel and Archeia Hope; the Elohim Astrea and Claire; and the Ascended Masters Serapis Bey, Paul the Devoted, Reya, the Lady Masters Venus and Se Ray, and the Group of Twelve.

Will: Choice.

Write and Burn Technique: An esoteric technique venerated by Ascended Master students and chelas to transmute any unwanted situation or circumstance, primarily dysfunctional life patterns. This technique involves hand-writing and then burning a letter—a petition—to the I AM Presence for Healing and Divine Intervention.

Appendix A

Saint Germain, the Holy Brother:
The Lord of the Seventh Ray and the Master of the Violet Flame, Saint Germain lived numerous noteworthy lifetimes, dating back thousands of years, before incarnating as the Comte de Saint Germain during Renaissance Europe. He lived as the Englishman Sir Francis Bacon, the sixteenth-century philosopher, essayist, and Utopian who greatly influenced the philosophy of inductive science. His most profound and well-known work on the restoration of humanity, the *Instauratio Magna* (Great Restoration), defined him as an icon of the Elizabethan era. Research also shows his co-authoring of many Shakespearean sonnets.

According to Esoteric historians, Queen Elizabeth I of England—The Virgin Queen—was his biological mother. Before Bacon's birth, the queen married Earl of Leicester, quieting ideas of illegitimacy. Elizabeth's lady in waiting, Lady Ann Bacon, wife of the Lord High Chancellor of England, adopted him following the stillbirth of her baby. Bacon was, therefore, the true heir to the crown and England's rightful king.[1] But his cousin James I of Scotland succeeded the throne. Sir Bacon described this turn of events in his book, Novum Organo, published in 1620: "It is an immense ocean that surrounds the island of Truth." And Saint Germain often reminds us to this day "there are no mistakes, ever, ever, ever."

Bacon's philosophies also helped define the principles of Free Masonry and democracy. As an adept leader of the Rosicrucians (a secret society of that time), he set out to reveal the obsolescence and oppression of European monarchies.

Eventually, Bacon's destiny morphed. He shed his physical form and sought the greatest gift of all: immortality. And that's what placed him in the most extraordinary circumstances throughout history. Even his death (or lack of) evokes controversy. Some say Bacon faked his demise in 1626—the coffin contained the carcass of a dog.

According to the author, ADK Luk, Saint Germain ascended on May 1, 1684 in Transylvania at the Rakoczy mansion. He was 123 years old. Some say Saint Germain spent the lost years—from 1626 to 1684—in Tibet. During this time he took (or may have been given) the name *Kajaeshra*. Interpreted as *God's helper of life* and *wisdom*, it was possibly a secret name and rarely used. Kaja has several interpretations: in Greek it means *pure*; Balinese, *toward the mountain*; early Latin (Estonian), *echo*; Hopi, *wise child*; Polish, *of the Gods*; and Hebrew, *life*. The second part of the name—Eshra (Ezra)—translates into *help* or *aid*.

Indeed, Bacon's work would impact centuries to follow. During his time in Tibet, tucked away in silent monasteries, Germain designed a society that eventually created a United Brotherhood of the Earth: Solomon's Temple of the Future. It's a metaphor used to describe the raising of consciousness as the greater work of democracy. Author Marie Bauer Hall studied the life of Francis Bacon. In her book, *Foundations Unearthed*, she described the legendary edifice: "This great temple was to be supported by the four mighty pillars of history, science, philosophy, and religion, which were to bear the lofty dome of Universal Fellowship and Peace."[2]

But Germain embraced an even deeper passion: the people and nation of America, christening it *New Atlantis*. He envisioned this land—present-day United States, Canada, Mexico, and South America—as part of the United Democracies of Europe and the People of the World. America, this growing society, held his hope for a future guided by a Democratic Brotherhood.

The Comte de Saint Germain emerged years later in the courts of pre-revolutionary France—his appearance, intelligence, and worldliness baffled members of the Court of Versailles. This gentleman carried the essence of eternal youth: he was a skilled artist and musician; he spoke fluent German, English, French, Italian, Portuguese, Spanish, Greek, Latin, Sanskrit, Arabic, and Chinese; and he was a proficient chemist. Meanwhile, literary, philosophic, and political aristocracy of the time sought his company. French philosophers Jean-Jacque Rousseau and Voltaire; the Italian adventurer Giacomo Casanova; and the Earl of Chatham and statesman Sir Robert Walpole of Britain were among his friends.

In courts throughout Europe, he dazzled royalty with his Mastery of Alchemy, removing flaws from gems and turning lead into Gold. And the extent of Germain's ken reached well into the theosophical realm. A guru of yogic and tantric disciplines, he possessed highly developed telepathic and psychic abilities. This preternatural knowledge led to the development of a cartographic Prophecy—the Map of Changes. This uncanny blueprint, now in the hands of the scion of Russian aristocracy, detailed an imminent restructuring of the political and social boundaries of Europe.[3]

But few grasped Germain's true purpose during this time of historic critical mass: not even the king and queen of France could comprehend his tragic forewarnings. The Great White Brotherhood—a fellowship of enlightened luminaries—sent the astute diplomat Saint Germain to orchestrate the development of the United States of Europe. Not only a harbinger of European diplomacy, he made his presence in America during the germinal days of this country. Esoteric scholars say he urged the signing of the Declaration of Independence in a moment of collective fear—a fear of treason and ultimately death. Urging the forefathers to proceed, a shadowed figure in the back of the room shouted: *Sign that document!*

To this day, the ironclad identity of this person remains a mystery, though some mystics believe it was Saint Germain. Nevertheless, his avid support spurred the flurry of signatures, sealing the fate of America—and the beginning of Sir Francis Bacon's democratic experiment.

The Comte de Saint Germain never could shape a congealed Europe, but he did form a lasting and profound relationship with America. Germain's present-day participation in U.S. politics reaches the Oval Office. Some theosophical mystics say Germain visits the president of the United States the day after the leader's inauguration; others suggest he's the fabled patriot Uncle Sam.

Saint Germain identifies with the qualities of Brotherhood and freedom. He is the sponsor of humanity and serves as a conduit of Violet Light—a force some claim is powerful enough to propel one into Ascension.

[1] Marie Bauer Hall, *Foundations Unearthed,* originally issued as *Francis Bacon's Great Virginia Vault,* Fourth Edition (Los Angeles: Veritas Press), page 9.

[2] Ibid., page 13.

[3] K. Paul Johnson, *The Masters Revealed: Madame Blavatsky and the Myth of the Great White Lodge (Suny Series in Western Esoteric Traditions)* (Albany, NY: State University of New York Press), page 19.

Appendix B

Lord Sananda:
During his paradigm-altering incarnation more than 2,000 years ago, Lord Sananda, also known as Sananda Kumara, embodied the Christ Consciousness, as Jesus, son of God. Some esoteric scholars say he's one of the four sons of Brahma—Sanaka, Sanatana, Sanat-Kumara, and Sanandana—his namesake. According to Vedic lore, the foursome possess eternally liberated souls and live in Tapaloka, the dimension of the great sages. Before manifesting in physical form, Jesus belonged to the Angelic Kingdom. His name was Micah—the Great Angel of Unity. Micah is the son of Archangel Michael who led the Israelites out of Egypt.[1] [For more information on the life story of Jesus' life, I recommend reading, "Twelve World Teachers," by Manly P. Hall.]

Sananda Kumara revealed his identity to the mystic Sister Thedra. Her Master first contacted her in the early 1960s and instructed her to move to Peru, specifically, to a hidden monastery in the Andes mountains. There, undergoing an intense spiritual training, she kept in constant contact with Sananda, and he shared with her prophecies of the coming Earth Changes. After leaving the abbey, Sister Thedra moved to Mt. Shasta, California where she founded the Association of Sananda and Sanat Kumara. She died in 1992. Sananda posed for a photograph on June 1, 1961 in Chichen Itza, Yucatan. He told Sister Thedra that though the image is valid, he is not limited by form of any kind; therefore, he may take on any appearance necessary. [See *Freedom Star, Prophecies that Heal Earth*].

---

[1] Papastavro, Tellis S., *The Gnosis and the Law* (Tucson, AZ: Group Avatar), page 358.

Appendix C

Inner Garden Meditation Technique:
This meditation technique is perhaps one of the best methods to learn meditation, especially if you are a beginner. First, select a comfortable location to sit, on the floor in a classic legs folded-in posture, or in an easy chair. Pick a time of day that you know is quiet, early morning or after lunch is often a good time. If you are away from home, you can sit quietly at your desk or in your car. Make sure you have at least fifteen minutes of uninterrupted time.

Close your eyes and focus on your breath. When you have reached a level of relaxation, begin this visualization process. First, see yourself sitting on a beautiful park bench. It may be built of rustic logs or beautiful marble – there is no limitation, remember, this is *your* garden. The temperature is perfect, you may hear birds sing, or a waterfall gently fall in the background. The air is filled with the perfume of flowers: lilac, rose, honeysuckle, or any other flower or wildflower you desire. There may be evergreens with the scents of pine, fir, or cedar; or flowering fruit trees with aromatic orange, apple, pear, or exotic tropical fruits. Again, this garden is comprised of your mental constructs and is filled with the visuals, sounds, and scents of your preference.

Once you have filled your garden with beauty and peace, sit and enjoy the tranquil setting. Feel the calm rhythm of your breath as you immerse yourself in the still perfection of your creation – the Inner Garden. Sit for as long as you wish in your Inner Garden, observing and experiencing the peaceful surroundings. Over time your garden may morph or change according to your creative desires, and it is like any other spiritual practice, the more you repeat this exercise, the more readily your garden appears for rest and serenity. Occasionally a spirit guide or Master Teacher may join you. Sometimes they share insight and spiritual knowledge, but more often they sit quietly beside you. In these instances they often emit healing energy that restores, soothes, and uplifts.

The ancient etymology of the word "garden" connects to an Old French term that literally means "guardian." May your Inner Garden offer you protection and quiet refuge during the often stressful and harried *Time of Change*.

Appendix D

El Morya:

El Morya incarnated from a long line of historical notables, including the fabled King Arthur of England; the Renaissance scholar Sir Thomas Moore, author of Utopia; the patron saint of Ireland, Saint Patrick; and a Rajput prince. El Morya is even linked to the Hebrew patriarch Abraham. But in spite of his illustrious lifetimes, El Morya is best known as Melchior, one of the Magi who followed the Star of Bethlehem to the Christ infant.

El Morya first revealed himself to the founder of the Theosophical Society Helena Petrovna Blavatasky—also known as Madame Blavatsky or H. P. B.—during her childhood in London; that mid-nineteenth century meeting forged a lifelong connection with her Master and other members of the Spiritual Hierarchy. Some esoteric scholars recount different, more dramatic scenarios of their initial introduction. Blavatsky herself claimed El Morya rescued her from a suicide attempt on Waterloo Bridge.[1] The gracious Master dissuaded her from plunging into the waters of the Thames River. Others say the two met in Hyde Park or on a London street. According to Blavatsky, El Morya appeared under a secret political cover as the Sikh prince Maharaja Ranbir Singh of Kashmir, who served as a physically incarnated prototype of Master M. Singh and died in 1885.

Metaphysical scholars credit Blavatsky's work as the impetus for present-day theosophical philosophy and the conception of the Great White Brotherhood. Devoted disciples learned of the Hindu teacher from Blavatsky's childhood visions, and later on in a series of correspondences known as the *Mahatma Letters*, which contained spiritual guidelines for humanity. El Morya's presence in H. P. B.'s life enriched her spiritual knowledge, and she shared this transformation in a prolific body of texts and writings, namely *Isis Unveiled* and *The Secret Doctrine*.

Master M. is associated with the Blue Ray of power, faith, and good will; the Golden City of Gobean; and the planet Mercury. A strict disciplinarian, El Morya dedicates his work to the development of the will. He assists many disciples in discovering personal truths, exploring self-development, and honing the practice of the esoteric discipline. El Morya passes this wisdom to his numerous chelas and students. The Maha Chohan—El Morya's guru, Lord of the Seven Rays and the Steward of Earth and its evolutions—educated him during his Earthly incarnations in India, Egypt, and Tibet. Declining the Ascension a number of times, it is said that El Morya finally accepted this divine passage in 1888, ascending with his beloved pet dog and horse. (Esoteric symbols of friendship and healing.)

[1] Johnson, K. Paul, *The Masters Revealed: Madame Blavatsky and the Myth of the Great White Lodge (Suny Series in Western Esoteric Traditions)* (Albany, NY: State University of New York Press), page 41.

Appendix E

The Violet Flame:
Simply stated, the Violet Flame stabilizes past karmas through Transmutation, Forgiveness, and Mercy. This leads to the opening of the spiritual heart and the development of bhakti—the unconditional love and compassion for others. Our Co-creative ability is activated through the Ascended Master's gift of the Unfed Flame in adjunct with the practice of the Law of Love, and the Power of Intention. But the Violet Flame, capable of engendering our greatest spiritual growth and evolution, is spiritual velocity pure and simple.

Invoking the flame's force often produces feelings of peace, tranquility, and inner harmony—its ability to lift the low-vibrating energy fields of blame, despair, and fear into forgiveness and understanding, paves the path to love.

The history of the Violet Flame reaches back thousands of years before the Time of Christ. According to Ascended Master legend, the Lords of Venus transmitted the Violet Flame as a spiritual consciousness during the final days of the pre-Atlantis civilization Lemuria. As one society perished and another bloomed, the power of the Violet Flame shifted, opening the way for Atlantean religiosity. This transfer of power initiated a clearing of the Earth's etheric and psychic realms, and purged the lower physical atmosphere of negative forces and energies. Recorded narratives of Atlantis claim that Seven Temples of Purification sat atop visible materializations of the Violet Flame. The archangels Zadkiel and Amethyst, representing freedom, forgiveness and joy, presided over an Atlantean Brotherhood known as the Order of Zadkiel, also associated with Saint Germain. These Violet Flame Temples still exist today in the celestial realm over Cuba.

The Violet Flame benefits humans and divinities equally. During spiritual visualizations, meditations, prayers, decrees, and mantras, many disciples seek the Violet Flame for serenity and wisdom. Meanwhile, the Ascended Masters always use it in inner retreats—

even Saint Germain taps into its power to perfect and apply its force with chelas and students

The Violet Flame, rooted in Alchemic powers, is sometimes identified as a higher energy of Saturn and the Blue Ray, a force leavened with justice, love, and wisdom. Ascended-Master lore explains the Violet Flame's ability to release a person from temporal concerns: Saturn's detachment from emotions and low-lying energies sever worldly connections. That's why the scientific properties of violet light are so important in metaphysical terms. The shortness of its wavelength and the high vibration of its frequency induce a point of transition to the next octave of light and into a keener consciousness.

Appendix F

Prayers from the Ascended Masters and Beings of Light:
The following collection of prayers have been given as part of the I AM America Spiritual Teachings.

The Awakening Prayer

This is the back story of the *Awakening Prayer*, excerpted from "Sisters of the Flame," by Lori Toye: "It was mid-summer in 1990 and I was biking on the trail along the river about two miles from Asotin, pedaling as fast as I could to outrun an ominous thunderstorm rolling in from the South. Lightning flashed and reflected on the water. Thunder resounded and then the conscious voice of Master Kuthumi spoke to me: 'Great Light of Divine Wisdom, stream forth to my being and through your right use let me serve mankind and the planet.' Requesting that he please hold that thought, I rushed home with the wind pelting me with large raindrops, and as soon as I got inside, penned several more verses, then went to bed only to be awakened late that night by Saint Germain—with what are now the final words of the *Awakening Prayer*. This prayer, a request and affirmation for worldwide Spiritual Awakening, has been offered in our conferences, our spiritual gatherings, and before channelings. It is printed on the Freedom Star World Map and is published in many of our books."

> Great Light of Divine Wisdom,
> Stream forth to my being,
> And through your right use
> Let me serve mankind and the planet.
> Love, from the Heart of God.
> Radiate my being with the presence of the Christ
> That I walk the path of truth.
> Great Source of Creation.

Empower my being,
My Brother,
My Sister,
And my planet with perfection
As we collectively awaken as one cell.
I call forth the Cellular Awakening.
Let wisdom, love, and power stream forth to this cell,
This cell that we all share.
Great Spark of Creation awaken the Divine Plan of Perfection.
So we may share the ONE perfected cell,
I AM.

Great White Lodge Prayer:
This prayer, from Master Kuthumi, is offered for the worldwide healing of Earth and humanity:

To the planes of form I send my prayer and intention
through the Light of All.
Let Light descend on Earth and
may humanity COOPERATE willingly through it.
Let Light DEVOTE those who are readied
to serve the greater plan.
Let Light INSPIRE our collective mind and
serve the Cause Divine.
Let Light ascend on Earth and EXPAND
the heart of love of all creation,
great and small, united in one service.
OM MANAYA PITAYA, HITAKA!
(I AM the Light of God, So Be It!)

The Middle Way Prayer:
This prayer, offered by Lady Nada and Serapis Bey, asks for the healing and balance of Earth and humanity.

> We call forth the healing balance of humanity,
> For only in the path of simplicity
> may the heart return to love.
> May love return to Earth through the Middle Way.
> OM MANAYA PATIYA HITAKA!

Babajeran's Prayer:
This prayer, from Babajeran the Earth Mother, focuses on thought, feeling, and action for personal balance and purification:

> Thought brings balance.
> All thought serves the next thought.
> All is as ONE.
> That is the thought, balance, harmony, and blending.

> The feeling is purification.
> Do not be afraid to allow your own change to erupt
> or to move.
> Perhaps that change is necessary.
> It is the feeling.

> Purify your being.
> Place yourself in the heart of intent.
> Action, let it come from the blend of these two.
> Action in service, as has been stated, breathes the breath that
> all may utilize.

Web of Creation Prayer:
Saint Germain offers this prayer to recognize and bless the creative forces of Mother Earth:

> I have returned.
> I AM peace.
> I have come this day in love and goodwill to mankind.
>
> I have returned.
> I AM the light.
> I have come this day to bond to you.
>
> I have returned.
> I AM Creation, the inner spark from which you came.
>
> I have returned.
> I AM.

The Prayer of a Thousand Suns:
Master Kuthumi suggests a simple prayer for harmony and to adjust humanity's vibratory rate and frequencies to the Gold Ray:

> Bring Harmony forth to my Brothers and Sisters,
> Let us be united as ONE,
> for we truly are.

Ascension Prayer:
Saint Germain shares this prayer to remove separation and initiate the Ascension Process:

> May the Violet Flame blaze in, through,
> and around all those who seek the Path of Ascension.
> May the Violet Flame move all into the
> Crystal Consciousness of greater understanding.
> So Be It!

Flower of Life Prayer:
Mother Mary gives this prayer for acceptance of the Oneness of Life:

> Come gently into your garden when you are troubled,
> And I am there for you.
>
> Come gently into the garden of your heart,
> And you will find you are never without this
> great Flower of Life.
>
> You are always ONE.

Golden Service Prayer:
The Earth Mother Babjeran offers this prayer for those who wish to offer their service to the Golden Age:

> Beloved being of light that I AM,
> Stream forth these Golden Rays into my being.
> I AM resonating with all my focus, all that I AM,
> Into the Golden Light that streams from Divine Creation.
> Together we dance in the joy of being ONE.

A Prayer for the New Children:
Mother Mary instructs to use this prayer at 6:00 am for, "14 to 21 days, depending on the movement of Equinox of 28 to 35 days, in the days of lesser light, do this for 21 days. In the days of heavier light, 14 is sufficient."

> Beloved being of the Christ,
> Stream forth your radiance to the Swaddling Cloth.
> Let the Diamond Heart now shine throughout the Christos
> And serve as a beacon of freedom to those who activate Unana.

The Gentle Revolution Prayer:

Master Kuthumi's prayer to assist the new cycle and usher in the New Times:

Let us join in wisdom to extinguish ignorance and inequity.
Let us join in love to extinguish suffering.
Let us join in service to extinguish greed and avarice.
Let us join in charity to extinguish poverty.
Let us join in harmony to extinguish disease.
As our ears are opened and our eyes begin to see,
Let us join as ONE LIGHT, in our hearts and minds.
May this light of wisdom serve all.
May this light of truth and justice prevail.
May the law be written in hearts and joined through harmony, Brotherhood, and love.

Appendix G

Decrees:
Similar to prayers and mantras, these statements of intent and power are often integrated with the use of the I AM and requests to the I AM Presence. And when it comes to activating these spiritual channels, the possibilities are endless. Some express decrees silently through prayer and meditation, while others opt for forceful pronouncements of intent. Rhythmic chanting and singing, therapeutic journaling, and write-and-burn techniques provide just a few conduits of worship.

Decrees form the foundation of Ascended Master teachings; these simple affirmations create a conscious contact with the I AM Presence, shifting consciousness, expanding awareness, and activating the Co-creation process.

A classic Ascended Master decree for the Violet Flame is as follows:

"Violet Flame I AM, God I AM Violet Flame!"

Decrees, are yet another form of verbal prayer; however, decrees differ because of the added element of visualization, the spoken word, and the spiritual stillness of meditation. Some claim that decrees are one of the most powerful forms of prayer because they unite four chakras: prayer (Heart Chakra); spoken word (throat chakra); visualization (third eye chakra); meditation (crown chakra).[1] Violet Flame decrees are used worldwide by thousands of Ascended Master students. They can be spoken individually or used in groups to generate the benefic qualities of the Violet Ray: mercy, compassion, and forgiveness. One of my favorites is the simple Violet Fire decree by Mark Prophet,

"I AM a being of Violet Fire! I AM the purity God desires!"

Decrees or mantras are often said rhythmically, in groups of seven, or in rounds of 108—the traditional Mala. [Editor's Note: A Mala is a prayer or rosary bead typically used in Hinduism and Buddhism, and a full Mala contains 108 beads with one final large bead often referred to as the guru bead.] Decrees and mantras are also repeated silently in the mind, similar to prayer, in preparation for meditation. El Morya lends further insight: "It is when this (decree) is consciously applied by the chela, through the work of the Violet Flame, or other mantra work they may engage . . . light is then bonded to sound. Ultimately, this is the intertwining of consciousness with action." Simply stated, sound activates light, and light and sound together command the Ray into a force of conscious activity.

[1] Craig Donaldson, *How to Get Great Results When You Pray*, http://www.ascension-research.org/prayer.html, (2010)

Appendix H

The Gold Ray

The Ascended Masters Kuthumi and Saint Germain both prophesy that the Gold Ray is the most important energy force currently present on Earth. While its presence catalyzes the spiritual growth of the HU-man, it is also associated with Karmic Justice and will instigate change at all levels: Earth Changes, economic and social change.

The Master Teachers prophesy that its appearance fosters the dawn of a New Consciousness for humanity, which ends the turbulence of Kali Yuga and ushers in a 10,000-year time of spiritual potential and opportunity for all—the Golden Age of Kali Yuga.

Saint Germain gives this decree to initiate the stream of the New Consciousness within:

> Mighty Golden Ray, stream forth now,
> into the heart of the consciousness of humanity.
> Mighty Golden Ray, bring forth new
> understanding.
> Bring forth a new Spiritual Awakening.
> Bring forth complete and total divinity
> In the name of I AM THAT I AM.
> So be it.

This decree allows the Brotherhood to give further aid and contact to individuals who desire the Masters' help and assistance for spiritual development.

The Gold Ray initiates and transforms through the spiritual principles of balance and harmony. Working through the Hermetic Principle of vibration, Saint Germain claims that the Gold Ray creates, "Absolute Harmony." This sublime Ray of Consciousness also helps the chela to shape and form the will and align our emotions and inevitably our actions to the Divine Will. It enters into the Seventh Chakra and its current flows alongside the Golden Thread Axis (Medullar Shushumna). The ideal of Unana—the ONE—is initiated and inevitably created through the presence of the Gold Ray. Saint Germain suggests this decree for the Violet Flame to prepare spiritual consciousness to receive and apply the influence of the Gold Ray.

> Mighty Violet Ray,
> Come forth in all transmuting action.
> Mighty Violet Ray,
> Come forth now and dissolve all discord
> and the cause and effect of all that is holding me
> from understanding and moving forward into the
> new Golden Age.
> I call this forth in the name of
> That mighty Christ I AM.
> So be it.

The Gold Ray assists humanity's evolution at this important time. This process is calibrated by the premise of vibration and is a developmental step associated with the use of the Violet Flame. Those who apply this teaching may notice a golden tinge in their light bodies, hear a high-pitch sound, or celestial music (the Harmony of the Spheres) before falling asleep or upon awakening. As the Gold Ray floods the Earth with energies to evolve human consciousness this energy is controlled by both the Galactic Center and further calibrated by the Spiritual Hierarchy for humanity.

Appendix I

Sunday Peace Meditation
In this turbulent Time of Change, Lord Sananda suggests a weekly Sunday Peace Meditation. He instructs:

> "It is important at this time for those who seek the Christ within to find it through inner meditation. First, it is important to silence the mind. This may be done with several decrees, one that the individual may choose. But bring within, an inner silence. Sit in contemplation. Gently close the eyes. Focus all energy upon the heart. In that moment of the focus of energy upon the heart, feel within the connection to all of life. Feel, as this heart is connected to all of life, the radiating pulse that is in all living creatures, that is in all living consciousness. This consciousness that permeates all living things is the consciousness of the ONE, Unana. Meditate upon this pulse. Work to hear this pulse within the inner ear. In this inner hearing comes a radiation. This radiation is the growth of a new energy body. This energy source is carried with you throughout the day. Bless all that you come in contact with throughout the day. Carry the radiance of this loving Christ throughout your day. This I encourage all to do."

Unana, or Unity Consciousness, is another name for the unified field of human consciousness. Major General Kulwant Singh of India explains, "This field of consciousness–termed the unified field in the language of quantum physics–is millions of times more fundamental and powerful than nuclear force." Major Singh, a 35-year career army veteran who helped to assemble thousands of meditation experts for peaceful defense explains, "This will produce an indomitable influence of peace and coherence in the country. No nation will ever be moved to attack

India, as it becomes a lighthouse of peace and coherence to its neighbors and the world."

The Stars of Golden City Vortices function with a unique similarity to a technique developed by the late Dr. David Hawkins whose research mapped states of human consciousness known as critical point analysis. In his book "Power Versus Force," Hawkins explains his process, "Critical point analysis is a technique derived from the fact that in any highly complex system there is a specific critical point at which the smallest input will result in the greatest change. The great gears of a windmill can be halted by lightly touching the right escape mechanism; it is possible to paralyze a giant locomotive if you know exactly where to put your finger."

All spiritual practice, especially prayer and meditation is extremely effective while located in any Star area of a Golden City Vortex for World Peace. The Ascended Masters' instruction focuses on Lord Sananda's Heart Meditation and recommends that a group of seven individuals focused on this meditation can effect personal change for global peace. In essence, this technique is a force field of light, especially when applied within the Star of a Golden City Vortex, where the least amount of energy exerts the greatest effect.

A partial list of towns and cities located in the United States Golden City Stars follows. [Editor's Note: For more information see *I AM America Atlas* and *I AM America United States Golden City Map*.]

Golden City Star of Gobean
Pinetop, AZ
Lakeside, AZ
Springerville, AZ
Eagar, AZ

Golden City Star of Malton
Mattoon, IL
Charleston, IL
Shelbyville, IL
Sullivan, IL
Humboldt, IL

Golden City Star of Wahanee
Augusta, GA
Grovetown, GA
Appling, GA
Harlem, GA
Gracewood, GA
Thompson, GA
Modeo, GA
North Augusta, SC
Trenton, SC
Eureka, SC
Parksville, SC
Kitchings Mill, SC
Williston, SC

Golden City Star of Shalahah
Lolo Pass, MT
Lolo, MT
Missoula, MT
Stevensville, MT

Golden City Star of Klehma
Cope, CO

Appendix J

Write and Burn Technique

The Write and Burn Technique helps students and chelas transmute any and all unwanted situations and circumstances, primarily undesirable dysfunctional life patterns. A venerated practice of the Ascended Masters, this type of journaling involves a handwritten letter—a petition—to the I AM Presence for Healing and Divine Intervention. The process encompasses two objectives: identifying and releasing unwanted and outdated energy or attracting and manifesting new and evolving energies. After the letter is written, it is then burned, either by fire or by light. Most students prefer to burn by fire. If, however, you choose to burn by light, place the document under a light source for twenty-four continuous hours. Insidious problems and complex-manifestation petitions may require up to one week of light exposure. The success of the light method and the subsequent acceptance of a petition depend on the reliability of the light source; the concentration of light must be continuous and without problems, e.g. blackouts, burnouts, and so on. If the issues are profound, you may need to probe deeper by identifying and addressing personal problem or life patterns. You may also want to consider rephrasing your approach to the problem, rewriting the letter, or both. Write and burn templates are provided below.

Transmute and Release Energy Patterns: Make one handwritten copy of this letter. In the name of I AM THAT I AM, I release this to the Universe to be transmuted. (List the energy or behavior patterns you have identified. Some students also insert various alchemic decrees to the Violet Flame to dissolve, consume, and transform the energy.) Sign and date the letter. Burn the letter by fire or by light.

Attract and Manifest New Energy Patterns: Make two handwritten copies of this letter. In the name of I AM THAT I AM, I release this to the Universe to be fulfilled, maintained, and sustained in perfect alignment to the Divine Will. (List the new energy or behavior pattern you would like to Co-create.) Sign and date the letter. Burn one copy by fire or by light. Keep the other copy in a sacred place (e.g. personal altar, family Bible, favorite spiritual book) until you have achieved your goal or desired behavior change, and then burn that copy by fire.

Appendix K

Step-down Transformer:
The processes instigated through the Cellular Awakening rapidly advance human light bodies. Synchronized with an Ascended Master's will, the awakened cells of light and love evolve the skills of a Step-down Transformer to efficiently transmit and distribute currents of Ascended Master energy—referred to as an Ascended Master Current (A.M. Current). This metaphysical form of intentional inductive coupling creates an ethereal power grid that can be used for all types of healing.

A.M. Currents release beneficially charged and sometimes spine-tingling rushes of energy throughout the human system. This energy current is often accompanied by an audible high-pitched ring and a visible translucent glow of white or Gold light. Step-down Transformers report sensations of time slowing down and a body-warming flush as hands, feet, and chakras conduct the high frequency energy.

According to the Master Teachers tuning your body and your consciousness as a Step-down Transformer resembles a high quality quartz crystal, emitting effulgent Rays of Light and energy from many directions.

Surprisingly, an A.M. Current is calming and soothing. Since the Vibration of fear is effectively extinguished in its wake, the curative and peaceful frequency influences all who come within contact. Transfers of Step-down energies create a remnant force field that is later detectable, and the frequency can change significantly in strength or weakness dependant on the purpose for the release of the A.M. Current.

Master Teachers often train students to purposely hold and direct Step-down energies of healing love and light on behalf of Earth and humanity. Primarily, Step-down Transformers work solely in private to perfect their craft and skill. When accomplished Step-down Transformers gather in groups the spiritual voltage significantly intensifies. These larger batteries of energy are often circuited into the Collective Consciousness to bring about positive political change, societal healing, and restorative balance to Mother Earth.

Appendix L

Mother Mary, the Western Goddess and Archetype of the Feminine

The Ascended Master and Western Goddess of the Feminine Archetype was an initiate of the ethereal Temples of Nature before her incarnation as Mary, Mother of Jesus Christ. It is claimed that as a child Mary was raised in the mystical traditions of the Essenes, and throughout her lifetime as Mother Mary, she was constantly overshadowed by the Angelic Kingdom. Some Ascended Master texts claim Mary was once a member of the heavenly realm.

Mary's lifetime as the mother of Jesus Christ was planned in-between lifetimes on Earth, "Her embodiment as Mother of Jesus was in the Divine Plan long before she entered the physical realm. She went through a severe initiation at inner levels to test her strength some time before taking embodiment." [1] Throughout her life as the Master's mother, Mary was attuned to the spiritual planes which gave her strength and insight to fulfill her role as the Mother of Jesus. And, no doubt, Mary or Maryam, as she is known in Aramaic, lived in perilous times. The Biblical story in the Book of Matthew accounts the Holy Family's flight to Egypt to avoid King Herod's Massacre of the Innocents. It is claimed that Mother Mary made a vow to assist anyone who had lost their life as a Christian martyr to obtain the Ascension in a future life.[2] Mary the Mother of Jesus became an archetype of the Cosmic Mother for all of humanity.

As an archetype of the Feminine, Mary is also a form of Isis, the Virgin of the World of Hermetic Teaching. The name Isis draws its meaning from Hebrew and Greek sources, which means wisdom or to serve.[3] However, the myth of the Virgin Goddess is contained in the ancient language of Scandinavia as Isa; and is similarly portrayed as the Eleusian Goddess Ceres and Queen Moo of the Mayans. Manly Hall writes, "She was known as the Goddess with ten-thousand appellations and was meta-morphosed by Christianity into the Virgin Mary, for Isis, although she gave birth to all living things—chief among them the Sun—still remained a virgin, according to legendary accounts." As the eldest daughter of Kronus the Ancient Titan, and the wife and sister to Osiris, Isis was the student of the great Master Hermes Trismegistus. Through this affiliation it is claimed the laws for humanity were developed, including an alphabet for written language, astronomy, and the science of seamanship. Isis helped humanity to overcome paternal tyranny through instructing men to love women and children to love and respect their elders through the philosophic teachings of beauty as truth, and the intrinsic value of justice. The teachings of Isis are not for the irreverent. The discipline of emotion and the acquisition of wisdom are required in order to access and understand the evolutionary energies of the Feminine. Ancient initiates were advised to keep silent their venerated knowledge of the spiritual truths underlying the vulgar and profane.[4]

In Christianity Mary is known as the Virgin Mother of Jesus; however, Catholics and Protestants differ regarding their worship of the Mother of the Son of God. In Islam, the Virgin Mary is esteemed as the mother to the Prophet Issa.[5] Jesus' birth was prophesied by the Archangel Gabriel in a visit to Mary during her betrothal to Joseph, and the Archangel declared, "She was to be the mother of the promised Messiah by conceiving him through the Holy Spirit."[6] The New Testament places Mary at Nazareth in Galilee, the daughter of Joachim and Anne. Apocryphal legend claims Mary's birth was also a miracle—her mother was barren. To many Roman Catholics, Mary was the perfect vessel to carry the Christ, and was "filled with grace from the very moment of her conception in her mother's womb and the stain of original sin."[7] This spiritual precept is known as the Immaculate Conception of Mary.

Contemporary interpretations of the Immaculate Concept state this spiritual practice is the Alchemy of holding the image of perfection through the use of prayer, meditation, and visualization. Thought-forms of "Beauty, poise, and grace on behalf of others," is claimed to create Divine Energies of purity and protection.[8] David C. Lewis writes regarding the spiritual exercise of holding the Immaculate Concept for ourselves:

> "Ultimately we must first hold the immaculate concept for ourselves by attuning to our own Higher Self and maintaining a vigil of Oneness through presence and awareness of our own Divine Nature. Once we have learned to live in this unified field of stillness and beingness and maintain our spiritual poise, especially during challenging times and situations, we can more easily practice the science of the immaculate concept on behalf of others."[9]

According to the Ascended Masters Mother Mary holds the Immaculate Concept for the incoming generations of the Seventh Manu through the energies of the Swaddling Cloth, located in Brazil, South America. In the I AM America teachings, Mother Mary often merges her energies with Kuan Yin, the Feminine Bodhisattva of Mercy and Compassion, and together they channel the energies of the Divine Mother to Earth. Divine Mother is an archetype of Feminine Unity and the ONE. Beloved Mary is known to appear at times of physical or emotional crisis, often to convey the healing power of wholeness and unconditional love. Mother Mary's Temple of the Sacred Heart, located in the Fifth Dimension, prepares souls for re-embodiment.[10] She is the Ascended Master sponsor of the Golden City of Marnero, located in Mexico. Marnero means the ocean of candles; its quality is Virtue; and this Golden City is affiliated with the Green Ray.[11]

[1] A. D. K. Luk, *Points Law of Life, Book II,* (ADK Luk Publications, 1989, Pueblo, CO), page 343.

[2] Ibid., page 344.

[3] Manly P. Hall, *The Secret Teachings of All Ages: An Encyclopedic Outline of Masonic, Hermetic, Qabbalistic and Rosicrucian Symbolical Philosophy,* (Philosophical Research Society, Inc., 1988, Los Angeles, CA), page 45.

[4] Ibid., page 44.

[5] *Wikipedia,* Mary (Mother of Jesus), http://en.wikipedia.org/wiki/Mary_(mother_of_jesus), (2009).

[6] Ibid.

[7] Ibid.

[8] David C. Lewis, "The Immaculate Concept: Creating Alchemical Change," http://www.theheartscenter.org, (2009).

[9] Ibid.

[10] A. D. K Luk, *Points Law of Life, Book II,* (ADK Luk Publications, 1989, Pueblo, CO), page 347.

[11] Lori Toye, *Freedom Star: Prophecies that Heal Earth,* (I AM America Seventh Ray Publishing, 1995, Payson, AZ), page 41.

Appendix M

Mantra
Certain sounds, syllables, and sets of words are deemed sacred and often carry the power to transmute Karma, purify the spirit, and transform an individual. These are known as a *mantras*. The mantra is a foundation of Vedic tradition and often treated as a devotional *upaye*—a remedial measure of difficult obstacles. Mantras, however, are not limited to Hinduism. Buddhists, Sikhs, and Jains also utilize mantras. The Ascended Masters occasionally provide mantras to chelas to improve resonation with certain Golden Cities.

My teacher of Vedic tradition gave this explanation regarding the anatomy of the mantra:

    MAM + TRA = MANTRA
    Chants + Protects = MANTRA

He was particularly avid about adding the sound HREEM before chanting the mantra to transmute difficult Karmas. His explanation:

    H = Sins
    REEM = Removes
    HREEM = Removal of Sins

Mantras for the Five Golden Cities of the United States
According to Saint Germain, individual mantras infuse Golden City Ray Forces into light bodies (auras), a practice that evolves the conscious life experience toward Ascension Consciousness. He suggests that the efficiency of a Ray is best understood when used in a Golden City Vortex, where the energy of a mantra works concurrently with the centrifugal force of the Golden City Star. Uttering mantras is most effective in the Star of a Golden City, but don't let that prevent you from the practice. If you can't make it to the Star, saying mantras in any part of a Golden City is beneficial. The following mantras should be used simultaneously with the initiatory Ray work in each Golden City.

Sacred Fire

GOBEAN	*Om Shanti*	Produces peace and harmony
MALTON	*Om Eandra*	Produces harmony and balance for the Nature Kingdoms. It is also associated with instant thought manifestation.
WAHANEE	*Om Hue*	Aligns the chakras with the Vertical Power Current, or Golden Thread Axis, and evokes the Sacred Fire—the Violet Flame. Since this mantra is a Vibration of Violet Flame Angels, it invokes their Healing presence, which helps purify and heal the body.
SHALAHAH	*Om Sheahah*	Evokes the consciousness of the ONE-SHIP—Unana. This mantra means, "I AM as ONE."
KLEHMA	*Om Eandra*	Used as a decree for Instant-Thought-Manifestation of Ascension, glory, and conclusion.

Discography

This list provides the recording session date and name of the original selected recordings cited in this work that provide the basis for its original transcriptions.

Toye, Lori

Courage to Heal, I AM America Seventh Ray Publishing International, Audiocassette and MP3, © June 3, 1993.

The Inner Garden, I AM America Seventh Ray Publishing International, Audiocassette and MP3, © July 2, 1993.

Perfect Plan of Purity, from *Freedom Message,* I AM America Seventh Ray Publishing International, Audiocassette, © July 2, 1993.

Earth Healing, I AM America Seventh Ray Publishing International, Audiocassette and MP3, © June 22, 1994.

Golden Ray Stream Forth, from *Flood of Consciousness,* I AM America Seventh Ray Publishing International, Audiocassette and MP3, © March 30, 2003.

Ascension of Consciousness, I AM America Seventh Ray Publishing International, Audiocassette and MP3, © September 1, 2000.

All is Love, I AM America Seventh Ray Publishing International, Audiocassette and MP3, © July 26, 2001.

The Master Within, I AM America Seventh Ray Publishing International, Audiocassette and MP3, © August 2, 2001.

The Mighty Violet Flame, I AM America Seventh Ray Publishing International, Audiocassette and MP3, © August 16, 2001.

The Heart of Peace, from *Lighting the Heart of Peace,* I AM America Seventh Ray Publishing International, Audiocassette, © September 16, 2001.

Unified Plane of Understanding, from *Lighting the Heart of Peace,* I AM America Seventh Ray Publishing International, Audiocassette. © September 20, 2001.

Science of Solutions, I AM America Seventh Ray Publishing International, Audiocassette and MP3, © October 18, 2001.

I AM Awareness, I AM America Seventh Ray Publishing International, Audiocassette and MP3, © December 12, 2001.

Eternal Balance, I AM America Seventh Ray Publishing International, Audiocassette and MP3, © December 13, 2001.

Index

A

Acceleration
 of energies 52
acceptance 45
active intelligence 113
Africa
 stabilized by Wahanee 184
Age of Cooperation 185
 definition 191
Age of Information 56
aggregate body of light 34
agreement 50
Akashic Records
 and the I AM 74
 definition 191
Alchemy
 and the number five 145
 definition 191
 through the Violet Flame 106
alignment
 definition 191
All-seeing Eye of God 24
 definition 191
A.M. Current 243
ancestors
 of the hidden planet 88
anger
 and vibration 167
anger and violence
 use of Sunday Peace Meditation 162
animal behavior
 in humans 73
animal consciousness
 and evolution of the emotional body 98
animalistic qualities
 and emotional response 129
Animal Kingdom 112
animals
 and the I AM Awareness 171
answers
 "All answers lie within." 158
Antarctica
 stabilized by Canadian Golden Cities 184
Archangel Crystiel 43
 Flower of Life prayer 46
Archangel Gabriel 246
Ascended Masters 149
 and the Golden Cities 185
 definition 192
 stand guard over their retreats 133
 their ancestral teachers 89
 will never tell you what to do 123
Ascension 32
 and Divine Love 72
 and help from the Ascended Masters 135
 and overcoming animalistic behavior 75
 and personal experience 70
 and review of karmic patterns 71
 and sponsorship through an Ascended Master 74
 as a "graduation of souls" 69
 definition 192
Ascension Prayer 230
Ascension Process
 definition 192
 prayer for Ascension 230
Asia
 stabilized by Shalahah 184

Sacred Fire 255

asteroid
  as a comet trail 92
  seven year warning 93
Astral Body
  definition 193
At-One-Ment
  definition 193
attention
  and consciousness 155
aura
  definition 193
Australia 184
  stabilized by Shalahah 184
avatar(s)
  the Paradigm of Twelve 160
  twelve always on Earth 160
awakening
  and consciousness 152
  and levels of consciousness 153
  divinity 159
  on the path 153
Awakening Prayer 227
awareness
  and consciousness of the I AM Presence 153
awareness of the environment 56

B

Babajeran 177
  and activation of the Golden Cities 185
  and Earth's Grid 129
  and the Earth Planet 112
  and the Golden Cities 185
  definition 193
  sponsoring new souls 130

Babajeran's Prayer 229
Bacon, Sir Francis 215
balance
  and non-judgment 167
  and the human condition 92
being
  ONE body of Being 42
belief(s)
  and religion 148
  definition 193
  power of 119
Blavatsky, H. P. 223
Blue Flame 121
  definition 194
Blue Ray
  definition 194
  for transformation of karmic patterns 70
brown dwarf star 116

C

calm
  calm the mind with meditation 129
camaraderie 154
  on the spiritual path 154
Cascade Mountains 50
Cause and effect
  definition 194
Cellular Awakening
  definition 195
ceremony
  and Golden City Stars 131
chakra(s)
  and breath 163
  and the Seventh Seal 145
  definition 195

change
  "A change of heart can change the world." 93
  and positive growth 83
Chela
  definition 195
chohan
  definition 195
choice 32, 33
  and change 82
  and development of the will 139
  and solution(s) 157
  and spiritual evolution 123
  and the Golden Ray 58
  and the I AM 168
  and the individual 149
  and the soul 62
  and thoughts 99
  "Choose, choose, and then choose again." 147
  the pefection of 41
Christ
  force as a Meissner Field 91
  overcomes duality 137
  the Christ Plane and higher consciousness 140
  the energy of 52
  trinity of ONE 156
Christ Consciousness 29, 81, 155
  beyond duality 86
  definition 195
  "Rest in the Christ." 124
Christ Plane
  and Alchemy 145
  and Unana 180
Clarity 178
  and the Eighth Ray 44

Co-creation 98, 173
  and vibration 167
  definition 195
  process 174
Collective Consciousness 60, 68
  quantum leap 51
  Step-down Transformer 244
comet trail
  of Nibiru 92
compassion 98, 179
  and the Law of Love 69
  definition 195
  Violet Flame Decree 107
conscience
  definition 195
conscious immortality
  decree 108
  definition 196
consciousness 52, 151
  and Ascension 76
  and duality 165
  and evolution 151
  and love 86
  and optimism 159
  and predictable consequences 167
  and prophecy 168
  and spiritual evolution 168
  and spiritual growth 168
  and spiritual practice 181
  and the Earth Plane 111
  and the Unified Plane 138
  and the Violet Flame 110
  and Unified Field Theory 114
  and vibration 165
  blocks 155
  definition 195
  higher vibration through group consciousness 130

moving into silicon-based consciousness 115
of choice 41
shift 34
the group consciousness of the I AM Awareness 170
universal 113
crisis 154
Cup
  definition 196
  Saint Germain's explanation 152
  the Cup of Neutrality 152
Cycle of the Yugas
  definition 196

D

darkness 178
  and the Violet Flame 125
"Death to the old way of doing things." 31
decree 233
  and chakras 233
  and two or more 141
  before entering sleep 118
  builds momentum on a daily basis 142
  Courage to Heal 31
  for Abundance 31
  for awareness of the I AM 169
  for drug use 118
  for problems 156
  for suffering 140
  for the Gold Ray 57
  for the I AM Awareness 172
  for the Violet Ray and assimilating the Golden Ray 61
  for the will 122
  for the World Leaders 126

groups of seven 141
"I AM eternal life." 108
"I AM the resurrection." 108
immortality 108
Spiritual Awakening 39
Star of Wahanee 182
to awaken the Master within 101
to empower the I AM THAT I AM 169
to heal the death urge 24
to out-picture perfection 98
to overcome duality 137
to raise vibration 166
Violet Flame for justice 107
Violet Flame for karmic burden 105
desire
  definition 196
  to know God 100
detachment 179
  and spiritual evolution 70
  move beyond duality 179
Deva Kingdom
  healing emotional energy 117
Deva(s)
  definition 196
dharma
  definition 196
diet
  and the schools of light 183
  Ascension and the emotional body 76
difference
  "Is experience." 173
  "The difference is experience." 178
dimensions
  and the Earth Plane 111
disease
  and healing 159

disharmony
   decree for 31
Divine Authority
   of the I AM Presence 23
Divine Complement
   definition 197
Divine Conception 52
Divine Heritage 101
Divine Intervention
   and the Violet Flame 109
   of the Golden Cities 186
Divine Love 77
   beyond illusion 72
Divine Mother 247
   and Earth 130
   definition 197
Divine Plan 121
   humanity and the Hidden Planet 106
Divine Will 124, 173
  60
   and change 83
   and Mastery of natural law 25
   and the chela's experience 26
   and the I AM Awareness 173
   and the mental body 73
   overcoming duality 167
divinity 173
   and the God Presence 153
   and the I AM Awareness 172
   and the Master within 153
doorways
  Golden City and energy disbursement 144
doubt 167
doubt and spiritual challenge 23
Dove of Peace 38

dream state
   working in 117
drugs
   "Experience without judgment." 119
dualistic consciousness
   and judging 165
duality 123
   and choice 136
   and consciousness 156
   and detachment 179
   and judging 165
   and perspective 154
   and problem-solution 156
   and separation 103
   and the I AM Awareness 171
   and the surrender of the will to the Divine Will 167
   the mirror of duality 136
Dvapara Yuga
   and the discovery of the hidden planet 90
   definition 197
   development of the mind 115
Dvapara-Yuga 196

E

Eabra 184
   holds the world in balance 184
Earth
   and the kingdoms of creation 112
   as a schoolroom 68
   as our Divine Mother 130
   astral body 117
   calmed through Sunday Peace Meditation 162
   "Is a blessing." 179

"Is set upon a path of construction and growth." 93
schoolroom 146
Earth Changes 130
and the comet trail of Nibiru 92
and the Law of Correspondence 177
and the Stars of Golden Cities 142
Earth Healing
through the Golden City Star Mudra 163
Earth Plane and Earth Planet
defined by Saint Germain 111
Eighth Ray 43
Eight-sided Cell of Perfection 108, 129, 170
and the Great I AM 168
and the I AM 168
decree for 108
definition 197
Elemental Kingdom 112
definition 197
healing emotional energy 117
Elementals 53
El Morya 68, 223
definition 197
Elohim 53
emotion 72
and physical activity 78
emotional body
and diet 76
and karmic patterns 80
and money 78
evolution of 98
energy
and reciprocity 95
"Energy goes where attention flows." 155
"Energy flows within and without." 99
energy for energy 79, 197
enlightenment
and compassion 98
and Western Doors 144
ethereal schools
and the Seven Rays 186
and the Violet Flame 182
and Wahanee 182
Europe
stabilized by Malton 184
Ever Present Now
definition 197
evil
and perception 127
evolution 107
and love 85
and the Golden Ray 62
and the Violet Flame 110
of humanity 54
expectation
and illusion 100
experience 123, 168, 173
and the soul's education 73
"Experience is the guide." 179

F

family 52
fear 151
a lower frequency 129
and love 84
Ascended Masters assist 135
moving out of 151
Fifth Dimension 51
definition 197
five
Alchemy and the Christ Plane 145

Flame of Love 124
Flower of Life Prayer 231
focus
   and Co-creation 174
forcefields
   and groups of seven 142
forgiveness 64, 180
   and perception 184
   of self 185
Fourth Dimension 51, 52
   and the paradigm of twelve 160
   definition 198
   movement to 160
freedom
   exchanges and expands energy 35
   the three spiritual paths 101
   through restriction 77
Freedom Star
   definition 198
frequency
   higher frequency on Earth 130

G

Galactic Center 87
   definition 198
Galactic Web
   definition 198, 209
garden 46
Gateway Point
   definition 198
genetics
   and animalistic behavior 73, 76
Gentle Revolution Prayer 232
global healing
   and Southern Doors 144
Gobean 184
   affiliated with Gobi 184
   definition 198

mantra 250
Gobi 184
   affiliated with Gobean 184
   definition 198
God
   God-like qualities in all things 178
God I AM
   within everyone 129
"God is everything. God is within all." 28
Golden Age 115, 130
   and the growth of consciousness 55
   and the protective grid 143
   and the Twelve Jurisdictions 160
   definition 199
Golden Age of Kali Yuga 235
   definition 199
Golden City (Cities)
   a Divine Intervention 186
   and activation 145, 185
   and Babajeran 185
   and consciousness 132
   and meditation 182
   and the service of many Masters 145
   divine intervention 186
   doorways 143
   Eastern Door 144
   gateway point and its Master 131
   interconnectivity 184
   Northern Doors 143
   of Wahanee 181
   retreats 133
   retreats at the gateway points 132
   Schools of Light 186
   Southern Door 144
   stabilize continents 184

Stars and their influence 131
Western Door 144
Golden City Doorway
  definition 200
Golden City Mantras 249
Golden City Star Mudra 162
Golden City Vortex 200
  and lei-lines 131
  and the Gold Ray 56
  of Gobean
    definition 198
  of Gobi
    definition 198
  of Klehma
    definition 204
  of Malton
    definition 206
  of Shalahah
    definition 210
  of Wahanee 181
    definition 214
  prayer 231
  Star
    definition 211
  the first seven 184
  their function 163
Gold(en) Ray 55
  and the Age of Information 56
  definition 200
  ends the limitations of Kali Yuga 56
  next step within the Violet Flame 63
Golden Thread Axis
  and the Golden Ray 60
  definition 201
Great Central Sun 107, 161
  definition 201
  guidance through the ancestors 89

Great Purification
  and possibility for humanity 107
Great Silence 123
  definition 201
  "To do, to dare, and to be silent." 97
Great White Brotherhood 146
  and their retreats 142
  definition 201
Great White Lodge Prayer 228
Green Ray
  definition 202
group mind
  and decree 141
  I AM Awareness 170
groups of seven
  and the use of decree 141
guru
  definition 202
guru and chela relationship 75

H

Hall, Manly P. 219
Hall, Marie Bauer 216
harmony 169
    and cultivation of tolerance 171
    and its influence on Collective Consciousness 68
    and the Law of Attraction 143
harmony among nations
  and Eastern Doors 144
Harmony of the Spheres 51
  definition 202
hate
  and doubt of God within 167
Hawkins, Dr. David 238
healing 34, 37
  and the Law of Rhythm 28
  choice and higher vibration 159

Inner Garden Meditation technique 221
thought and Alchemy 27
heart
  and the Flame of Love 124
  opening 99, 179
Heart Chakra
  definition 202
Heart of Compassion 179
Heavenly Lords
  definition 202
  spiritually liberated 112
Helios and Vesta 54
Hermetic Law 113, 122
Hidden Planet 90
  and the Divine Plan of humanity 106
  definition 203
higher frequencies 54
higher mind
  identifying emotions 79
high-pitched ring 183
HU-man
  definition 203

I

I AM 109, 152
  and choice 168
  and God perfection 108
  and harmony 157
  and the consciousness of Unana 138
  and the Great White Brotherhood 146
  and the power of choice 147
  and the spiritual awakening 74
  and the teachings of choice 168
  and the use of God I AM 137
  and Unana 168
  decree for 169
  definition 203
  empowerment through the I AM 157
  interconectivity of the I AM Awareness 170
  release of the energies of the Great I AM 152
I AM America
  dispensation through the Rays 67
  purpose of prophecy 168
I AM America Map 273
I AM Awareness 169, 174, 183
  commanding 172
  definition 203
I AM Presence 152, 178
  and Divine Authority 23
  and the I AM Awareness 171
  and the Master within 152
  and the ONE 152
  calling into activity 153
  calling upon 172
  definition 203
I AM THAT I AM 169
  and Divine Order 73
  definition 203
illusion 71, 178
  and expectation 100
  and tests 178
  and the Earth Plane 111
Immaculate Conception of Mary 246
immortality
  decree for 108
  definition 203
India
  stabilized by Shalahah 184
Industrial Age 56
infectious optimism 159

Sacred Fire 263

Information Age
  definition 191
initiation
  definition 203
inner activity 126
Inner Garden 124
  meditation technique 221
inner marriage
  definition 203
inner spark 54
inner voice 24
intention 68
  and money 78
  and the Law of Love 30
  definition 204
interconnectivity
  through the I AM Awareness 170
Involution of Consciousness 54
Isis
  "Virgin of the World" 245

J

Jesus Christ 245
  Prophet Issa 246
Jiva 54
  definition 204
joy 153
judgment 39
  and dualistic consciousness 165
  and the emotional body 80
  definition 204
  "Is a trap." 119
  move beyond 148

K

Kali Yuga 196
  and the awakening 114
  and use of drugs 118
  definition 204
  ends 55
karma 53, 70, 84
  and illusion 111
  and mantra 249
  and the Earth's ancestors 89
  definition 204
  past 225
  transmuting through the Violet Flame 122
karmic patterns 70
Klehma 184
  definition 204
  Golden City of 52
  mantra 250
  stabilizes North America 184
knowledge
  moves one beyond animal behavior 99
  the Path of Knowledge 101
Krita Yuga 196
Kuan Yin 35, 51, 189
  definition 204
kundalini
  definition 204
Kuthumi
  Awakening Prayer 227

L

Law of Attraction 26, 83, 143, 147, 177
  and Earth Healing 164
  and loss 125

"Know the difference." 136
"When the student is ready, the
    Master appears." 178
Write and Burn Technique 241
Law of Correspondence 177
  and Earth Changes 177
  definition 205
Law of Forgiveness 180
  and the Violet Flame 180
  definition 205
Law of Love 29, 69
  and spiritual growth 84
  and the Earth's ancestors 88
  definition 205
  follow the Law of Love 133
Law of Nature
  and the Earth Planet 112
  and the Violet Flame 109
Law(s) of
  Abundance 31
  Acceptance 45
  Attraction and Repulsion
    definition 204
  Balance 59
  Cause and Effect 53
  Compassion
    and higher consciousness 69
  Cooperation 52
  Freedom 35
  Grace 49
  Harmony 50, 106
  Non-Judgment 45
  Reciprocity 95
  Rhythm 28
    definition 205
  Surrender and Non-Judgment 28

lei-line 131
  adjustment 163
  adjustment through Earth Healing
    163
  definition 205
Lemuria 184
lessons 178
Lewis, David C. 247
light
  increases from the Great Central
    Sun 161
  ONE body of Light 42
light bodies
  and the Violet Flame 111
Lords of Venus 54, 225
  and ancestral guidance 91
  definition 205
loss
  and perception 138
love 30, 68
  and evolution 85
  and spiritual growth 180
  and Unana 153
  definition 205
  "Love for all." 180
  Path of Love 101
"Love has brought me here." 102
Luk, A. D. K. 216

M

Mala 234
Maltese Cross
  and Golden Cities 132
  definition 206
Malton 184
  definition 206
  mantra 250
  stabilizes Europe 184

Sacred Fire 265

mankind
  and the Temple Divine 147
mantra
  definition 206, 249
  for the Violet Flame 119
Marnero
  Golden City of 247
Master
  and chela 154
  finding the Master within at a Golden City Star 131
  "It takes work to reveal this Master." 159
  "Lies within." 149
  within 101, 152
    and the I AM Presence 157
    definition 206
Master Teacher 100, 183
  and energy for energy 79
  and gateway points 131
  definition 206
  lifts the burdens of the student 96
  "Many more are coming." 144
  "Never tells the student what to do." 97
  "When the student is ready." 133
Mastery 174
  and choices 100
  definition 206
  of natural law 24
medicine
  changes through Dvapara Yuga 115
meditation 140
  and Golden Cities 182
  benefits 158
  builds energy 158
  definition 206
  Inner Garden 221

  instructions from Saint Germain 140
  in the Garden with Sananda 37
  preparation through mantra or decree 234
  Sunday Peace Meditation 162
  The Loving Christ 128
Meissner Field 91
  definition 206
mental body
  and Divine Love 77
  and karmic patterns 71
  and the Violet Ray 151
  definition 207
Micah
  Great Angel of Unity 219
Middle Way Prayer 229
mind
  and the Ascension 71
  and the Violet Ray 85
  calming through meditation 129
Mineral Kingdom 112
mistake
  "No mistake ever, ever, ever." 127, 149
momentum
  and groups of seven 142
Monad 41, 51, 53
  and the Law of Attraction 26
  definition 207
  "What is freedom?" 34
money
  and emotional experiences 78
Mother Mary 52
mudra
  definition 207
  Golden Star 162
  to direct energy to the Stars of Golden Cities 162

N

neutrality
  the center point 139
  the plane of neutrality 156
  "There is no mistake ever, ever, ever." 167
New Atlantis 216
new children
  A Prayer for the New Children 231
New Consciousness
  decree for the Gold Ray 235
New Day
  definition 207
Nibiru 91
North America
  stabilized by Klehma 184

O

obstacles
  and mantra 249
ONE
  and Ascension 75
  and Saint Germain's teachings 38
  and teachings on love 30
  and the I AM Awareness 171
  and the I AM Presence 152
  and the new consciousness 111
  and Unana 180
  definition 207
  problem and solution 154
  the I AM Presence and the I AM Awareness 171
  "We are always ONE." 103
Oneness 41
  definition 207

Oneship 51
  and Christ Consciousness 29
  and the I AM 38
  definition 207
  mantra 250
  teachings by Sananda 36
one-world experience
  not one-world government 181
optimism 157
  "Infectious optimism." 159
out-picturing 73, 174
  and the Violet Flame 166
Outpicturing
  definition 207

P

pain 174
  forgetting 69
  "Is often the greatest teacher." 175
Paradigm of Twelve
  definition 207
Pashacino 184
  stabilizes Antarctica 184
past life
  reciprocity of mental energies 96
peace 126
  "Carry peace within." 135
  Sunday Peace Meditation 162
perception 116
  and evil 127
  and forgiveness 185
  and juxtaposition 155
  and mind 27
  and prophecy 158, 177
  and the Violet Ray 81
  beyond loss and duality 139
  definition 208
  shift through prophecy 158

Sacred Fire 267

perfection 98, 108
  and the I AM Presence 152
  "Hold the vibration of perfection." 38
perfect thought 52
physical activity
  discharges emotion 78
Pink Ray
  definition 208
Pluto 161
Point of Perception 98
  definition 208
polarization 123
Portia 184
positive thoughts 157
prana
  definition 208
prayer
  A Prayer for the New Children 231
  Ascension Prayer 230
  Awakening Prayer 227
  Golden City Purification
    definition 231
  Great White Lodge Prayer 228
  The Flower of Life Prayer 231
  The Gentle Revolution Prayer 232
  The Middle Way 229
  The Prayer of a Thousand Suns 230
  Thought, Feeling, and Action 229
  Web of Creation Prayer 230
Prayer for Ascension 230
preparation
  readied to receive 100
Presence of God
  and the I AM Presence 152
probability
  and the collective will 93

problem(s) 157
  and attention 155
  and consciousness 155
  and solution(s) 154
  and solutions 154
  the answer is also present 156
Prophecies of Change
  and technology 56
  definition 208
Prophecies of Peace 49
  definition 208
Prophecy 158
  and choice 123
  and human consciousness 168
  and the Green Ray 67
  contains keys to circumventing disasters 92
  definition 208
  "Greatest of spiritual teachings." 158
  possibility and probability 93
Prophet, Mark 233
Protective Grid 142
  definition 209
psychedelic drugs
  use of 118
purification
  definition 209
purifying a room
  with the Violet Flame 141

Q

quality of consciousness
  and vibration 165
quartz crystal
  and the Step-down Transformer 243
questions
  and evolution 107

R

Ray Force(s)
  and the Golden City Star 131
  calling into action 72
Ray(s)
  and the ethereal schools 186
  definition 209
  Eighth 43
reciprocity 95
religion
  and beliefs 148
restriction and freedom 77
revealing the Master within
  "There is no quick fix." 159
Rosicrucians 215
Ruby and Gold Ray
  definition 209

S

sacred architecture 187
sacred geometry
  and the Schools of Light 187
Saint Germain 38
  and the Violet Flame 189
  and the Wahanee School of Light 183
  and vibration 165
  Awakening Prayer 227
  definition 209
  Holy Brother 215
  Kajaeshra 216
  Map of Political Changes 217
  on Mastery 149
  on meditation 140
  Portia, Twin Flame 184
  teachings on the I AM Awareness 170
  teachings on vibration 166
Sananda 29, 36, 70, 179
  and the Loving Christ 128
  biography 219
  definition 209
  Sunday Peace Meditation 237
Saturn 226
schools of light 183
science
  and consciousness 113
Seamless Garment 36
  definition 209
security and emotion 79
self-examination 137
self-realization 109
separation
  and duality 103
  dissolves through acceptance 45
Serapis Bey
  definition 210
service
  and Ascended Beings 130
  Path of Service 101
Seven Rays of Light and Sound
  and ancient astrology 196
  definition 210
Seventh Manu 53, 54
  definition 210
Seventh Ray 35
Seventh Seal
  and chakras 145
Shalahah 184
  definition 210
  mantra 250
  stabilizes India 184

Sacred Fire 269

Shamballa
  definition 210
Sierra Madres 50
silence 97
silicon-based consciousness 115
simultaneous reality
  definition 210
Singh, Major Kulwant 237
Sister Thedra 219
sleep
  decree of protection 118
sojourn of the soul 62
solar system
  Paradigm of Twelve 160
Solomon's Temple 216
solution(s)
  and choice 157
  and higher states of consciousness 156
  lie within 158
spirit guide
  Inner Garden Meditation 221
Spiritual Awakening 33, 45
  and Kali Yuga 114
  definition 211
spiritual growth
  and Earth Changes 177
Spiritual Hierarchy
  and the Gold Ray 57
spiritual liberation
  and the Heavenly Lords 112
  definition 211
spiritual path
  and camaraderie 154
  and freedom 101
spiritual practice 181
spiritual preparedness
  definition 211

spiritual stagnation 84, 181
Star(s)
  and spiritual practice 141
  critical points 238
  disbursement of the energies of the doorways 144
  forcefields 142
  mudra 143
  of a Golden City
    definition 211
  of the Golden Cities 131
  United States cities and towns 238
Star seed
  and animalistic behavior 76
  definition 211
Step-down Transformer 187
  definition 212
storms
  calming through Earth Healing 163
stuck 82
student
  "When the student is ready, the Master indeed appears." 133
suffering
  and the Violet Flame 111
  use of Violet Flame 140
Sun
  solar storms 163
  the two Suns 88, 116
  the two Suns illuminate 161
  two Suns 161
Sunday Peace Meditation 162
surrender to God
  Path of Surrender 102

T

teaching
  lifting emotional burden of the student 96
technology 56
telepathy 183
Temple of Mercy 189
Temple of the ONE 108
Temples of Consciousness 132, 182
tests
  "The student is ready." 147
Third Dimension 52
  and the Law of Attraction 83
  definition 212
Third Eye
  definition 212
  opening 82
thought
  and the I AM 27
  and transforming for Ascension 71
  ONE body of Thought 42
Thought, Feeling, and Action Prayer 229
thousand eyes
  definition 212
Time
  of Awakening 54
  of Peace 54
Time Compaction
  definition 212
Time of Change
  definition 212
Time of Testing 122, 154, 178, 181
  and spiritual stagnation 181
  definition 213

Time of Transition 53
  and humanity's potential transformation 106
  work completed 146
"To do, to dare, and to be silent." 74
tolerance 149, 167, 174
  cultivating tolerance and patience 171
  without judgment 167
Toye, Lenard
  about 274
Toye, Lori
  about 273
  Awakening Prayer 227
transgression 185
transmute energy patterns
  Write and Burn Technique 241
Treta Yuga 196
True Memory 70
  definition 213
Tube of Light 122
  and the Violet Flame 110
twelve
  paradigm of twelve 160
Twelve Jurisdictions 160
  definition 213
  their purpose 160
Twin Flame
  definition 213
"Two Suns" 88

U

Unana 37, 102, 107, 159, 168
  and Golden City Stars 141
  and love 153
  and the Christ Consciousness 124
  and the Golden City of Wahanee 181
  and the Golden Ray 58
  and the I AM 168
  and the I AM Presence 153
  as a Meissner Field 91
  definition 213
  Plane of Unana 138
  Sunday Peace Meditation 237
Unfed Flame 25
  definition 213
Unified Field Theory 113
United Brotherhood
  and Wahanee 181
United States
  Declaration of Independence 217
Unity Consciousness 75, 138
  unified field of human consciousness 237
universal
  and the I AM 152
universal consciousness
  and the I AM Awareness 170
upaye
  and mantra 249

V

Vedic
  Rishis 196
Vegetable (Plant) Kingdom 112
Vertical Power Current
  definition 213

vibration
  and consciousness 165
  and group consciousness 131
  and quality of consciousness 165
  and the Hidden Planet 90
  and the Violet Flame 110
  and the Yugas 57
  decree to shift vibration 169
  "You create your own vibration." 166
victim mentality
  healing 26
Violet Flame 78, 109, 182
  and humanity's karmic burden 105
  and justice 107
  and karma 83
  and Portia 184
  and the darkest hour 125
  and the Gold Ray 64
  and the Law of Attraction 136
  and the Law of Forgiveness 180
  and the Star of Wahanee 181
  and the use of the I AM 109
  and use of drugs 119
  decree before meditation 182
  Decrees 233
  definition 214, 225
  for compassion 125
  for judgment 166
  for problems 156
  for removing blocks 156
  for suffering 140
  for the will 122
  for the world leaders 126
  invocation at sunrise, sunset 190
  Spiritual Lineage 189
  to overcome duality 137
  to prepare for meditation 182

   to raise vibration 166
   transmuting karma 122
   use before meditation 141
Violet Flame Decree
   for compassion 107
   for difficult and trying situations 106
   immersion into the divine 119
   to eliminate karma 105
   Violet Flame Mantra 119
Violet Ray 85, 110
   and Divine Intervention 61
   and emotional responses 79
   and perception 81
   and the Ascension 71
   and write and burn techniques 78
   for preparing the mind 151
   opens humanity's heart of compassion 151
   to quiet the mind 71
   use to overcome attachments 78
Virgin Goddess 245
Vortex (Vortices)
   Oklahoma 116
   older 51

W

Wahanee 184
   and the Violet Flame 181
   definition 214
   mantra 250
   Violet Flame Decree 182
Web of Creation
   Prayer
      definition 230
White Ray
   and healing for Ascension 69
   definition 214

will
   and non-judgment 167
   decree for 122
   definition 214
   development of 139
world economies
   and Northern Doors 144
World Trade Center and 9-11
   and the Law of Attraction 126
Write and Burn Technique 78, 241
   definition 214

Y

Yuga(s)
   Cycle of 196
   four 196
Yugas, cycle of 57
Yukon Territory 184

Z

Zadkiel
   Order of 225

About Lori and Lenard Toye

Lori Toye is not a Prophet of doom and gloom. The fact that she became a Prophet at all is highly unlikely. Reared in a small Idaho farming community as a member of the conservative Missouri Synod Lutheran church, Lori had never heard of meditation, spiritual development, reincarnation, channeling, or clairvoyant sight.

Her unusual spiritual journey began in Washington State, when, as advertising manager of a weekly newspaper, she answered a request to pick up an ad for a local health food store. As she entered, a woman at the counter pointed a finger at her and said, "You have work to do for Master Saint Germain!"

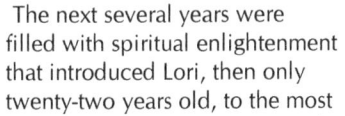

The next several years were filled with spiritual enlightenment that introduced Lori, then only twenty-two years old, to the most exceptional and inspirational information she had ever encountered. Lori became a student of Ascended Master teachings.

Awakened one night by the luminous figure of Saint Germain at the foot of her bed, her work had begun. Later in the same year, an image of a map appeared in her dream. Four teachers clad in white robes were present, pointing out Earth Changes that would shape the future United States.

Five years later, faced with the stress of a painful divorce and rebuilding her life as a single mother, Lori attended spiritual meditation classes. While there, she shared her experience, and encouraged by friends, she began to explore the dream through daily meditation. The four Beings appeared again, and expressed a willingness to share the information. Over a six-month period, they gave over eighty sessions of material, including detailed information that would later become the I AM America Map.

Clearly she had to produce the map. The only means to finance it was to sell her house. She put her home up for sale, and in a depressed market, it sold the first day at full asking price.

She produced the map in 1989, rolled copies of them on her kitchen table, and sold them through word-of-mouth. She then launched a lecture tour of the

Sacred Fire 275

Northwest and California. Hers was the first Earth Changes Map published, and many others have followed, but the rest is history.

From the tabloids to the *New York Times*, *The Washington Post*, television interviews in the U.S., London, and Europe, Lori's Mission was to honor the material she had received. The material is not hers, she stresses. It belongs to the Masters, and their loving, healing approach is disseminated through the I AM America Publishing Company operated by her husband and spiritual partner, Lenard Toye.

Lenard Toye, originally from Philadelphia, PA, was born into a family of professional contractors and builders, and has a remarkable singing voice. Lenard's compelling tenor voice replaced many of the greats at a moment's notice—Pavarotti and Domingo, including many performances throughout Europe. When he retired from music, he joined his family's business yet pursued his personal interests in alternative healing.

He attended *Barbara Brennan's School of Healing* to further develop the gift of auric vision. Working together with his wife Lori, they organized free classes of healing techniques and the channeled teachings. Their instructional pursuits led them to form the *School of the Four Pillars* which includes holistic and energy healing and Ascended Master Teachings. In 1995 and 1996 they sponsored the first Prophecy Conferences in Philadelphia and Phoenix, Arizona. His management and sales background has played a very important role in his partnership with his wife Lori and their publishing company. Other publications include three additional Prophecy maps, thirteen books, a video, and more than sixty audio tapes based on sessions with Master Teacher Saint Germain and other Ascended Masters.

Spiritual in nature, I AM America is not a church, religion, sect, or cult. There is no interest or intent in amassing followers or engaging in any activity other than what Lori and Lenard can do on their own to publicize the materials they have been entrusted with.

They have also been directed to build the first Golden City community. A very positive aspect of the vision is that all the maps include areas called, "Golden Cities." These places hold a high spiritual energy, and are where sustainable communities are to be built using solar energy alongside classical feng shui engineering and infrastructure. The first community, Wenima Village, is currently being planned for development.

Concerned that some might misinterpret the Maps' messages as doom and gloom and miss the metaphor for personal change, or not consider the spiritual teachings attached to the maps, Lori emphasizes that the Masters stressed that this was a Prophecy of choice. Prophecy allows for choice in making informed decisions and promotes the opportunity for cooperation and harmony.
Lenard and Lori's vision for I AM America is to share the Ascended Masters' prophecies as spiritual warnings to heal and renew our lives.

Books by Lori Toye

Books:

NEW WORLD WISDOM SERIES: *Book One, Two, and Three*

FREEDOM STAR: *Prophecies that Heal Earth*

THE EVER PRESENT NOW: *A New Understanding of Consciousness and Prophecy*

I AM AMERICA ATLAS: *Based on the Maps, Prophecies, and Teachings of the Ascended Masters*

GOLDEN CITIES AND THE MASTERS OF SHAMBALLA: *The I AM America Teachings*

GOLDEN CITY SERIES
  Book One: Points of Perception
  Book Two: Light of Awakening
  Book Three: Divine Destiny
  Book Four: Sacred Energies of the Golden Cities
  Book Five: Temples of Consciousness
  Book Six: Awaken the Master Within
  Book Seven: Soul Alchemy (Advanced students only)

I AM AMERICA TRILOGY
  Book One: A Teacher Appears
  Book Two: Sisters of the Flame
  Book Three: Fields of Light

I AM AMERICA COLLECTION
  Sacred Fire
  Building the Seamless Garment

Maps by Lori Toye

Maps:
  I AM America Map
  Freedom Star World Map
  United States 6-Map Scenario
  United States Golden City Map

I AM
AMERICA

I AM AMERICA PUBLISHING & DISTRIBUTING
P.O. Box 2511, Payson, Arizona, 85547, USA. (928) 978-6435

For More Information:
www.iamamerica.com
www.loritoye.com

I AM America Online Bookstore:
www.iamamerica.com

About I AM America

I AM America is an educational and publishing foundation dedicated to disseminating the Ascended Masters' message of Earth Changes Prophecy and Spiritual Teachings for self-development. Our office is run by the husband and wife team of Lenard and Lori Toye who hand-roll maps, package, and mail information and products with a small staff. Our first publication was the I AM America Map, which was published in September 1989. Since then we have published three more Prophecy maps, thirteen books, and numerous recordings based on the channeled sessions with the Spiritual Teachers.

We are not a church, a religion, a sect, or cult and are not interested in amassing followers or members. Nor do we have any affiliation with a church, religion, political group, or government of any kind. We are not a college or university, research facility, or a mystery school. El Morya told us that the best way to see ourselves is as, "Cosmic Beings, having a human experience."

In 1994, we asked Saint Germain, "How do you see our work at I AM America?" and he answered, "I AM America is to be a clearinghouse for the new humanity." Grabbing a dictionary, we quickly learned that the term "clearinghouse" refers to "an organization or unit within an organization that functions as a central agency for collecting, organizing, storing, and disseminating documents, usually within a specific academic discipline or field." So inarguably, we are this too. But in uncomplicated terms, we publish and share spiritually transformational information because at I AM America there is no doubt that, "A Change of Heart can Change the World."

With Violet Flame Blessings,
Lori & Lenard Toye

For more information or to visit our online bookstore, go to:
www.iamamerica.com
www.loritoye.com
To receive a catalog by mail, please write to:
I AM America
P.O. Box 2511
Payson, AZ 85547

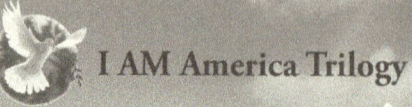

I AM America Trilogy
The contemporary Spiritual Journey

A Teacher Appears
ISBN: 9781800050446
254 pages

Sisters of the Flame
ISBN: 9781800050262
216 pages

Fields of Light
ISBN: 9781800050613
310 pages

This series of insightful books, written by the creator of the acclaimed *I AM America Maps* shares a fresh and personal viewpoint of the contemporary spiritual journey. Lori Toye was just twenty-two years old when she first encountered Ascended Master teaching. The *I AM America Trilogy* takes us back to the beginning of her experiences with her spiritual teachers and includes insights that have never been disclosed in any previous books or writings. In "A Teacher Appears," learn how true wisdom and the inner teacher is within all of us. "Sisters of the Flame," continues an initiatory passage into the feminine with the Cellular Awakening. "Fields of Light," explains how to integrate and Master our spiritual light through soul-transcending teachings of Ascension. Lori's personal story is interwoven throughout the I AM America Trilogy in a rich tapestry of spiritual techniques, universal wisdom, and knowledge gained through a life-changing spiritual journey.

our next evolution ...

Golden City Series

The Science of the Golden Cities and the Ascension Process

1. **POINTS OF PERCEPTION:** *Prophecies and Teachings from Saint Germain*

2. **LIGHT OF AWAKENING:** *Prophecies and Teachings from the Ascended Masters*

3. **DIVINE DESTINY:** *Prophecies and Teachings from the Ascended Masters*

4. **SACRED ENERGIES:** *Of the Golden Cities*

5. **TEMPLES OF CONSCIOUSNESS:** *Ascended Master Teaching of the Golden Cities*

6. **AWAKEN THE MASTER WITHIN:** *Golden Age Teaching of Saint Germain*

7. **SOUL ALCHEMY:** *Teaching on Golden City Community*

loritoye.com
iamamerica.com

Navigating the New Earth

I AM America Map
US Earth Changes
Order #001

Freedom Star Map
World Earth Changes
Order #004

Since 1989, I AM America has been publishing thought-provoking information on Earth Changes. All of our Maps feature the compelling cartography of the New Times illustrated with careful details and unique graphics. Professionally presented in full color. Explore the prophetic possibilities!

Retail and Wholesale prices available.

Purchase Maps at:
www.IAMAMERICA.com

6-Map Scenario
US Earth Changes Progression
Order #022

Golden Cities Map
United States
Order #110

I AM AMERICA
P.O. Box 2511
Payson, Arizona
(928) 978-6435